Enterprise PowerShell Scripting Bootcamp

Focused, intensive, and effective enterprise PowerShell Scripting

Brenton J.W. Blawat

BIRMINGHAM - MUMBAI

Enterprise PowerShell Scripting Bootcamp

First published: May2017

Production reference: 1160517

Published by Packt Publishing Ltd.
Livery Place
35 Livery Street
Birmingham B32PB, UK.

ISBN 978-1-78728-828-7

www.packtpub.com

Credits

Author
Brenton J.W. Blawat

Reviewer
Tim Amico

Commissioning Editor
Kartikey Pandey

Acquisition Editor
Namrata Patil

Content Development Editor
Amrita Noronha

Technical Editor
Jovita Alva

Copy Editors
Safis Editing
Laxmi Subramanian

Project Coordinator
Shweta H Birwatkar

Proofreader
Safis Editing

Indexer
Tejal Daruwale Soni

Graphics
Tania Dutta

Production Coordinator
Nilesh Mohite

Cover Work
Nilesh Mohite

About the Author

Brenton J.W. Blawat is an entrepreneur, strategic technical advisor, multi-published author, and enterprise architect who has a passion for the procurement of technology in profit-based organizations. Brenton is business-centric, while technology minded, and has many years of experience bridging the gap between technical staff and decision makers in organizations. He takes pride in his ability to effectively communicate to a diverse audience and provide strategic direction for large and small organizations alike.

Since 2013, he has authored and published multiple books with Packt Publishing, including:

- *PowerShell 3.0 WMI Starter*
- (Co-authored) *PowerShell: Automating Administrative Tasks*
- *Mastering Windows PowerShell Scripting*

Brenton currently works at CDW as an enterprise architect in Strategic Solutions and Services. CDW is a leading multibrand technology solutions provider to business, government, education, and healthcare organizations in the United States, Canada, and the United Kingdom. A Fortune 500 company with multinational capabilities, CDW was founded in 1984 and employs approximately 8,500 workers. For the year ending December 31, 2016, the company generated net sales of nearly $14 billion. For more information about CDW, visit www.CDW.com.

As the author of this book, Brenton always extends himself to the PowerShell community. You can follow Brenton on Twitter at @brentblawat or his blog at http://www.masteringposh.com. The author is always open for discussions on the book and will provide feedback to readers, as time allows. If you are an academic institution, Brenton engages with multiple colleges for guest speaking. You can contact Brenton on Twitter for more information.

Happy coding!

About the Reviewer

Tim Amico is a passionate technology leader with years of consulting experience around designing, implementing, and managing Endpoint and Mobility management infrastructures for small organizations to large global enterprise environments. He has continued to define technology solutions that help solve complex business problems and deliver highly customized solutions to clients.

He currently works at LMI as a systems engineer, managing their System Center Configuration Manager, Active Directory, and Azure IaaS environments. LMI is a not-for-profit government consulting firm that designs and implements solutions to some of the toughest problems facing government managers in logistics, information technology, and resource allocation. For more information about LMI, visit www.lmi.org.

You can follow Tim on twitter at @tim_amico or his blog at http://www.deploymentlife.com.

www.PacktPub.com

eBooks, discount offers, and more

Did you know that Packt offers eBook versions of every book published, with PDF and ePub files available? You can upgrade to the eBook version at www.PacktPub.com and as a print book customer, you are entitled to a discount on the eBook copy. Get in touch with us at customercare@packtpub.com for more details.

At www.PacktPub.com, you can also read a collection of free technical articles, sign up for a range of free newsletters and receive exclusive discounts and offers on Packt books and eBooks.

https://www.packtpub.com/mapt

Get the most in-demand software skills with Mapt. Mapt gives you full access to all Packt books and video courses, as well as industry-leading tools to help you plan your personal development and advance your career.

Why subscribe?

- Fully searchable across every book published by Packt
- Copy and paste, print, and bookmark content
- On demand and accessible via a web browser

Customer Feedback

Thanks for purchasing this Packt book. At Packt, quality is at the heart of our editorial process. To help us improve, please leave us an honest review on this book's Amazon page at `https://www.amazon.com/dp/1787288285`.

If you'd like to join our team of regular reviewers, you can e-mail us at `customerreviews@packtpub.com`. We award our regular reviewers with free eBooks and videos in exchange for their valuable feedback. Help us be relentless in improving our products!

I would like to dedicate this book to my wife, Rachel, whose love and support drives me to be a better person every day.

Table of Contents

Preface

PowerShell is quickly becoming the language of choice to support Microsoft systems in organizations. With Microsoft's deep integration of PowerShell in all of their software and cloud services, scripting knowledge will be a required skill set in the years to come. Even third-party vendors are creating modules or plugins to extend the PowerShell manageability of their systems. As a result, organizations are relying on their cross-platform engineers to automate systems through the use of PowerShell.

When you are implementing PowerShell scripts in enterprise environments, there are many common challenges that need to be solved. Robust logging functions, for example, are typically required to ensure that the script ran successfully and as intended. You may also need to implement a string encryption strategy to encrypt credentials, server host names, IP addresses, or other sensitive data. Further more, script execution speed may also take some consideration when processing large sets of data. You will want to ensure you are leveraging the fastest coding methods possible to optimize your scripting performance.

All of these challenges, and many more, can be solved by leveraging PowerShell. Through both native cmdlets and the .NET Framework, you can create sophisticated scripts to solve almost any problem. The PowerShell community of developers is very passionate about sharing their knowledge and providing information on how to solve problems. Through code sharing websites, social media, and Microsoft's TechNet, there is always a constant stream of examples that you can implement in your code. Also, now that PowerShell is open source and available on Linux, it deepens the relationships with the open source community. It provides a much wider set of open source developers to solve enterprise problems.

This book has been designed to teach you the ins and outs of enterprise PowerShell scripting. It is geared towards real-world scenarios of how Fortune 500 companies leverage PowerShell to solve problems. It provides a scripting framework that you can easily follow to start integrating the examples into your own scripts. At the end of this book, you will have learned many techniques to secure, optimize, and deliver PowerShell scripts that are ready to be deployed in the enterprise.

What this book covers

Chapter 1, Getting Started with Enterprise PowerShell Scripting, introduces the Windows server scanning script and performance considerations, and helps you create your own PowerShell scripting templates.

Chapter 2, Script Structure, Comment Blocks, and Script Logging, explores how to structure your PowerShell scripts, how to properly comment your script, and how to create a robust logging function.

Chapter 3, Working with Answer Files, explains the purpose of XML-based answer files and displays how to leverage them in your scripts.

Chapter 4, String Encryption and Decryption, dives into advanced string encryption and encoding methodologies. It shows you how to securely store encrypted data in scripts, and a how to decrypt and decode values during runtime.

Chapter 5, Interacting with Services, Processes, Profiles, and Logged-on Users, evaluates different Windows server components for nonstandard configurations. It also evaluates logged-on users and user profiles to identify what users have been interacting with a particular system.

Chapter 6, Evaluating Scheduled Tasks, displays how to interact with scheduled tasks on a system. It helps identify the different processes that may be invoked on a scheduled basis on a system.

Chapter 7, Determining Disk Statistics, explores how to interact with the disks on a system to retrieve and record disk information.

Chapter 8, Windows Features and Installed Software Detection, explains how to review the installed Windows features and installed software on a system.

Chapter 9, File Scanning, dives into scanning for file types in directories on a server. It also displays the process to scan for strings in files.

Chapter 10, *Optimizing Script Execution Speed*, evaluates how to increase server performance through the use of different scripting techniques. It also evaluates how to measure command execution time for benchmarking script performance.

Chapter 11, *Improving Performance Using Regular Expressions*, displays how to leverage regular expressions to significantly increase the performance of your PowerShell scripts.

Chapter 12, *Overall Script Workflow, Termination Files, and Merging Data Results*, evaluates the overall Windows server scanning script workflow and the full answer file creation. It also explores when and why you would use termination files and how to merge the results from the Windows server scanning script.

Chapter 13, *Creating the Windows Server Scanning Script and Post Execution Cleanup*, provides an in-depth explanation of all of the components in the Windows server scanning script. It also provides cleanup considerations for postscript execution on systems.

What you need for this book

To work through the examples provided in *Enterprise PowerShell Scripting Bootcamp*, you will need access to two Server 2012 R2, or greater, Windows Server operating systems. Preferably, both systems will be joined to a domain. The chapters in this book highly rely on Windows Management Framework and it is recommended to leverage version 5.0 for PowerShell 5.0. You will need to download and install Windows Management Framework on the systems you are running these examples on.

Who this book is for

Enterprise PowerShell Scripting Bootcamp has been designed for PowerShell scripters that are both beginner- and advanced-level coders. After reading this book, you will have in-depth knowledge of PowerShell scripting in enterprises and will create a working script to execute in your environment. Previous scripting and basic coding experience is required to understand the concepts presented in this book.

Conventions

In this book, you will find a number of styles of text that distinguish between different kinds of information. Here are some examples of these styles, and an explanation of their meaning.

Code words in text, database table names, folder names, filenames, file extensions, pathnames, dummy URLs, user input, and Twitter handles are shown as follows: "The get-service cmdlet is used to retrieve detailed information about Windows Services."

A block of code is set as follows:

```
$sid = "S-1-5-18"
$usersid = New-Object System.Security.Principal.
SecurityIdentifier("$SID")
$usersid.Translate( [System.Security.Principal.NTAccount]).Value
```

New terms and **important words** are shown in bold. Words that you see on the screen, in menus or dialog boxes for example, appear in the text like this: "clicking the **Next** button moves you to the next screen".

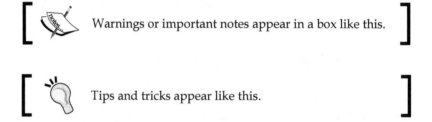

Warnings or important notes appear in a box like this.

Tips and tricks appear like this.

Reader feedback

Feedback from our readers is always welcome. Let us know what you think about this book—what you liked or may have disliked. Reader feedback is important for us to develop titles that you really get the most out of.

To send us general feedback, simply send an e-mail to feedback@packtpub.com, and mention the book title via the subject of your message.

If there is a topic that you have expertise in and you are interested in either writing or contributing to a book, see our author guide on www.packtpub.com/authors.

Customer support

Now that you are the proud owner of a Packt book, we have a number of things to help you to get the most from your purchase.

Downloading the example code

You can download the example code files for all Packt books you have purchased from your account at http://www.packtpub.com. If you purchased this book elsewhere, you can visit http://www.packtpub.com/support and register to have the files e-mailed directly to you.

You can download the code files by following these steps:

1. Log in or register to our website using your e-mail address and password.
2. Hover the mouse pointer on the **SUPPORT** tab at the top.
3. Click on **Code Downloads & Errata**.
4. Enter the name of the book in the **Search** box.
5. Select the book for which you're looking to download the code files.
6. Choose from the drop-down menu where you purchased this book from.
7. Click on **Code Download**.

Once the file is downloaded, please make sure that you unzip or extract the folder using the latest version of:

- WinRAR / 7-Zip for Windows
- Zipeg / iZip / UnRarX for Mac
- 7-Zip / PeaZip for Linux

The code bundle for the book is also hosted on GitHub at https://github.com/PacktPublishing/Enterprise-PowerShell-Scripting-Bootcamp. We also have other code bundles from our rich catalog of books and videos available at https://github.com/PacktPublishing/. Check them out!

Downloading the color images of this book

We also provide you with a PDF file that has color images of the screenshots/diagrams used in this book. The color images will help you better understand the changes in the output. You can download this file from https://www.packtpub.com/sites/default/files/downloads/EnterprisePowerShellScriptingBootcamp_ColorImages.pdf.

Errata

Although we have taken every care to ensure the accuracy of our content, mistakes do happen. If you find a mistake in one of our books—maybe a mistake in the text or the code—we would be grateful if you would report this to us. By doing so, you can save other readers from frustration and help us improve subsequent versions of this book. If you find any errata, please report them by visiting http://www.packtpub.com/submit-errata, selecting your book, clicking on the **errata submission form** link, and entering the details of your errata. Once your errata are verified, your submission will be accepted and the errata will be uploaded on our website, or added to any list of existing errata, under the Errata section of that title. Any existing errata can be viewed by selecting your title from http://www.packtpub.com/support.

Piracy

Piracy of copyright material on the Internet is an ongoing problem across all media. At Packt, we take the protection of our copyright and licenses very seriously. If you come across any illegal copies of our works, in any form, on the Internet, please provide us with the location address or website name immediately so that we can pursue a remedy.

Please contact us at copyright@packtpub.com with a link to the suspected pirated material.

We appreciate your help in protecting our authors, and our ability to bring you valuable content.

Questions

You can contact us at questions@packtpub.com if you are having a problem with any aspect of the book, and we will do our best to address it.

1
Getting Started with Enterprise PowerShell Scripting

The PowerShell language was developed to provide engineers with a method to quickly automate the provisioning and management of environments. In the last decade, PowerShell's use has greatly expanded, to encompass the setup and configuration of a myriad of hardware and software systems. Since third-party manufacturers are creating PowerShell modules to control their systems, PowerShell is becoming the automation language of choice. It is being used to configure multiple systems from multiple manufacturers, with a single set of PowerShell code.

Creating scripts for enterprise environments requires a robust scripting framework. A scripting framework consists of reusable code that you can leverage for a large majority of your scripts. This framework needs to be efficient, reliable, and secure. It must also provide logging capabilities, leverage answer files, and be flexible for execution on a wide variety of systems.

As you are exploring this book, you will learn a large number of tested and industry-proven scripting techniques. The examples you create will be applied at the end of the book in a Windows server scanning script. This will enable you to quickly integrate new sections of code into your own scripts, and will provide a trusted platform you can confidently deploy in your environment.

In this chapter, you will:

- Learn about the Windows server scanning script created throughout this book

- Explore performance optimizations implemented throughout each chapter

- Review different components you should include in all of your PowerShell scripts

Windows server scanning script

There can be times in large enterprises where you need to determine the functionality of systems. If you don't have large asset management software, you will need the ability to perform a discovery. This book was designed to provide a significant jumpstart for the creation of a Windows server scanning script. The script takes into consideration the limitations of Windows components and provides extremely detailed information about systems.

Some of the items that you will be scanning for include:

- **Disk configuration**: You will be able to query the disk layout for a particular system and determine device type, drive letters, free space, and total disk size.

- **Scheduled task scanning**: You will discover the scheduled tasks that are not running as built-in accounts, providing visibility into non-standard configurations.

- **Windows processes**: You will identify the Windows processes on the system to determine what processes are running with alternate user credentials. This will help identify systems that have service accounts for process execution.

- **Windows services**: You will review the Windows services on the system to discover what services are not running as built-in accounts. This will further identify service account usage in your enterprise.

- **Installed software**: You will learn how to safely scan a system for software to identify software titles installed on a system.

- **User profiles**: You will evaluate all of the user profiles created on a system to determine the last login usernames and times. This will help identify teams that own the management of the servers.

- **Windows features**: You will determine the installed Windows features and roles on a system to help identify what role the server has in your enterprise.

- **Scanning files**: You will scan individual files on a system for strings. This provides the ability to identify items such as user credentials and configured server names.

This script is designed to provide a robust platform to scan your enterprise. Variations of this script have been used in multiple Fortune 500 companies and executed on well over 10,000 systems. The chapters in this book have been designed to enable you to quickly learn the core components to integrate this PowerShell tool into your personal repository.

Performance considerations

This book dives into important performance considerations for your scripts. Since PowerShell is an extremely flexible language, you can complete the same activity in multiple ways. While both sets of code get the script to create the same results, there are ways to optimize your code to make it much more efficient. This becomes increasingly important as you evaluate large amounts of data.

Execution time for file scanning, for example, exponentially grows with the quantity of files and the file sizes. 100 files with 100 lines of code can quickly create 10,000 evaluations. Now, if you scale that to 6 million files in a storage volume times 100 lines of code, you are performing 600 million evaluations. Small code performance improvements can significantly optimize your scanning of scripts at scale.

Some of the performance considerations include:

- **Measuring commands**: You will evaluate a technique to measure the execution time for commands.

- **Cmdlet considerations**: You will learn which cmdlets are more efficient than others and how to avoid common cmdlet mistakes.

- **Regular expressions over arrays**: Regular expressions can be difficult to learn, but they provide significant performance improvements to your scripts. You will learn how to properly implement dynamic regular expressions in your scripts.

- **Switch statements**: You will evaluate how to perform data sorting with switches and why switch statements are significantly faster.

PowerShell scripting templates

As you develop different scripts for your enterprise environment, you will have a core set of functions that you tend to use in all of your scripts. Some enterprise scripters create their own functions, while others leverage scripts from the vast community of PowerShell developers. With either method, you will need a solid foundation to build your scripts on.

Some of the most common items this book provides for scripting templates include:

- **Encryption and decryption technologies**: Probably the most common requirement in enterprise environments is security. It's no secret that you should not have clear text administrative-level credentials in scripts. Providing an encryption and decryption function in your scripts is essential to maintaining a secure enterprise.

- **Logging mechanisms**: The second most common requirement in enterprise environments is logging script actions. Since scripts are typically executed on a large number of systems at the same time, you will need the ability to track exactly what is being performed on these systems. Creating a logging function will provide the ability to log script actions to both the event log and a log file.

- **Answer file logic**: One of the more advanced methods for PowerShell scripting is leveraging an answer file for script variables. The core to the answer file is that you can add, remove, and modify the values in the answer file without having to modify your script. This provides the ability to have flexibility in your scripts without needing to touch any lines of code.

- **Standardized comment blocks**: When you are creating scripts, it's essential to give yourself and others reminders of what the script's function is. Comment blocks enable the ability to provide details about the script, revision history, and execution parameters of the script.

Whether you are new to PowerShell scripting or you have been scripting for a long time, this book provides thought-inspiring methods to improve your scripting abilities. As you work through this book, it's strongly encouraged to incorporate these examples in your own scripts. This applied learning methodology will significantly help in your retention of the content, and provide a very robust enterprise scripting platform.

Summary

In this chapter, you explored the different components that will be implemented in the Windows server scanning script. You continued to learn about the different performance optimizations that you will be implementing in the book. Finally, you reviewed the individual components that should be included in most of your PowerShell Scripts.

In the next chapter, you will begin your journey by learning script structure, comment blocks, and script logging techniques.

2
Script Structure, Comment Blocks, and Script Logging

The Windows server scanning script requires three core components to make the script suitable for enterprise environments. These components include developing a strict scripting structure, creating the comment block, and developing a flexible logging solution. Strict scripting structures ensure that all your scripts are created in the same order. This means that each section of the code is defined in the same place in all your scripts. A uniform structure helps others understand your code quickly and enables them to follow a standardized format for changes.

You will also learn how to create a comment block at the beginning of the script. The comment block ensures that you fully document the purpose, the requirements, the bug fixes, and change history for the script. It also provides details on how to execute the script leveraging command line parameters.

The final core component discussed in this chapter is logging mechanisms. Logging mechanisms provide the ability to record information about what is being performed during the execution of the script. This information is typically written to log files, event logs, and data collection files.

In this chapter, you will:

- Learn the overall structure of a PowerShell Script
- Create a comment block to describe the script's function
- Develop a logging platform for your scripts

 The examples in this chapter build upon each other. You will need to execute the script sequentially to have the final script in this chapter work properly.

Overall script structure

When you are creating scripts, you should adhere to a strict script structure. The structure of the script dictates the order of execution and how things are processed. The following diagram displays the proper method for organizing your script:

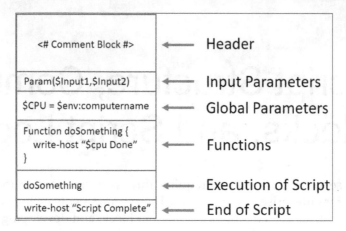

It is recommended that you structure your scripts as follows:

1. **Declare the comment block**: To start the scripting process, declare a comment block and include everything that is pertinent to the script. This may include a description, revision information, author, editor, and additional notes.

2. **Declare the input parameters**: After the header, declare your input parameters, if required by the script. The input parameters are required to be directly after the comment block. Input parameters help the developers identify what is being inputted into the script, and what fields are required for proper execution of the script.

3. **Declare the global variables**: You should declare your global variables after the input parameters. Since variables declared in a function only stay within the boundary of the function, the variables you need to use globally should be defined here.

4. **Declare the functions in order**: The next portion of the structure is declaring your functions. If you have functions that call each other, you will want to declare the functions that are needed first in the script. This ensures that your scripts will not error out due to the function not being declared prior to execution.

5. **Start the execution of the script**: After declaring the functions, you can start the execution of the script. This section will call the other functions used by the global variables, and parameters to complete the tasks for the script.

6. **Declare the end of the script**: After execution, it is recommended that you create an indicator that specifies that the script has run successfully. Whether it is a logging of exit codes to a file or pausing the script at the end, it is important for you to create logic to declare proper or improper execution of your script.

Comment blocks

The first recommendation is to create comment blocks for detailed tracking information about the PowerShell script itself. Comment blocks can track information about the script's creation, authors, changes, and other useful information that will enable you to quickly determine what the script is doing. PowerShell has built-in comment block support which integrates with the get-help cmdlet.

The required components include the following:

1. **Comment block location**: The comment block must be the first item defined at the top of your script. If you use parameter blocks, you specify the parameter blocks after the comment block.

2. **Start comment block**: In order to integrate with the help system, you need to specify the starting of the comment block. To start a comment block, you type <#.

3. .SYNOPSIS: To create a synopsis for the script, type .SYNOPSIS on a line, and then on a subsequent line type a one-line description of why the script is being created.

4. .DESCRIPTION: To create a full description for the script, type .DESCRIPTION on a line, and then on a subsequent line type a description of the script's functions so that any editor of the script will know the script's basic function. If it is a complicated script or a script that invokes other scripts, describe the overall process for it. You may also want to include author information that contains the author's name, author's position, author's company, contact information, initial release number, and date of the initial release.

5. .PARAMETER: To provide parameter information that can be used while running the script, you can type .PARAMETER, and specify the parameter name. On a subsequent line, type a description of that parameter. If you have multiple parameters, you can define multiple .PARAMETER statements referencing parameter names.

6. `.EXAMPLE`: To provide an example of usage for your script, you can type `.EXAMPLE` and provide an example on how to run the script from a command line. If you have multiple examples, you can define multiple `.EXAMPLE` statements.

7. `.NOTES`: To provide notes for execution caveats, you can type `.NOTES`, and on a subsequent line type a usage note to execute the script.

8. `.LINK`: If you have other help topics you want to link to, you can type `.LINK`, and on a subsequent line provide a URL to another help topic.

9. `Ending comment block`: In order to integrate with the help system, you need to specify the ending of the comment block. To end a comment block, you type #>.

The following screenshot displays a proper comment block that will integrate with the help system:

```
<#
.SYNOPSIS
This is a server discovery script which will scan different server components to determine
the current configuration.

.DESCRIPTION
This script will scan processes, Windows services, scheduled tasks, server features, disk information,
registry, and files for pertinent server information.

Author: Brenton J.W. Blawat / Packt Publishing / Author / email@email.com
Revision: 2.1a - Initial Release of Script / 6-22-2018
Revision: 2.5 - Paul Brandes / Company XYZ / Consultant / email@company.com / 11-21-2018
R2.5 details: Updated script to support systems still running PowerShell 2.0.

.PARAMETER SDD
This script requires a server side decryptor as a parameter to the script.

.EXAMPLE
powershellscript.ps1 /SDD "ServerSideDecryptor"

.NOTES
You must have administrative rights to the server you are scanning. Certain functions will not work properly
without running the script as system or administrator.
#>
```

This properly shows the syntax of a comment block that is usable via the PowerShell help system. You start by first defining the commend block with `<#`. You then create a `.SYNOPSIS` section with a synopsis of the script. Then you create a `.DESCRIPTION` section and provide a detailed description of the script. You also provide details regarding the author, revision, and editing revisions to the script. Following that section, you define a `.PARAMETER PATH` section, which provides detailed information about the `.PARAMETER PATH` in the script. Next, you create an `.EXAMPLE` section, to provide an example for usage, and you create a `.NOTES` section to provide information about the required execution environment. You then close the comment block by issuing #>.

Script logging

As you create your enterprise script template, you will need to incorporate a logging mechanism. Logging allows you to capture script output, including informational, warning, and error messages. In typical logging scenarios, you will need to record script actions to either the event log, a `log` file, or a data collection file, like a **Comma Separated Values** (**CSV**) file. While PowerShell has a transcript which you can invoke, leveraging the start-transcript and stop-transcript cmdlets, it only allows you to record output to a single `log` file. This doesn't provide for writing to the event log or data collection files.

A popular logging mechanism is to create your own PowerShell logging function. This enables you to pass in parameters into the `logging` function to tell the script to either write to the event log, `log` file, or append data to the data collection file. It can also write the actions to the PowerShell window to view progress. This avoids having to write multiple lines of code each time you want something to be displayed in either the event log, `log` file, or the data collection file. You just need to call the `logging` function and pass in the required parameters, and it will write to the locations you specify.

Creating the logging files

To start, you will need to create the files for logging. Enterprises typically include both the server name and a date timestamp for log files. This allows for a clear identity of log files and execution times in large environments.

To create a time-stamped `log` file, you can perform the following:

```
$date = (Get-Date -format "yyyyMMddmmss")
$compname = $env:COMPUTERNAME
$logname = $compname + "_" + $date + "_ServerScanScript.log"
$scanlog = "c:\temp\logs\" + $logname
new-item -path $scanlog -ItemType File -Force
```

The output of creating the `log` file is shown in the following screenshot:

```
PS C:\> $date = (Get-Date -format "yyyyMMddmmss")
PS C:\> $compname = $env:COMPUTERNAME
PS C:\> $logname = $compname + "_" + $date + "_ServerScanScript.log"
PS C:\> $scanlog = "c:\temp\logs\" + $logname
PS C:\> new-item -path $scanlog -ItemType File -Force

    Directory: C:\temp\logs

Mode                LastWriteTime         Length Name
----                -------------         ------ ----
-a----        1/23/2017   11:54 PM             0 DESKTOP-VJ71805_201701235440_ServerScanScript.log
```

The preceding script displays how to create a .log file for script logging. To start, you leverage the Get-Date cmdlet with the -format parameter set to "yyyyMMddmmss" and place it into the $date variable. The $date variable will then have sequentially the four-digit year, two-digit month, two-digit day, two-digit minute, and two-digit seconds, from when the script was executed, contained in it. You then gather the computer name by leveraging the $env:COMPUTERNAME environment variable and placing the value into the $compname variable. You then combine the $compname variable with a plus symbol, an underscore for separation with a plus symbol, the date timestamp with a plus symbol, and log file name of "ServerScanScript. log", and store it in the $logname variable. You then create the full log path by specifying "c:\temp\logs\" with a plus symbol and the $logname directory and store it in the $scanlog variable. Finally, you leverage the new-item cmdlet with the -path parameter set to $scanlog, -ItemType set to File, and the -Force parameter. After execution, you will have a log file in c:\temp\logs\ with the filename of computername_datetimestamp_ServerScanScript.log.

To create a time-stamped data collection file in the format of a CSV file, you can perform the following:

```
$date = (Get-Date -format "yyyyMMddmmss")

$compname = $env:COMPUTERNAME

$logname = $compname + "_" + $date + "_ScanResults.csv"

$scanresults = "c:\temp\logs\" + $logname

new-item -path $scanresults -ItemType File -Force


# Add Content Headers to the CSV File

$csvheader = "ServerName, Classification, Other Data"

Add-Content -path $scanresults -Value $csvheader
```

The output of creating the CSV file is shown in the following screenshot:

```
PS C:\> $date = (Get-Date -format "yyyyMMddmmss")
PS C:\> $compname = $env:COMPUTERNAME
PS C:\> $logname = $compname + "_" + $date + "_ScanResults.csv"
PS C:\> $scanresults = "c:\temp\logs\" + $logname
PS C:\> new-item -path $scanresults -ItemType File -Force
    Directory: C:\temp\logs

Mode                LastWriteTime         Length Name
----                -------------         ------ ----
-a----        1/24/2017  12:23 AM              0 DESKTOP-VJ71805_201701242303_ScanResults.csv

PS C:\>
PS C:\> # Add Content Headers to the CSV File
PS C:\> $csvheader = "ServerName, Classification, Other Data"
PS C:\> Add-Content -path $scanresults -Value $csvheader
```

The preceding script displays how to create a data collection file in the format of a .csv file for script logging. To start, you leverage the Get-Date cmdlet with the -format parameter set to "yyyyMMddmmss" and place it into the $date variable. The $date variable will then have sequentially the four-digit year, two-digit month, two-digit day, two-digit minute, and two-digit seconds, from when the script was executed, contained in it. You then gather the computer name by leveraging the $env:COMPUTERNAME environment variable and placing the value into the $compname variable. You then combine the $compname variable with a plus symbol, an underscore for separation with a plus symbol, the date timestamp with a plus symbol, and log file name of _ScanResults.csv, and store it in the $logname variable. You then create the full log path by specifying "c:\temp\logs\" with a plus symbol and the $logname directory, and store it in the $scanresults variable. You will then leverage the new-item cmdlet with the -path parameter set to $scanlog, the -ItemType set to File, and the -Force parameter. After execution, you will have a .csv file in c:\temp\logs\ with the filename of computername_datetimestamp_ScanResults.csv.

Finally, to add the headers to the CSV file, you specify the header names separated by values as "ServerName, Classification, Other Data" and store it in the $csvheader variable. You then add the header to the CSV file by leveraging the Add-content cmdlet with the -path parameter set to $scanresults and the -value parameter set to $csvheader. The computername_datetimestamp_ScanResults.csv file will have the headers of ServerName, Classification, and Other Data.

When opening the CSV file in excel, it displays the headers as follows:

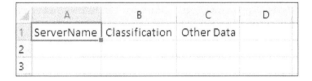

You may choose to optimize this code by not adding the computer name using the $compname variable. Alternatively, you can call the $env:COMPUTERNAME variable directly when setting the $logname variable. The script was written to display the progression of the log file string with the computer name, date timestamp, and script filename.

Creating a windows event log source

In the instance that you want to write to the Windows event log, one of the prerequisites is to register the script as an event source with the Windows event log system. This is done with the use of the New-EventLog cmdlet. You start by specifying the New-EventLog cmdlet, followed by the -LogName parameter followed by an event log name. You can either select your own event log or specify one of the built-in event logs, such as Application or system. Finally, you specify the -Source parameter with the name of the script you are executing.

You can only register the event log source once, which may lead to errors when executing a script multiple times on the same system. You can retrieve the event log sources by specifying the get-eventlog cmdlet with the -LogName parameter, and piping the results to Select-object Source -Unique. This is not very desirable as it requires the system to query all the log events to determine if a source is already registered. Since Windows systems have a large number of event logs and log events, the query is very CPU and memory intensive.

The fastest way to get around a duplicate event log source error message is to suppress the error message itself. This is done through leveraging the -ErrorAction parameter set to SilentlyContinue with the New-Eventlog cmdlet. The -ErrorAction parameter with SilentlyContinue specified will capture the error and silently continue with the script, suppressing the error messages.

To register a new event log source suppressing error messages, you can perform the following:

```
New-EventLog -LogName Application -Source "WindowsServerScanningScript"
-ErrorAction SilentlyContinue
```

The output of the PowerShell window will look like the following:

```
PS C:\> New-EventLog -LogName Application -Source "WindowsServerScanningScript" -ErrorAction SilentlyContinue
```

The preceding script displays how to register a new event log source with the Windows event log system. You first start by using the New-EventLog cmdlet with the -LogName parameter set to Application. You then specify the -Source argument and set it to the script name of "WindowsServerScanningScript". Finally, you suppress error messages by using the -ErrorAction argument and setting it to SilentlyContinue. After executing this command, you will be able to write to the Application event log with the event source of WindowsServerScanningScript.

When you create an event log source, it provides the ability to use that source for logging of messages. You need to write something to that event log source to have it appear in the Application event log.

The Windows event log cmdlets require that the PowerShell Window is Run as administrator. When testing this code, you will want to right-click the PowerShell icon and Run as administrator. If you are remotely executing this code, you may want to ensure the user credentials you are using have administrative rights to the system.

Creating the logging function

After creating the log files and registering the event log source, you are now able to create a custom logging function. The logging function will be flexible in that it can accept arguments for three types of data writes. These include event logs, log files, and the data collection .csv file.

The logging function is declared with functionlog {. You will then need to leverage a parameter block to accept arguments into the function. The parameter block is declared with param() and includes the variables $string, $scnlg, and $evntlg. $string will be the string value for the informational, warning, error, or data collection content. The $scnlg variable dictates if the content is written to the scan log file. The $evntlg variable dictates if the content is written to the event log.

To create the beginning of the logging function, type the following:

```
function log { param($string, $scnlg, $evntlg)
```

Using a variation of the arguments with the logging function, you can write log information to different locations. You can set the following:

- If $scnlg is set to Y and no value is specified for $evntlg, the script will only write to the scanning log file.

- If $scnlg is set to N and $evntlg is set to Y, the script will write only to the event log.

- If $scnlg is set to Y and $evntlg is set to Y, the script will write to both the scanning log file and the event log.

- If no parameters other than `$string` are passed into the function, it will write the contents to the data collection CSV file.
- In all cases, the `logging` function will leverage the `write-host` cmdlet with the contents of the `$string` variable. This will verbose print all the logging variations.

To create the full `logging` function, you can perform the following:

```
function log { param($string, $scnlg, $evntlg)
    # If Y is populated in the second position, add to log file.
    if ($scnlg -like "Y") {
        Add-content -path $scanlog -Value $string
    }
    # If Y is populated in the third position, Log Item to Event Log As
well
    if ($evntlg -like "Y") {
        write-eventlog -logname Application -source
"WindowsServerScanningScript" -eventID 1000 -entrytype Information
-message "$string"
    }
    # If there are no parameters specified, write to the data collection
file (CSV)
    if (!$scnlg) {
        $content = "$env:COMPUTERNAME,$string"
        Add-Content -path $scanresults -Value $content
    }
    # Verbose Logging
    write-host $string
}


$date = Get-Date
log "Starting WindowsServerScanningScript at $date ..." "Y" "Y"
log "Writing a message to the Event Log Only." "N" "Y"
log "ScriptStart,$date"
```

The output of this script will look like the following screenshot:

```
PS C:\> function log { param($string, $scnlg, $evntlg)
>>      # If Y is populated in the second position, add to log file.
>>      if ($scnlg -like "Y") {
>>          Add-content -path $scanlog -Value $string
>>      }
>>      # If Y is populated in the third position, Log Item to Event Log As well
>>      if ($evntlg -like "Y") {
>>          write-eventlog -logname Application -source "WindowsServerScanningScript" -eventID 1000 -entrytype Informatio
n -message "$string"
>>      }
>>      # If there are no parameters specified, write to the data collection file (CSV)
>>      if (!$scnlg) {
>>          $content = "$env:COMPUTERNAME,$string"
>>          Add-Content -path $scanresults -Value $content
>>      }
>>      # Verbose Logging
>>      write-host $string
>> }
PS C:\>
PS C:\> $date = (Get-Date -format "yyyyMMddmmss")
PS C:\> log "Starting WindowsServerScanningScript at $date ..." "Y" "Y"
Starting WindowsServerScanningScript at 201701242748 ...
PS C:\> log "Writing a message to the Event Log Only." "N" "Y"
Writing a message to the Event Log Only.
PS C:\> log "ScriptStart,$date"
ScriptStart,201701242748
```

This example displays how to create a `logging` function and log information to a `log` file, event log, and data collection CSV file. To start, you first declare `function log {`. You then accept three parameters into the function with the `param($string, $scnlg, $evntlg)` section of code. You then create an IF statement to determine if the `$scnlg` contents are `-like "Y"`. If it returns true, you then execute the `Add-content` cmdlet with the `-path` parameter set to `$scanlog`, and the `-Value` parameter set to `$string`. The contents of the string will now be in the `$scanlog` file.

The second IF statement evaluates if the `$evntlg` contents are `-like "Y"`. If it returns `True`, you then leverage the `write-eventlog` cmdlet with the `-logname` parameter set to `Application`. You also include the `-source` parameter set to `"WindowsServerScanningScript"`, the `-eventID` parameter set to the event ID number of 1000, the `-entrytype` parameter set to `Information`, and the `-message` attribute set to `$string`. The contents of the string will now be in the `Application` event log under the source of `WindowsServerScanningScript` and the event ID of 1000.

Some Enterprise environments have monitoring solutions that can parse the event log and trigger actions based on the event IDs. As an alternative to passing in a `"Y"`, you can pass in an event ID which can automatically trigger alerts with those monitoring systems. You would have to update the `if` statement to read `if ($evntlg) {}`, which will return `True` if data is contained in the variable. You can then set the `-eventID` parameter to `$evntlg` in the script, and you have the ability to change the event ID as needed.

The third `if` statement determines if there is any data in the `$scnlg` variable. This means the default action will be to write to the data collection CSV file. You leverage the `if` statement with an exclamation point preceding the `$scnlg` variable. This specifies `if NOT True`, or if there is not any data being passed in that variable, to proceed to the next steps. You then specify the environment variable of `$env:COMPUTERNAME`, followed by a comma, followed by the `$string` variable, and set the value in the `$content` variable. You then write the `$content` variable to the CSV file by leveraging the `Add-content` cmdlet with the `-path` parameter set to `$scanresults`, and the `-value` parameter set to `$content`.

The final step in the function is to display the content by using the `write-host` cmdlet with `$string` as the content.

To test the script, you then obtain the date timestamp by using the `Get-Date` cmdlet and setting the value in the `$date` variable. You then call the `log` function with the first argument of `"Starting WindowsServerScanningScript at $date"`, the second argument of `"Y"`, and the third argument of `"Y"`. This writes the content in the first argument to both the `log` file and the event log.

The following displays the contents of the created `log` file:

The following displays the contents of the event log generated by the script:

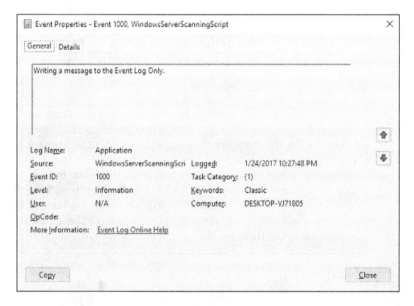

You then call the `log` function again with the first argument of `"Writing A Message to the Event Log Only."`, with the second argument of `"N"`, and the third argument set to `"Y"`. This writes to the `Application` log with the source of `WindowsServerScanningScript` and the Event ID of 1000.

The following displays the contents of the event log generated by the script:

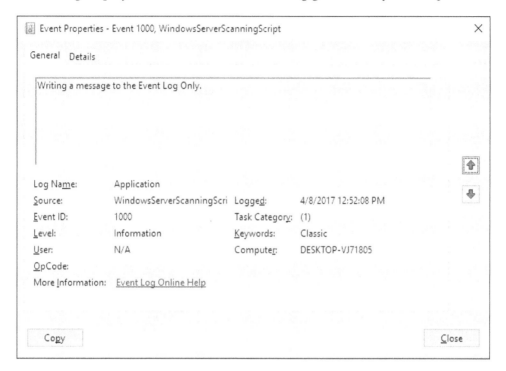

Finally, you call the `log` function with the first argument set to `"Script,$date"`. No other arguments are specified with this function. The script will then write to the data collection CSV file with the following syntax—`"computer name, ScriptStart, DateTimestamp"`.

The following displays the contents of the created data collection CSV file:

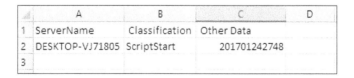

Summary

In this chapter, you successfully learned the three core components of the scripting template. The first component is defining a script structure. You learned of all the required locations for the individual scripting components. You then learned how to write a comment block and the proper documentation to include in the comment block itself. Finally, you learned how to create a logging mechanism for your scripts. You started by learning how to create a time-stamped `log` file, followed by learning how to create a data collection CSV file, and then how to create a new event log source. Finally, you put all the components together to create a function named `log`.

In the next chapter, you will explore answer files and exclusion lists for your scripts.

3

Working with Answer Files

As you continue developing the Windows server scanning script, you may run into scenarios where you need to modify your script to run in different environments. While it's fairly low risk to modify code in a one or two-line script, large enterprise scripts require a better structure and process. The general rule of thumb is that if you need to adjust values in your script for different scenarios, you should put those values into an answer file. The contents of the answer file are read during runtime, and those values are used as input into the script. This provides another layer of stability to your scripts because you're not adding risk by modifying code in the script itself.

There are many different formats for answer files. The industry standard with .NET programs are XML-based answer files. This is due to their ability to have file format integrity built into the standards for XML. If the answer file is not formatted properly, it will not be possible for it to be used by applications. PowerShell has built-in XML support to be able to create, read, modify, and utilize XML files, which makes it perfect for script answer files.

In this chapter, you will:

- Explore different ways you can leverage answer files
- Learn the structure of XML-based files
- Read the individual tags, attributes, and attribute values of XML-based answer files
- Create a function to pull different elements from the XML file, and store them in variables

 The examples in this chapter build upon each other. You will need to execute the script sequentially to have the examples in this chapter work properly.

Answer files

As you develop your enterprise scripting templates, you will find that you may need to modify small portions of code for running in different environments. For example, if you are using the same script in multiple non-trusted Active Directory forests, you most likely would have to store information about those respective forests in your script. This creates complexity as you would have to manage multiple scripts for multiple forests. Not only is this inefficient, but changing a validated script introduces a great amount of risk for scripting errors.

A common way to reduce this risk is to leverage answer files. Answer files are separate files that contain information you will use in your script. This allows you to modify parameters for your script, without having to touch the code in the script itself.

Some of the most common items to include in an answer file are:

- **Script logging location**: This defines where you want all your log files to be stored. This typically is locally to the system or a UNC path.

- **Data sources**: This defines the connection string information for connecting to different data source types. This could include server information, usernames, passwords, port numbers, and driver information.

- **Data output information**: This defines where you want the output from the script to be stored. This could be email server information, database information, or a UNC path to store files.

- **Encrypted data**: Any encrypted usernames, passwords, server names, security keys, and other secure data can be stored in the answer file. Since you can easily delete the answer file after execution within your script, this is a common place for this type of data.

- **Inclusion/Exclusion lists**: Inclusion and exclusion lists are lists of data that you want to use in your script. Typically, these lists are stored as an array or a regular expression.

- **Enable/Disable script features**: It is a common need for administrators to quickly turn on and off portions of a script. Instead of commenting out the code, you can leverage your answer file to quickly enable and disable blocks of code.

 It is strongly recommended to not use clear text usernames and passwords in your scripts or in your answer files. Since PowerShell scripts and answer files are written in human readable clear text, it is recommended to only leverage secure methods for storing credentials. This will be discussed in later chapters.

XML answer files

There are many different types of answer file formats used with scripting languages. Languages like .NET leverage `.config` formatted files for application configurations, while languages like Java leverage `.properties` formatted files for configuration data. While you can use **comma separated value** (**CSV**) files for answer files with PowerShell, it is highly recommended to use **eXtensible Markup Language** (**XML**) formatted files.

XML was created by the **World Wide Web Consortium** (**W3C**) to standardize the encoding of documents to make them both legible to humans and usable by computer systems. The XML format is very similar to **Hypertext Markup Language** (**HTML**). If you know the basics of HTML, you should be able to pick up XML rather quickly.

There are four main components to the syntax of XML files:

- **XML declaration**: The XML declaration is a mandatory line at the very beginning of the XML document itself. The declaration tells the XML parser what XML specification version to use and what encoding format (optional) to use.

- **XML comments**: Comments are data and are just like comments in PowerShell. They provide developers with information about each of the sections or individual items in an XML file.

- **XML tags**: As you build multiple tags in your XML files, you will need to follow the XML W3C **Document Object Model** (**DOM**) tree structure. In simple terms, the XML DOM tree structure consists of a parent, child, and siblings. The parent is a grouping tag which groups the child tags. If there are multiple child tags in the parent tag, the individual child tags are siblings.

- **XML attributes and elements**: There are two methods to define data about the individual XML tag. The first method is leveraging attributes and attribute values. An attribute is a unique name that describes an item related to the XML tag. The attribute value is whatever data you want stored for that attribute. The second method is to leverage elements, or inner XML data. This data is also associated with the tag. When the XML parser calls a tag in a script, the element is returned for use.

An example of an XML answer file would look like the following:

```
<?xml version="1.0"?>
<!-- XML Comment -->
<!-- XML Declaration -->


<!-- XML Parent Tag-->
<ScriptAnswers>

    <!-- XML Child Tag-->
    <ports port="21" name="FTP"></ports>

    <!-- XML Sibling Tags-->
    <ports port="25" name="SMTP"></ports>
    <ports port="53" name="DNS"></ports>
    <ports port="80" name="HTTP"></ports>
    <ports port="443" name="HTTPS"></ports>

<!-- XML Parent Closing Tag-->
</ScriptAnswers>
```

The preceding graphic displays a properly formatted XML answer file. The file opens by specifying the XML declaration. This has to be the first line in an XML file, or you will receive a syntax error. It opens with `<?xml` and with the attribute version set to the attribute value of `1.0`. The declaration then closes with `?>`. The script then displays the use of XML comments. The syntax for the comments opens with `<!--` followed by the comments, and closes with `-->`.

The answer file continues to declare a parent tag of `<ScriptAnswers>`. After the parent tag, a child tag of `<ports` is declared. This tag has the port attribute set to the attribute value of `21`, and the name attribute set to `FTP`. The tag is closed by declaring `</ports>`. The script continues with sibling tags of ports. It displays ports `25` for `SMTP`, `53` for `DNS`, `80` for `HTTP`, and `443` for `HTTPS`. Finally, the XML file closes with a parent closing tag of `</ScriptAnswers>`.

To complete the examples in this chapter, you will need to create a new XML file named `Answers.xml` in the location of `C:\Temp\POSHScript\`. Leveraging the text editor of your choice, insert the preceding data inside the `Answers.xml` file. The examples also build on each other, so you will want to execute this chapter sequentially, to ensure all the code samples work appropriately.

 You may also refer to this chapter's code file to quickly create the previously described content.

Reading XML answer files

PowerShell has the ability to natively read and parse the data in XML files. This is done by loading an XML file into an XML document object, leveraging the `get-content` cmdlet. You first start by defining a variable like `$xmlfile` with the data type set to `[xml]`. You then call the `get-content` cmdlet with the –path parameter set to the location of an XML file. If you omit the `[xml]` data type while defining the variable, it will interpret the file as a text file. This means that you will not be able to leverage any of the built-in XML support.

To load the XML answer file you created earlier, you can perform the following:

```
[xml] $xml = get-content "C:\temp\POSHScript\Answers.xml"
$xml
```

The output of this command will look as follows:

```
PS C:\> [xml] $xml = get-content "C:\temp\POSHScript\Answers.xml"
>> $xml

xml                 #comment                                    ScriptAnswers
---                 --------                                    -------------
version="1.0" { XML Comment ,  XML Declaration ,  XML Parent Tag} ScriptAnswers
```

This example displays how to properly obtain the contents of an XML file and place them into an XML formatted variable. The command starts by declaring the `[xml]` data type followed by the variable of `$xml`. You then leverage the `get-content` cmdlet and declare the content path of `"C:\temp\POSHScript\Answers.xml"` and contents are stored in the `$xml` variable. Finally, you call the `$xml` variable to display the XML formatted contents.

After retrieving the contents of the XML file, you will want to retrieve the individual XML tags to store the configuration information in memory for the script. The `.GetElementsByTagName("TagName")` method enables you to search the XML file for tags named with specific values. This will return the attributes and elements of an XML tag. In the instance that there are tags named the same, or the child tag has siblings, the method will return all values that equal the tag value specified in the method.

To retrieve the contents of an XML file and retrieve specific tag information, you can perform the following:

```
[xml] $xml = get-content "C:\temp\POSHScript\Answers.xml"
$ports = $xml.GetElementsByTagName("ports")
$ports | Select Name, Port
```

The output of this command will look as follows:

```
PS C:\> [xml] $xml = get-content "C:\temp\POSHScript\Answers.xml"
PS C:\> $ports = $xml.GetElementsByTagName("ports")
PS C:\> $ports | Select Name, Port

name   port
----   ----
FTP    21
SMTP   25
DNS    53
HTTP   80
HTTPS  443
```

This example displays how to obtain the contents of an XML file, place it into an XML formatted variable, and retrieve data by XML tag names. The command starts by declaring the `[xml]` data type followed by the variable of `$xml`. You then leverage the `get-content` cmdlet and declare the content path of `"C:\temp\POSHScript\Answers.xml"` and contents are stored in the `$xml` variable.

You then leverage the `.GetElementsByTagName()` method on the `$xml` variable with the `"ports"` argument to obtain the XML tags named `"ports"`. After this command is executed, you will have the child and sibling information that matches the tag name of `"ports"` in the `$ports` variable. You then pipe `$ports` to `Select Name, Port`, which will display the attribute values for the attributes `Name` and `Port`.

 Once you call the `get-content` cmdlet and place the XML data into a variable, you are no longer working with the data contained in the XML file. You will be working with an in-memory copy of the XML file. If you change any of the contents in the XML file, you will need to re-run the `get-content` cmdlet to have an updated copy in memory.

XML also supports dot notation for retrieving XML tag data. Using dot notation, you can retrieve all the parent, child, and sibling tags simply by calling the tag names and attributes, separated by a period. For the previous example, you could call `$ports.Name` to return FTP, SMTP, DNS, HTTP, and HTTPS. You can also reference the `$xml` content directly and specify `$xml.ScriptAnswers.Ports.Name` to return FTP, SMTP, DNS, HTTP, and HTTPS.

Using dot notation to view the port names, you can type the following:

$ports.Name

$xml.ScriptAnswers.Ports.Name

The output of this command would look like the following:

```
PS C:\> $ports.Name
FTP
SMTP
DNS
HTTP
HTTPS
PS C:\> $xml.ScriptAnswers.Ports.Name
FTP
SMTP
DNS
HTTP
HTTPS
```

The preceding example displays how to leverage dot notation in PowerShell to view different attributes in XML content. The first example leverages the $ports variable referencing the Name attribute using dot notation. This returned FTP, SMTP, DNS, HTTP, and HTTPS. The second example displays using the top-level XML content to reference child and sibling attributes. This is done by using dot notation between the $xml content, the parent ScriptAnswers, the child of Ports, and the attribute of Name. This returned FTP, SMTP, DNS, HTTP, and HTTPS.

XML tag function

As you start building more complex scripts, you will likely add more tags into your answer files. You can leverage the .GetElementsByTagName() method with the argument of the tag names to gather additional data from the answer file. This enables you to call each of the tags individually and store the contents into a variable.

When you leverage the .GetElementsByTagName() method, it only reads the data once and stores the data in the variable. This means that if the XML file changes, the data will not automatically update in the variable. You will need to call the method a second time to gather an updated copy of the data in the XML file.

Alternatively, you may also choose to create a function to read the individual XML tags. This function can refresh the XML content in memory each time it is called. This enables the function to be called in multiple parts of the script, and to always have the current XML data.

Consider the following answer file (`Scan_Answers.xml`) for use with the XML tag function:

```xml
<?xml version="1.0"?>

<ScriptAnswers>

  <!-- This section enables and disables features in the script -->
  <!-- To Enable Logging For Each Step, Set To True. To Disable Logging, Set to False -->
  <verboselog id="False"></verboselog>
  <!-- Scan Disks -->
  <scndisks id="True"></scndisks>
  <!-- Scan Scheduled Tasks -->
  <scnschtsks id="True"></scnschtsks>
  <!-- Scan Processes -->
  <scnproc id="True"></scnproc>
  <!-- Scan Services -->
  <scnsvcs id="True"></scnsvcs>
  <!-- Scan Software -->
  <scnsoft id="True"></scnsoft>
  <!-- Scan User Profiles -->
  <scnuprof id="True"></scnuprof>
  <!-- Scan Windows Features -->
  <scnwfeat id="True"></scnwfeat>
  <!-- Scan Files -->
  <scnfls id="True"></scnfls>
  <!-- Scan Windows Updates -->
  <scnwupd id="True"></scnwupd>

</ScriptAnswers>
```

The preceding XML file and data will be used in the remainder of this chapter. To complete the examples in this chapter, you will need to create a new XML file named `Scan_Answers.xml` in the location of `c:\Temp\POSHScript\`. Leveraging the text editor of your choice, insert the previous data inside the `Scan_Answers.xml` file.

 You may also refer to this chapter's code file to quickly create the earlier described content.

To create an XML `tag` reading function, you can do the following:

```powershell
# Answer File Location
$xmlfile = "c:\temp\POSHScript\Scan_Answers.xml"
Function read-xmltag { param($xmlanswers, $xmlextract)
    # Validate that the XML file still exists
    $test = test-path $xmlanswers
    if (!$test) {
        Write-Error "$xmlanswers not found on the system. Select any key to exit!"
        # Stop the Script for reading the Error Message
        PAUSE
```

```
        # Exit the Script

        exit

    }
    # Read XML Data

    [xml] $xml = (get-content $xmlanswers)

    return $xml.GetElementsByTagName("$xmlextract")

}
# Determine Features of Script

$logging = (read-xmltag $xmlfile "verboselog").id

$scanDisks = (read-xmltag $xmlfile "scndisks").id

$scanSchTasks = (read-xmltag $xmlfile "scnschtsks").id

$scanProcess = (read-xmltag $xmlfile "scnproc").id

$scanServices = (read-xmltag $xmlfile "scnsvcs").id

$scanSoftware = (read-xmltag $xmlfile "scnsoft").id

$scanProfiles = (read-xmltag $xmlfile "scnuprof").id

$scanFeatures = (read-xmltag $xmlfile "scnwfeat").id

$scanFiles = (read-xmltag $xmlfile "scnfls").id

$scanWinUpdates = (read-xmltag $xmlfile "scnwupd").id

#Display Features

Write-host "Script Scanning Settings: Verbose Logging: $logging
| Scan Disks: $scanDisks | Scan Scheduled Tasks: $scanSchTasks |
Scan Processes: $scanProcess | Scan Services: $scanServices | Scan
Software: $scanSoftware | Scan Profiles: $scanProfiles | Scan Features:
$scanFeatures | Scan Files: $scanFiles | Scan Windows Updates:
$scanWinUpdates"

# Intentional Wrong Answer File Path to Display Error

read-xmltag "C:\Temp\POSHScript\DOES_NOT_EXIST.xml" "scndisks"
```

The output of this script would look like the following:

This example displays how to properly create an XML `reading` function that will read the XML file each time it is called. It also shows how to display the gathered XML data in the script. The script completes by displaying error handling for missing XML answer files.

To start, you define the XML file location by setting the `$xmlfile` variable to `c:\temp\POSHScript\Scan_Answers.xml`. You then continue to declare the new function by stating the function `read-xmltag {`. Since you will be providing the XML file location and the tag names as you call the function, you create a parameter block by declaring `param($xmlanswers, $xmlextract)`. When used, `$xmlanswers` will contain a filename and `$xmlextract` will contain an XML tag name.

You continue to leverage the `test-path` cmdlet to determine if the file declared in `$xmlanswers` exists on the system and set the value to `$test`. You then create the statement `if (!$test) {`, or if not true, use the `Write-error` cmdlet to throw an error of `$xmlanswers` not found on the system. Select any key to exit! You then execute the command `PAUSE`, to pause the script and provide an opportunity for a user to read the error message. You then provide the command `exit` to close the PowerShell script. This is done to ensure that if the answer file is not present, the script will not function properly.

If `$test` is equal to true, or the answer file exists, you continue to read the data in the answer file. You leverage the `get-content` cmdlet with the argument of `$xmlanswers` to store the content in the variable of `$xml`, which has a forced data type of `[xml]`. Finally, you leverage the `$xml.GetElementsByTagName()` method with the `$xmlextract` argument to gather the tag information. Instead of storing the result in a variable, you leverage `return`, which returns the values back to the original calling function. By executing this function, you've effectively passed parameters into the function, manipulated data, and returned a result back to the script for future use.

You then continue to store the script setting data, from the XML answer file, in individual variables. You start by declaring a variable and executing the `read-xmltag` function with the first argument of `$xmlfile`, and the second argument of the XML tag you want to extract from the `answer` file. When the function executes, it returns all the tag elements, including attributes and attribute values. Since you only want the attribute data of the `id` attribute, you use parentheses around the `read-xmltag` statement and use dot notation specifying `id`. The `Settings` variable will now contain the setting information from the XML `answer` file. This is repeated a number of times until you have all the settings from the XML `answer` file in variables.

You then leverage the `write-host` cmdlet to display the different setting values from the XML file. When you execute the commands, the script returns `Script Scanning Settings: Verbose Logging: False | Scan Disks: True | Scan Scheduled Tasks: True | Scan Processes: True | Scan Services: True | Scan Software: True | Scan Profiles: True | Scan Features: True | Scan Files: True | Scan Windows Updates: True`.

The very last command used in the script specifies an invalid XML answer file of
"C:\temp\POSHScript\DOES_NOT_EXIST.xml". Since this is an invalid file, the
script throws an error message of read-xmltag: C:\Temp\POSHScripts\DOES_NOT_
EXIST.xml not found on system. Select any key to exit! When you press any key on
the keyboard, the script exits.

> In certain instances, PowerShell 2.0 may not be able to use dot
> notation. To work around this issue, you can use the same
> function call but instead of the dot notation of .id, you can pipe
> the result to Select id instead.

Summary

In this chapter, you learned the basics of answer files and why they are used in
combination with scripts. You learned the structure of XML and how to create
XML-based answer files. You continued to explore how to read tag data from the
files. You then created a function named read-xmltag that reads the tag data from
answer file. Finally, you learned how to store the XML answer file data in variables
for use later in the script. In the next chapter, you will learn about string encryption
and decryption leveraging RijndaelManaged 256-bit encryption.

4
String Encryption and Decryption

Large enterprises often have very strict security standards that are required by industry-specific regulations. When you are creating your Windows server scanning script, you will need to approach the script carefully with certain security concepts in mind. One of the most common situations you may encounter is the need to leverage sensitive data, such as credentials, in your script. While you could prompt for sensitive data during runtime, most enterprises want to automate the full script using zero-touch automation.

Zero-touch automation requires that the scripts are self-contained and have all of the required credentials and components to successfully run. The problem with incorporating sensitive data in the script, however, is that data can be obtained in clear text. The usage of clear text passwords in scripts is a bad practice, and violates many regulatory and security standards.

As a result, PowerShell scripters need a method to securely store and retrieve sensitive data for use in their scripts. One popular method to secure sensitive data is to encrypt the sensitive strings. This chapter explores RijndaelManaged symmetric encryption, and how to use it to encrypt and decrypt strings using PowerShell.

In this chapter, we will cover the following topics:

- Learn about RijndaelManaged symmetric encryption
- Understand salt, init, and password for the encryption algorithm
- Script a method to create randomized salt, init, and password values
- Encrypt and decrypt strings using RijndaelManaged encryption
- Create an encoding and data separation security mechanism for encryption passwords

The examples in this chapter build upon each other. You will need to execute the scripts sequentially to have the final script in this chapter work properly.

RijndaelManaged encryption

When you are creating your scripts, it is best practice to leverage some sort of obfuscation or encryption for sensitive data. There are many different strategies that you can use to secure your data. One is leveraging string and script encoding. Encoding takes your human readable string or script, and scrambles it to make it more difficult for someone to see what the actual code is. The downsides of encoding are that you must decode the script to make changes to it and decoding does not require the use of a password or passphrase. Thus, someone can easily decode your sensitive data using the same method you would use to decode the script.

The alternative to encoding is leveraging an encryption algorithm. Encryption algorithms provide multiple mechanisms to secure your scripts and strings. While you can encrypt your entire script, it's most common to encrypt the sensitive data in the scripts themselves, or answer files.

One of the most popular encryption algorithms used with PowerShell is RijndaelManaged. RijndaelManaged is a symmetric block cipher algorithm, which was selected by **United States National Institute of Standards and Technology (NIST)** for its implementation of **Advanced Encryption Standard (AES)**. When using RijndaelManaged for the AES standard, it supports 128-bit, 192-bit, and 256-bit encryption.

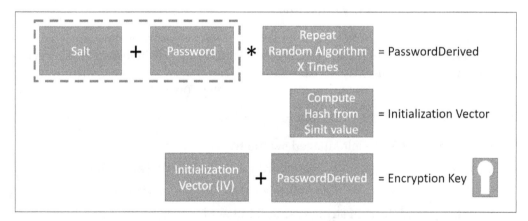

In contrast to encoding, encryption algorithms require additional information to properly encrypt and decrypt the string. When implementing RijndaelManaged in PowerShell, the algorithm requires **salt**, a **password**, and the **InitializationVector (IV)**. **Salt** is typically a randomized value that changes each time you leverage the encryption algorithm. The purpose of **salt** in a traditional encryption scenario is to change the encrypted value each time the encryption function is used. This is important in scenarios where you are encrypting multiple passwords or strings with the same value. If two users are using the same password, the encryption value in the database would also be the same. By changing the **salt** each time, the passwords, though the same value, would have different encrypted values in the database. In this chapter, we will be leveraging a static salt value.

The **password** typically is a value that is manually entered by a user, or fed into the script using a parameter block. You can also derive the password value from a certificate, Active Directory attribute values, or a multitude of other sources. In this chapter, we will be leveraging three sources for the password.

The **InitializationVector (IV)** is a hash generated from the IV string and is used for the **EncryptionKey**. The IV string is also typically a randomized value that changes each time you leverage the encryption algorithm. The purpose of the IV string is to strengthen the hash created by the encryption algorithm. This was created to thwart a hacker who is leveraging a rainbow attack using precalculated hash tables using no IV strings, or commonly used strings. Since you are setting the IV string, the number of hash combinations exponentially increases and it reduces the effectiveness of a rainbow attack. In this chapter, we will be using a static initialization vector value.

The implementation of randomization of the salt and initialization vector strings becomes more important in scenarios where you are encrypting a large set of data. An attacker can intercept hundreds of thousands of packets, or strings, which reveals an increasing amount of information about your IV. With this, the attacker can guess the IV and derive the password.

 The most notable hack of IVs were with **WiredEquivalentPrivacy (WEP)** wireless protocol that used a weak, or small, initialization vector. After capturing enough packets, an IV hash could be guessed and a hacker could easily obtain the passphrase used on the wireless network.

Creating random salt, initialization vector, and passwords

As you are creating your scripts, you will want to make sure you use complex random values for the salt, IV string, and password. This is to prevent dictionary attacks where an individual may use common passwords and phrases to guess the salt, IV string, and password. When you create your salt and IVs, make sure they are a minimum of 10 random characters each. It is also recommended that you use a minimum of 30 random characters for the password.

To create random passwords in PowerShell, you can do the following:

```
Function create-password {
    # Declare password variable outside of loop.
    $password = ""
    # For numbers between 33 and 126
    For ($a=33;$a -le 126;$a++) {
        # Add the Ascii text for the ascii number referenced.
        $ascii += , [char] [byte] $a
    }
    # Generate a random character form the $ascii character set.
    # Repeat 30 times, or create 30 random characters.
1..30 | ForEach { $password += $ascii | get-random }


    # Return the password
return $password
}
# Create four 30 character passwords
create-password
create-password
create-password
create-password
```

The output of this command would look like the following:

```
PS C:\> Function create-passwor i
>>>
>>>     # Declare password variable outside of loop.
>>>     $password = ""
>>>
>>>     # For numbers between 33 and 126
>>>     For ($a=33;$a -le 126;$a++) {
>>>         # Add the Ascii text for the ascii number referenced.
>>>         $ascii += ,[char][byte]$a
>>>     }
>>>     # Generate a random character form the $ascii character set.
>>>     # Repeat 30 times, or create 30 random characters.
>>>     1..30 | ForEach { $password += $ascii | get-random }
>>>
>>>     # Return the password
>>>     return $password
>>> }
PS C:\> # Create four 30 character passwords
PS C:\> create-password
WZqru/jfhLKz1)8r'Y;pG#qH,'2vX[
PS C:\> create-password
!s?`LUU\[5dA"'[kPQMR&NpvP[i&sF
PS C:\> create-password
uRb?,&KG%~U>+L?2H!RL@nArw!'Fo\
PS C:\> create-password
mz6_;Vqp?WuoVQ|t4;HG,XiYrWi?Bz
```

This function will create a string with 30 random characters for use with random password creation. You first start by declaring the create-password function. You then declare the $password variable for use within the function by setting it equal to "".

The next step is creating a For command to loop through a set of numbers. These numbers represent ASCII character numbers that you can select from for the password. You then create the For command by writing For ($a=33; $a -le 126;$a++). This means starting at the number 33, increasing the value by one ($a++), and continuing until the number is less than or equal to 126. You then declare the $ascii variable and construct the variable using the += assignment operator. As the For loop goes through its iterations, it adds a character to the array values. The script then leverages the [char] or character value of the [byte] number contained in $a. After this section, the $ascii array will contain an array of all the ASCII characters with the byte values between 33 and 126.

You then continue to the random character generation. You declare the 1..30 command, which means, for numbers 1 to 30, repeat the following command. You pipe this to ForEach {, which will designate for each of the 30 iterations. You then call the $ascii array and pipe it to | get-random cmdlet. The get-random cmdlet will randomly select one of the characters in the $ascii array. This value is then joined to the existing values in the $password string using the assignment operator +=. After the 30 iterations, there will be 30 random values in the $password variable. Lastly, you leverage return $password, to return this value to the script. After declaring the function, you call the function four times using create-password. This creates four random passwords for use.

To create strings that are less than 30 random characters in length, you can modify the 1..30 to be any value that you want. If you want 15 random character Salts and Initialization Vectors, you use 1..15 instead.

Encrypting and decrypting strings

To start using RijndaelManaged encryption, you need to import the .NET System. Security Assembly into your script. Much like importing a module to provide additional cmdlets, using .NET assemblies provide an extension to a variety of classes you wouldn't normally have access to in PowerShell. Importing the assembly isn't persistent. This means you will need to import the assembly each time you want to use it in a PowerShell session, or each time you want to run the script.

To load the .NET assembly, you can use the Add-Type cmdlet with the -AssemblyName parameter with the System.Security argument. Since the cmdlet doesn't actually output anything to the screen, you may choose to print to the screen after successful importing of the assembly.

To import the System.Security Assembly with display information, you can do the following:

```
Write-host "Loading the .NET System.Security Assembly For Encryption"
Add-Type -AssemblyNameSystem.Security -ErrorActionSilentlyContinue
-ErrorVariable err
if ($err) {
Write-host "Error Importing the .NET System.Security Assembly."
    PAUSE
    EXIT
}
```

```
# if err is not set, it was successful.

if (!$err) {

    Write-host "Succesfully loaded the .NET System.Security Assembly For
Encryption"

}
```

The output from this command looks like the following:

```
PS C:\> Write-host "Loading the .NET System.Security Assembly For Encryption"
Loading the .NET System.Security Assembly For Encryption
PS C:\> Add-Type -AssemblyName System.Security -ErrorAction SilentlyContinue -ErrorVariable err
PS C:\> if ($err) {
>>>     Write-host "Error Importing the .NET System.Security Assembly."
>>>     PAUSE
>>>     EXIT
>>> }
PS C:\> # if err is not set, it was successful.
PS C:\> if (!$err) {
>>>     Write-host "Succesfully loaded the .NET System.Security Assembly For Encryption"
>>> }
Succesfully loaded the .NET System.Security Assembly For Encrytion
```

In this example, you successfully import the `.NET System.Security Assembly` for use with PowerShell. You first start by writing "Loading the .NET System.Security Assembly for Encryption" to the screen using the `Write-host` command. You then leverage the `Add-Type` cmdlet with the `-AssemblyName` parameter with the `System.Security` argument, the `-ErrorAction` parameter with the `SilentlyContinue` argument, and the `-ErrorVariable` parameter with the `err` argument. You then create an `if` statement to see if `$err` contains data. If it does, it will use `Write-host` cmdlet to print "Error Importing the .NET System.Security Assembly." to the screen. It will PAUSE the script so the error can be read. Finally, it will exit the script. If `$err` is `$null`, designated by `if (!$err) {`, it will use the `Write-host` cmdlet to print "Successfully loaded the .NET System.Security Assembly for Encryption" to the screen. At this point, the script or PowerShell window is ready to leverage `System.Security Assembly`.

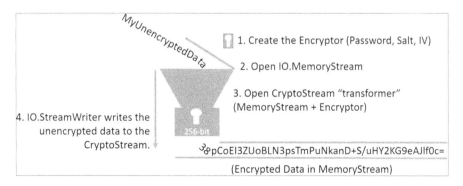

After you load `System.Security Assembly`, you can start creating the encryption function. RijndaelManaged encryption requires a four-step process to encrypt the strings, which is represented in the preceeding diagram.

The RijndaelManaged encryption process is as follows:

1. The process starts by creating the **encryptor**. The **encryptor** is derived from the encryption key (**password** and **salt**) and initialization vector.

2. After you define the **encryptor**, you will need to create a new memory stream using the `IO.MemoryStream` object. A memory stream is what stores values in memory for use by the encryption assembly.

3. Once the memory stream is open, you define a `System.Security.Cryptography.CryptoStream` object. The `CryptoStream` is the mechanism that uses the memory stream and the **encryptor** to transform the unencrypted data to encrypted data. In order to leverage the `CryptoStream`, you need to write data to the `CryptoStream`.

4. The final step is to use the `IO.StreamWriter` object to write the unencrypted value into the `CryptoStream`. The output from this transformation is placed into `MemoryStream`. To access the encrypted value, you read the data in the memory stream.

 To learn more about the `System.Security.Cryptography.RijndaelManaged` class, you can view the following MSDN article: `https://msdn.microsoft.com/en-us/library/system.security.cryptography.rijndaelmanaged(v=vs.110).aspx`.

To create a script that encrypts strings using RijndaelManaged encryption, perform the following:

```
Add-Type -AssemblyNameSystem.Security
function Encrypt-String { param($String, $Pass,
$salt="CreateAUniqueSalt", $init="CreateAUniqueInit")
try{
        $r = new-Object System.Security.Cryptography.RijndaelManaged
    $pass = [Text.Encoding]::UTF8.GetBytes($pass)
        $salt = [Text.Encoding]::UTF8.GetBytes($salt)
        $init = [Text.Encoding]::UTF8.GetBytes($init)
```

```
        $r.Key = (new-Object Security.Cryptography.PasswordDeriveBytes
$pass, $salt, "SHA1", 50000).GetBytes(32)
        $r.IV = (new-Object Security.Cryptography.SHA1Managed).
ComputeHash($init)[0..15]


        $c = $r.CreateEncryptor()
        $ms = new-Object IO.MemoryStream
        $cs = new-Object Security.Cryptography.CryptoStream
$ms,$c,"Write"
        $sw = new-Object IO.StreamWriter $cs
        $sw.Write($String)
        $sw.Close()
        $cs.Close()
        $ms.Close()
        $r.Clear()
        [byte[]]$result = $ms.ToArray()
    }
catch {
        $err = "Error Occurred Encrypting String: $_"
    }
if($err) {
        # Report Back Error
return $err
    }
else {
return [Convert]::ToBase64String($result)
    }
}
Encrypt-String "Encrypt This String""A_Complex_Password_With_A_Lot_Of_
Characters"
```

The output of this script would look like the following:

```
PS C:\> Add-Type -AssemblyName System.Security
PS C:\> function Encrypt-String { param($String, $Pass, $salt="CreateAUniqueSalt", $init="CreateAUniqueInit")
>>     try{
>>         $r = new-Object System.Security.Cryptography.RijndaelManaged
>>         $pass = [Text.Encoding]::UTF8.GetBytes($pass)
>>         $salt = [Text.Encoding]::UTF8.GetBytes($salt)
>>         $init = [Text.Encoding]::UTF8.GetBytes($init)
>>
>>         $r.Key = (new-Object Security.Cryptography.PasswordDeriveBytes $pass, $salt, "SHA1", 50000).GetBytes(32)
>>         $r.IV = (new-Object Security.Cryptography.SHA1Managed).ComputeHash($init)[0..15]
>>
>>         $c = $r.CreateEncryptor()
>>         $ms = new-Object IO.MemoryStream
>>         $cs = new-Object Security.Cryptography.CryptoStream $ms,$c,"Write"
>>         $sw = new-Object IO.StreamWriter $cs
>>         $sw.Write($String)
>>         $sw.Close()
>>         $cs.Close()
>>         $ms.Close()
>>         $r.Clear()
>>         [byte[]]$result = $ms.ToArray()
>>     }
>>     catch {
>>         $err = "Error Occurred Encrypting String: $_"
>>     }
>>     if($err) {
>>         # Report Back Error
>>         return $err
>>     }
>>     else {
>>         return [Convert]::ToBase64String($result)
>>     }
>> }
PS C:\> Encrypt-String "Encrypt This String" "A_Complex_Password_With_A_Lot_Of_Characters"
1K7GHaDD1FxknHu03TYAPxbFAAZeJ6KTSH1nSCPpJ7c=
```

This function displays how to encrypt a string leveraging the RijndaelManaged encryption algorithm. You first start by importing the System.Security assembly by leveraging the Add-Type cmdlet, using the -AssemblyName parameter with the System.Security argument. You then declare the function of Encrypt-String. You include a parameter block to accept and set values into the function. The first value is $string, which is the unencrypted text. The second value is $pass, which is used for the encryption key. The third is a predefined $salt variable set to "CreateAUniqueSalt". You then define the $init variable, which is set to "CreateAUniqueInit".

After the parameter block, you declare try { to handle any errors in the .NET assembly. The first step is to declare the encryption class using the new-Object cmdlet with the System.Security.Cryptography.RijndaelManaged argument. You place this object inside the $r variable.

You then convert the $pass, $salt, and $init values to the character encoding standard of UTF8 and store the character byte values in a variable. This is done by specifying [Text.Encoding]::UTF8.GetBytes($pass) for the $pass variable, [Text.Encoding]::UTF8.GetBytes($salt) for the $salt variable, and [Text.Encoding]::UTF8.GetBytes($init) for the $init variable.

After setting the proper character encoding, you proceed to create the encryption key for the RijndalManaged encryption algorithm. This is done by setting the RijndaelManaged `$r.Key` attribute to the object created by `(new-Object Security.Cryptography.PasswordDeriveBytes $pass, $salt, "SHA1", 50000).GetBytes(32)`. This object leverages the `Security.Cryptography.PasswordDeriveBytes` class and creates a key using the `$pass` variable, `$salt` variable, `"SHA1"` hash name, and iterating the derivative `50000` times. Each iteration of this class generates a different key value, making it more complex to guess the key. You then leverage the `.Get-Bytes(32)` method to return the 32-byte value of the key.

 RijndaelManaged 256-bit encryption is a derivative of the 32 bytes in the key. 32 bytes times 8 bits per byte is 256 bits.

To create the initialization vector for the algorithm, you set the RijndaelManaged `$r.IV` attribute to the object created by `(new-Object Security.Cryptography.SHA1Managed).ComputeHash($init)[0..15]`. This section of the code leverages `Security.Cryptography.SHA1Managed` and computes the hash based on the `$init` value. When you invoke the `[0..15]` range operator, it will obtain the first 16 bytes of the hash and place them into the `$r.IV` attribute.

 The RijndaelManaged default block size for the initialization vector is 128 bits. 16 bytes times 8 bits per byte is 128bits.

After setting up the required attributes, you are now ready to start encrypting data. You first start by leveraging the `$r` RijndaelManaged object with the `$r.Key` and `$r.IV` attributes defined. You use the `$r.CreateEncryptor()` method to generate the encryptor.

Once you've generated the encryptor, you have to create a memory stream to do the encryption in memory. This is done by declaring the `new-Object` cmdlet, set to the `IO.MemoryStream` class, and placing the memory stream object in the `$ms` variable.

Next, you create `CryptoStream`. `CryptoStream` is used to transform the unencrypted data into the encrypted data. You first declare the `new-Object` cmdlet with the `Security.Cryptopgraphy.CryptoStream` argument. You also define the memory stream of `$ms`, the encryptor of `$c`, and the operator of `"Write"` to tell the class to write unencrypted data to the encryption stream in memory.

After creating `CryptoStream`, you are ready to write the unencrypted data into `CryptoStream`. This is done using the `IO.StreamWriter` class. You declare a new-Object cmdlet with the `IO.StreamWriter` argument, and define `CryptoStream` of `$cs` for writing.

Last, you take the unencrypted string stored in the `$string` variable, and pass it into the `StreamWriter$sw` with `$sw.Write($String)`. The encrypted value is now stored in the memory stream. To stop the writing of data to the `CryptoStream` and `MemoryStream`, you close the `StreamWriter` with `$sw.Close()`, close the `CryptoStream` with `$cs.Close()` and the memory stream with `$ms.Close()`. For security purposes, you also clear out the encryptor data by declaring `$r.Clear()`.

After the encryption process is done, you will need to export the memory stream to a byte array. This is done by calling the `$ms.ToArray()` method and setting it to the `$result` variable with the `[byte[]]` data type. The contents are stored in a byte array in `$result`.

This section of the code is where you declare your `catch {` statement. If there were any errors in the encryption process, the script will execute this section. You declare the variable of `$err` with the `"Error Occurred Encrypting String: $_"` argument. The `$_` will be the pipeline error that occurred during the `try {}` section. You then create an `if` statement to determine whether there is data in the `$err` variable. If there is data in `$err`, it returns the error string to the script.

If there were no errors, the script will enter the `else {` section of the script. It will convert the `$result` byte array to `Base64String` by leveraging `[Convert]::ToBase 64String($result)`. This converts the byte array to string for use in your scripts.

After defining the encryption function, you call the function for use. You first start by calling `Encrypt-String` followed by `"Encrypt This String"`. You also declare the second argument as the password for the encryptor, which is `"A_Complex_ Password_With_A_Lot_Of_Characters"`. After execution, this example receives the encrypted value of `hK7GHaDD1FxknHu03TYAPxbFAAZeJ6KTSHlnSCPpJ7c=` `generated` from the function. Your results will vary depending on your salt, init, and password you use for the encryption algorithm.

While this example uses the `$salt` of `"CreateAUniqueSalt"`, the `$init` of `"CreateAUniqueInit"`, and the password of `"A_Complex_Password_With_A_Lot_Of_Characters"`, it is strongly recommended to change these values for your own scripts. These should use randomly generated strong values as described in the *Creating random salt, initialization vector, and passwords* section. Failure to use strong values and failure to keep these values in a safe location may compromise your encrypted data.

Decrypting strings

The decryption of strings is very similar to the process you performed when encrypting strings. Instead of writing data to the memory stream, the function reads the data in the memory stream. Also, instead of using the `.CreateEncryptor()` method, the decryption process leverages the `.CreateDecryptor()` method.

To create a script that decrypts encrypted strings using RijndaelManaged encryption, perform the following:

```
Add-Type -AssemblyNameSystem.Security

function Decrypt-String { param($Encrypted, $pass,
$salt="CreateAUniqueSalt", $init="CreateAUniqueInit")


if($Encrypted -is [string]){

    $Encrypted = [Convert]::FromBase64String($Encrypted)

  }


  $r = new-Object System.Security.Cryptography.RijndaelManaged

  $pass = [System.Text.Encoding]::UTF8.GetBytes($pass)

  $salt = [System.Text.Encoding]::UTF8.GetBytes($salt)

  $init = [Text.Encoding]::UTF8.GetBytes($init)


  $r.Key = (new-Object Security.Cryptography.PasswordDeriveBytes $pass,
$salt, "SHA1", 50000).GetBytes(32)
  $r.IV = (new-Object Security.Cryptography.SHA1Managed).
ComputeHash($init)[0..15]


  $d = $r.CreateDecryptor()

  $ms = new-Object IO.MemoryStream@(,$Encrypted)

  $cs = new-Object Security.Cryptography.CryptoStream $ms,$d,"Read"

  $sr = new-Object IO.StreamReader $cs


try {

    $result = $sr.ReadToEnd()

    $sr.Close()

    $cs.Close()

    $ms.Close()

    $r.Clear()
```

```
        Return $result
    }
    Catch {
        Write-host "Error Occurred Decrypting String: Wrong String Used In
Script."
    }
}
Decrypt-String "hK7GHaDD1FxknHu03TYAPxbFAAZeJ6KTSHlnSCPpJ7c=""A_Complex_
Password_With_A_Lot_Of_Characters".
```

The output of this script would look like the following:

```
PS C:\> Add-Type -AssemblyName System.Security
PS C:\> function Decrypt-String { param($Encrypted, $pass, $salt="CreateAUniqueSalt", $init="CreateAUniqueInit")
>>>
>>>     if($Encrypted -is [string]){
>>>         $Encrypted = [Convert]::FromBase64String($Encrypted)
>>>     }
>>>
>>>     $r = new-Object System.Security.Cryptography.RijndaelManaged
>>>     $pass = [System.Text.Encoding]::UTF8.GetBytes($pass)
>>>     $salt = [System.Text.Encoding]::UTF8.GetBytes($salt)
>>>     $init = [Text.Encoding]::UTF8.GetBytes($init)
>>>
>>>     $r.Key = (new-Object Security.Cryptography.PasswordDeriveBytes $pass, $salt, "SHA1", 50000).GetBytes(32)
>>>     $r.IV = (new-Object Security.Cryptography.SHA1Managed).ComputeHash($init)[0..15]
>>>
>>>     $d = $r.CreateDecryptor()
>>>     $ms = new-Object IO.MemoryStream @(,$Encrypted)
>>>     $cs = new-Object Security.Cryptography.CryptoStream $ms,$d,"Read"
>>>     $sr = new-Object IO.StreamReader $cs
>>>
>>>     try {
>>>         $result = $sr.ReadToEnd()
>>>         $sr.Close()
>>>         $cs.Close()
>>>         $ms.Close()
>>>         $r.Clear()
>>>         Return $result
>>>     }
>>>     Catch {
>>>         write-host "Error Occurred Decrypting String: Wrong String Used In Script."
>>>     }
>>> }
PS C:\> Decrypt-String "hK7GHaDD1FxknHu03TYAPxbFAAZeJ6KTSHlnSCPpJ7c=" "A_Complex_Password_With_A_Lot_Of_Characters"
Encrypt This String
```

This function displays how to decrypt a string leveraging the RijndaelManaged encryption algorithm. You first start by importing the System.Security assembly by leveraging the Add-Type cmdlet, using the -AssemblyName parameter with the System.Security argument. You then declare the Decrypt-String function. You include a parameter block to accept and set values for the function. The first value is $Encrypted, which is the encrypted text. The second value is $pass, which is used for the encryption key. The third is a predefined $salt variable set to "CreateAUniqueSalt". You then define the $init variable, which is set to "CreateAUniqueInit".

After the parameter block, you check to see if the encrypted value is formatted as a string by using if ($Encrypted -is [string]) {. If this evaluates to True, you convert the string to bytes using [Convert]::FromBase64String($Encrypted) and place the encoded value in the $Encrypted variable. Next, you declare the decryption class using new-Object cmdlet with the System.Security.Cryptography. RijndaelManaged argument. You place this object inside the $r variable.

You then convert the $pass, $salt, and $init values to the character encoding standard of UTF8 and store the character byte values in a variable. This is done by specifying [Text.Encoding]::UTF8.GetBytes($pass) for the $pass variable, [Text.Encoding]::UTF8.GetBytes($salt) for the $salt variable, and [Text. Encoding]::UTF8.GetBytes($init) for the $init variable.

After setting the proper character encoding, you proceed to create the encryption key for the RijndaelManaged encryption algorithm. This is done by setting the RijndaelManaged $r.Key attribute to the object created by (new-Object Security.Cryptography.PasswordDeriveBytes $pass, $salt, "SHA1", 50000).GetBytes(32). This object leverages the Security.Cryptography. PasswordDeriveBytes class and creates a key using the $pass variable, $salt variable, "SHA1" hash name, and iterating the derivative 50000 times. Each iteration of this class generates a different key value, making it more complex to guess the key. You then leverage the .get-bytes(32) method to return the 32-byte value of the key.

To create the initialization vector for the algorithm, you set the RijndaelManaged $r.IV attribute to the object created by (new-Object Security.Cryptography. SHA1Managed).ComputeHash($init)[0..15]. This section of the code leverages the Security.Cryptography.SHA1Managed class and computes the hash based on the $init value. When you invoke the [0..15] range operator, the first 16 bytes of the hash are obtained and placed into the $r.IV attribute.

After setting up the required attributes, you are now ready to start decrypting data. You first start by leveraging the $r RijndaelManaged object with the $r.key and $r.IV attributes defined. You use the $r.CreateDecryptor() method to generate the decryptor.

Once you've generated the decryptor, you have to create a memory stream to do the decryption in memory. This is done by declaring the new-Object cmdlet with the IO.MemoryStream class argument. You then reference the $encrypted values to be place in the memory stream object with @(,$Encrypted), and store the populated memory stream in the $ms variable.

Next, you create `CryptoStream`, which is used to transform the encrypted data into the decrypted data. You first declare `new-Object` cmdlet with the `Security.Cryptopgraphy.CryptoStream` class argument. You also define the memory stream of `$ms`, the decryptor of `$d`, and the operator of `"Read"` to tell the class to read the encrypted data from the encryption stream in memory.

After creating `CryptoStream`, you are ready to read the decrypted data from `CryptoStream`. This is done using the `IO.StreamReader` class. You declare `new-Object` with the `IO.StreamReader` class argument, and define `CryptoStream` of `$cs` to read from.

At this point, you use `try {` to catch any error messages that are generated from reading the data in the `StreamReader`. You call `$sr.ReadToEnd()`, which calls the `StreamReader`, reads the complete decrypted value, and places the data in the `$result` variable. To stop the reading of data to `CryptoStream` and `MemoryStream`, you close `StreamWriter` with `$sw.Close()`, close the `CryptoStream` with `$cs.Close()`, and the memory stream with `$ms.Close()`. For security purposes, you also clear out the decryptor data by declaring `$r.Clear()`. If the decryption is successful, you return the value of `$result` to the script.

After defining the decryption function, you call the function for use. You first start by calling `Decrypt-String` followed by `"hK7GHaDD1FxknHu03TYAPxbFAAZeJ6KTSHlnSCPpJ7c="`. You also declare the second argument as the password for the decryptor, which is `"A_Complex_Password_With_A_Lot_Of_Characters"`. After execution, you will receive the decrypted value of `"Encrypt This String"` generated from the function.

Securing the password

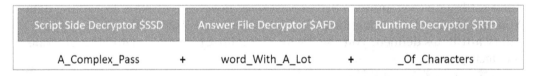

Script Side Decryptor $SSD		Answer File Decryptor $AFD		Runtime Decryptor $RTD
A_Complex_Pass	+	word_With_A_Lot	+	_Of_Characters

One of the most important parts of your encryption methodology is securing the password used for your encryption. A recommended methodology for securing your password is to break the password into three or more locations. The preceding diagram takes the password of **A_Complex_Password_With_A_Lot_Of_Characters** and breaks it into three separate segments. The purpose is to have the password data partially in the script itself, partially in the answer file, and the remainder fed into the script as an argument during runtime. If any of the three password sections are not provided, the encryption process would fail due to an incorrect password.

The purpose of this methodology is to provide multiple data points for passwords. The **Runtime Decryptor** requires user intervention, the **Answer File Decryptor** requires the answer file to be present for execution, and the **Script Side Decryptor** ensures that a password can't be solely determined from an answer file.

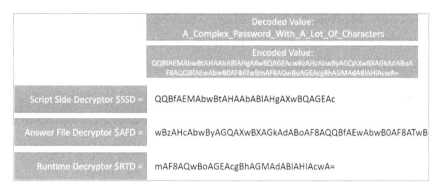

	Decoded Value: A_Complex_Password_With_A_Lot_Of_Characters
	Encoded Value: QQBfAEMAbwBtAHAAbABIAHgAXwBQAGEAcwBzAHcAbwByAGQAXwBXAGkAdABoA F8AQQBfAEwAbwB0AF8ATwBmAF8AQwBoAGEAcgBhAGMAdABlAHIAcwA=
Script Side Decryptor $SSD =	QQBfAEMAbwBtAHAAbABIAHgAXwBQAGEAc
Answer File Decryptor $AFD =	wBzAHcAbwByAGQAXwBXAGkAdABoAF8AQQBfAEwAbwB0AF8ATwB
Runtime Decryptor $RTD =	mAF8AQwBoAGEAcgBhAGMAdABlAHIAcwA=

An added layer of security to this methodology is to leverage encoding the password input. While encoding may not be great for encrypting the actual passwords in your script, it provides a very valuable obfuscation for storing a password in multiple locations. When you generate the encoded value for the password, it increases the character quantity and greatly obstructs brute-forcing of the encoding and password used in the encryption process.

To encode a password, do the following:

```
$pass = "A_Complex_Password_With_A_Lot_Of_Characters"
$encodedpass = [System.Text.Encoding]::Unicode.GetBytes($pass)
$encodedvalue = [Convert]::ToBase64String($encodedpass)
$encodedvalue
```

The output of this command would look like the following:

```
PS C:\> $pass = "A_Complex_Password_With_A_Lot_Of_Characters"
PS C:\> $encodedpass = [System.Text.Encoding]::Unicode.GetBytes($pass)
PS C:\> $encodedvalue = [Convert]::ToBase64String($encodedpass)
PS C:\> $encodedvalue
 QBfAEMAbwBtAHAAbAB1AHgAXwBQAGEAcwBzAHcAbwByAGQAXwBXAGkAdABoAF8AQQBfAEwAbwB0AF8ATwBmAF8AQwBoAGEAcgBhAGMAdABlAHIAcwA=
```

This example displays how to encode a password broken into multiple data points. You first start by defining the $pass variable with the value of "A_Complex_ Password_With_A_Lot_Of_Characters". You then encode the password leveraging the [System.Text.Encoding]::Unicode.GetBytes($pass) method and store the value in the $encodedpass variable. You then convert the encoded value into a string by leveraging [Convert]::ToBase64String($encodedpass) and storing the value in the $encodedvalue variable. At the end of this example, you call the $encodedvalue variable to display the encoded string.

To decode a string, you would do the following:

```
$encvalue = "QQBfAEMAbwBtAHAAbABlAHgAXwBQAGEAcwBzAHcAbwByAGQAXwBXAGkAdAB
oAF8AQQBfAEwAbwB0AF8ATwBmAF8AQwBoAGEAcgBhAGMAdABlAHIAcwA="

$encbytes = [System.Convert]::FromBase64String($encvalue)

$decodedvalue = [System.Text.Encoding]::Unicode.GetString($encbytes)

$decodedvalue
```

The output of decoding the string would look like the following:

```
PS C:\> $encvalue = "QQBfAEMAbwBtAHAAbABlAHgAXwBQAGEAcwBzAHcAbwByAGQAXwBXAGkAdABoAF8AQQBfAEwAbwB0AF8ATwBmAF8AQwBoAGEAcgBhAGMAdABlAHIAcwA="
PS C:\> $encbytes = [System.Convert]::FromBase64String($encvalue)
PS C:\> $decodedvalue = [System.Text.Encoding]::Unicode.GetString($encbytes)
PS C:\> $decodedvalue
_Complex_Password_With_A_Lot_Of_Characters
```

This example displays how to decode a password for use in your script. You first start by defining the `$encvalue` variable with the value of `"QQBfAEMAbwBtAHAAbABlAHgAXwBQAGEAcwBzAHcAbwByAGQAXwBXAGkAdAB oAF8AQQBfAEwAbwB0AF8ATwBmAF8AQwBoAGEAcgBhAGMAdABlAHIAcwA="`. You then convert the string to bytes by performing `[System.Convert]::FromBase64St ring($encvalue)` and storing the output in `$encbytes`. You then decode the bytes by calling `[System.Text.Encoding]::Unicode.GetString($encbytes)` and storing the output in `$decodedvalue`. At the end of this example, you call the `$decodedvalue` variable to display the decoded password of `"A_Complex_ Password_With_A_Lot_Of_Characters"`.

Decryption with encoded password

The final script in this chapter ties together multiple components you learned in the last two chapters. You will learn how you can combine the Answer File Decryptor, the Script Side Decryptor, and the Runtime Decryptor to decrypt an encrypted string. You will need to create an `Example.xml` file and an `Example.ps1` file in the `c:\ temp\` directory of your system to follow this example.

 It is helpful to refer to this chapter's code files to quickly create the content described next.

Create an `Example.xml` file with the decryptor value set to `wBzAHcAbwByAGQAXwBXAGkAdABoAF8AQQBfAEwAbwB0AF8ATwB` in the `c:\temp\` directory:

```
Example.xml - Notepad                                    —
File  Edit  Format  View  Help
<?xml version="1.0"?>

<ScriptAnswers>
  <AFD name="wBzAHcAbwByAGQAXwBXAGkAdABoAF8AQQBfAEwAbwB0AF8ATwB"></AFD>
</ScriptAnswers>
```

You will want to create an `Example.ps1` script in `c:\temp\` of your system. The contents of this script should be as follows:

```
# The script is invoked with the command line of:

# powershell.exe -file "c:\temp\Example.ps1""c:\temp\Example.xml""mAF8AQw
BoAGEAcgBhAGMAdABlAHIAcwA="

param($xmlfile, $RTD)

##################################################################

# Example On How To Decrypt a String

##################################################################

Add-Type -AssemblyNameSystem.Security

function Decrypt-String { param($Encrypted, $pass,
$salt="CreateAUniqueSalt", $init="CreateAUniqueInit")

if($Encrypted -is [string]){

    $Encrypted = [Convert]::FromBase64String($Encrypted)

  }

  $r = new-Object System.Security.Cryptography.RijndaelManaged

  $pass = [System.Text.Encoding]::UTF8.GetBytes($pass)

  $salt = [System.Text.Encoding]::UTF8.GetBytes($salt)

  $init = [Text.Encoding]::UTF8.GetBytes($init)

  $r.Key = (new-Object Security.Cryptography.PasswordDeriveBytes $pass,
$salt, "SHA1", 50000).GetBytes(32)

  $r.IV = (new-Object Security.Cryptography.SHA1Managed).
ComputeHash($init)[0..15]

  $d = $r.CreateDecryptor()

  $ms = new-Object IO.MemoryStream@(,$Encrypted)

  $cs = new-Object Security.Cryptography.CryptoStream $ms,$d,"Read"

  $sr = new-Object IO.StreamReader $cs
```

```
try {
        $result = $sr.ReadToEnd()
        $sr.Close()
        $cs.Close()
        $ms.Close()
        $r.Clear()
        Return $result
    }
    Catch {
        Write-host "Error Occurred Decrypting String: Wrong String Used In
Script."
    }
}
# Read the XML file for the Answer File Decryptor
[xml] $xml = (get-content $xmlfile)
$AFD = $xml.GetElementsByTagName("AFD").Name
# Define the Script Side Decryptor
$SSD = "QQBfAEMAbwBtAHAAbABlAHgAXwBQAGEAc"
# Combine the Decryptors
$encvalue = $SSD + $AFD + $RTD
# Decode the values
$encbytes = [System.Convert]::FromBase64String($encvalue)
$decrypt = [System.Text.Encoding]::Unicode.GetString($encbytes)
# Decrypt the string.
Decrypt-String "hK7GHaDD1FxknHu03TYAPxbFAAZeJ6KTSHlnSCPpJ7c=" $decrypt
PAUSE
```

To execute this script, you will want to perform the following command in PowerShell:

```
powershell.exe -file "c:\temp\Example.ps1""c:\temp\Example.xml""mAF8AQwBo
AGEAcgBhAGMAdABlAHIAcwA="
```

The output of this script is as follows:

```
PS C:\> powershell.exe -file "c:\temp\Example.ps1" "c:\temp\Example.xml" "mAF8AQwBoAGEAcgBhAGMAdABlAHIAcwA="
Encrypt This String
Press Enter to continue...:
```

This example displays how you can combine `Answer File Decryptor`, `Script Side Decryptor` and `Runtime Decryptor` to decrypt an encrypted string. At the beginning of the chapter, you encrypted a string of `"Encrypt This String"`. This generated the encrypted value of `hK7GHaDD1FxknHu03TYAPxbFAAZeJ6KTSHlnSCPpJ7c=`. Later in this chapter, we learned how to decrypt the encrypted value by leveraging the password of `"A_Complex_Password_With_A_Lot_Of_Characters"`. You then learned that you should encode the password and separate the value into three locations. This script encompasses decrypting a string and leveraging an encoded password from three data sources.

You first start by defining the parameter block with `param($xmlfile,$RTD)`. When you executed the script, you fed in the xml file location of `c:\temp\` `example.xml`, which is stored in `$xmlfile`, and the runtime decryptor as `"mAF8AQwBoAGEAcgBhAGMAdABlAHIAcwA="`, which is stored in `$RTD`. After the parameter block is populated, you add the `System.Security` assembly leveraging the `Add-Type` cmdlet with the `-AssemblyName` parameter set to the `System.Security` argument. You then define the `Decrypt-String` function, which is explained in detail earlier in this chapter.

The next step is to retrieve the XML file contents. You perform this using the `get-content` cmdlet with the path of `$xmlfile` and storing the value in the `$xml` variable with the `[xml]` data type. You then call the `$xml.GetElementsByTagName()` method set to `AFD`. You utilize dot notation to retrieve the answer file decryptor with the attribute value of Name and store this in the `$AFD` variable.

After retrieving `Answer File Decryptor`, you specify the `Script Side Decryptor` setting the `$SSD` variable to `"QQBfAEMAbwBtAHAAbABlAHgAXwBQAGEAc"`. You then combine the strings of the Script Side Decryptor, or `$SSD`, followed by `Answer File Decryptor`, or `$AFD`, and the final `Runtime Decryptor`, or `$RTD`. You proceed to decode the combined values by converting them to bytes and storing the value in the `$encbytes` variable. You then decode the `$encbytes` variable to reveal the script password stored in `$decrypt`.

Once you have the encryption password, you execute the `Decrypt-String"hK7GHaDD1FxknHu03TYAPxbFAAZeJ6KTSHlnSCPpJ7c="$decrypt` command, from the previous example, to return a result of `"Encrypt This String"`. You also issue a pause command to halt the script from closing. After execution, you have successfully decoded a password, and decrypted a string.

Summary

In this chapter, we learned about RijndaelManaged 256-bit encryption. We first started with the basics of the encryption process. Then, we proceeded to learn how to create randomized salt, init, and passwords in scripts. We then learned how to encrypt and decrypt strings. We ended the chapter by learning how to encode passwords and leverage multiple sources to derive an encoded password.

In the next chapter, we will learn how to interact with services, processes, profiles, and logged on users.

5
Interacting with Services, Processes, Profiles, and Logged on Users

The Windows server scanning script provides enterprises with visibility into the overall function of the system being scanned. While you may be able to evaluate installed Windows features and roles, doing so often does not provide enough information to be able to determine the full function of a server. Further, without deeper inspection, you won't be able to determine whether there are business-critical services and processes running on a system.

When you evaluate identities on a system, however, you can gain very valuable information about a system's function. Typically, in enterprise environments, service accounts are used to run different services and processes on a system. These service accounts are similar to normal users; however, they have restricted privileges. When you identify services or processes that are not running as the default built-in users, there is a high possibility that the system was configured that way for a reason. This will reveal nonstandard configurations for a system, which are excellent callouts for review with the Window server scanning script.

In addition to determining service account usage, scanning processes reveal the users logged into a particular system. Since every user account logged in to the system has its own processes assigned to its session, you can quickly dissect why a user is logged in. Also, there are legacy software solutions that are known to require an interactive login to properly run services, shells, and programs. Evaluating logged in users will enable you to better understand how user accounts are interacting with a system.

Lastly, you will want to evaluate user profiles. In large enterprise environments, there can be few traces of what user or department owns a particular system. Since user profiles contain the usernames of individuals who logged into the system, scanning the profiles will provide guidance for system ownership.

In this chapter, you will:

- Understand how to get, stop, start, and set Windows services
- Leverage different cmdlets to interact with Windows processes
- Identify logged on users on a system
- Gather data about the user profiles on a system

The examples in this chapter build upon each other. You will need to execute the scripts sequentially to have the final script in this chapter work properly.

It is also recommended you execute these examples on Windows 2012 R2 server (or greater) with PowerShell installed. This server must be joined to a Windows domain.

Windows services

When you are working with Microsoft-based systems, there may be times where you need to interact with Windows services. PowerShell offers a variety of cmdlets that enable you to work with these services. To start, you can review the services on a system by leveraging the Get-service cmdlet. By calling the Get-service cmdlet, you can retrieve the full list of Windows services on a system. If you want to obtain a filtered view into a specific service, you can leverage the -name parameter referencing a specific name of a service. After executing this command, you will see the Status, Name, and DisplayName of the service. You may also issue the -RequiredServices parameter to display the services that are required to be running for that particular service to be functional. You can query dependent Windows services by executing the -DependentServices parameter.

To use the Get-service cmdlet to query the Windows Audio Service, you could do the following:

```
Get-service -DisplayName "Windows Audio"
Get-service -DisplayName "Windows Audio" -RequiredServices
(Get-service -DisplayName "Windows Audio").Status
```

The output of this is shown in the following screenshot:

```
PS C:\> Get-service -DisplayName "Windows Audio"

 tatus   Name                 DisplayName
 ------   ----                 -----------
.unning  Audiosrv             Windows Audio


PS C:\> Get-service -DisplayName "Windows Audio" -RequiredServices

 tatus   Name                 DisplayName
 ------   ----                 -----------
.unning  AudioEndpointBu...   Windows Audio Endpoint Builder
.unning  RpcSs                Remote Procedure Call (RPC)


PS C:\> (Get-service -DisplayName "Windows Audio").Status
.unning
```

This example displays how to get information about the Windows Audio Service. You first start by calling the Get-service cmdlet, leveraging the -DisplayName parameter, and referencing the Windows Audio Windows service. After executing, you see the Status, Name and DisplayName fields printed to the PowerShell window. You then use the Get-service cmdlet with the -DisplayName parameter referencing Windows Audio, and the -RequiredServices parameter. After executing the Get-service command, you will see the Status, Name, and DisplayName of all the services that are required for the Windows Audio Windows Service to function properly. The last call you make leverages the Get-service cmdlet, with the -DisplayName parameter referencing the Windows Audio. This whole statement is wrapped in parentheses followed by the dot notation of .Status. This returns the current status of the Windows Audio Windows Service, which is Running.

In instances where you want to start, restart, and stop services, you may also leverage the start-service, restart-service, and stop-service cmdlets. To start a service, you can call the start-service cmdlet, followed by the -name or -DisplayName parameters with the corresponding service name. After execution, the service will change status from Stopped to StartPending; when it's successfully started, it will change the status to Running.

To stop a service, you can call the stop-service cmdlet, followed by the -name or -DisplayName parameters with the corresponding service name. After execution, the service will change status from Running to StopPending, and when it's successfully stopped, it will change the status to Stopped.

To restart a service, you can call `restart-service` cmdlet, followed by the `-Name` or `-DisplayName` parameters with the corresponding service name. After execution, the service will change status from `Running` to `StopPending`, `StopPending` to `Stopped`, `Stopped` to `StartPending`; when it's successfully started, it will change the status to `Running`.

> To start and stop Windows services requires a PowerShell window running with elevated privileges. You will need to open PowerShell with the **Run as administrator** parameter.

To stop and start the Windows Audio service, you can do the following:

```
stop-service -DisplayName "Windows Audio"

(Get-service -DisplayName "Windows Audio").Status

start-service -DisplayName "Windows Audio"

(Get-service -DisplayName "Windows Audio").Status
```

The output of this is shown in the following screenshot:

```
PS C:\> stop-service -DisplayName "Windows Audio"
PS C:\> (Get-service -DisplayName "Windows Audio").Status
Stopped
PS C:\> start-service -DisplayName "Windows Audio"
PS C:\> (Get-service -DisplayName "Windows Audio").Status
Running
```

This example displays how to start and stop Windows Services. You first stop the Windows Audio Service by leveraging the `stop-service` cmdlet with the `-DisplayName` parameter referencing the `Windows Audio` display name. You then get the current status of the service by executing `Get-service` with the `-DisplayName` parameter, referencing the `Windows Audio` display name. You encapsulate that in parentheses and leverage the dot notation of `.Status` to print the current status to the screen. The console will return the status of `Stopped`.

You then start the Windows Audio Service by leveraging the `start-service` cmdlet with the `-DisplayName` parameter referencing the `Windows Audio` display name. You then get the current status of the service by executing `Get-service` with the `-DisplayName` parameter, referencing the `Windows Audio` display name. You encapsulate that in parentheses and leverage the dot notation of `.Status` to print the current status to the screen. The console will return the status of `Running`.

You also have the ability to modify different aspects of the Windows services by using the `set-service` cmdlet. The `set-service` cmdlet can modify the service descriptions, start-up types, and even the display names for services. Since Windows does not allow you to modify running services, you first have to leverage the `stop-service` cmdlet to stop the service for editing.

If you want to modify the start-up type for a service, you can leverage the `set-service` cmdlet with the `–Name` parameter with the corresponding service name. You then include the `–startup` type parameter with `Automatic` for automatic start-up, `Manual` for manual start-up, or `Disabled` to disable the service start-up. To view the changes to the service start-up type, you will need to leverage the `get-wmiobject` cmdlet referencing the `win32_service` class, and the `–filter` parameter referencing `DisplayName='Display Name'`.

> While in most cases you can leverage the `Get-service` cmdlet to display the properties of a service, there are certain properties that are not made available to the cmdlet. As a result, you may have to directly query WMI using the `get-wmiobject` to view all of the properties for that service. To view all of the properties available to `Get-service` or through WMI, you can pipe | the results to `get-member`, and it will display all the available properties you can view.

To change the `Windows Audio –startup` type parameter, you can do the following:

```
(get-wmiobject win32_service -filter "DisplayName='Windows Audio'").
StartMode
stop-service -name "Audiosrv"
set-service -name "Audiosrv" -startup "Manual"
(get-wmiobject win32_service -filter "DisplayName='Windows Audio'").
StartMode
set-service -name "Audiosrv" -startup "Automatic"
(get-wmiobject win32_service -filter "DisplayName='Windows Audio'"
).StartMode
Start-service -name "Audiosrv"
```

The output of this is shown in the following screenshot:

```
PS C:\> (get-wmiobject win32_service -filter "DisplayName='Windows Audio'").StartMode
Auto
PS C:\> stop-service -name "Audiosrv"
PS C:\> set-service -name "Audiosrv" -startup "Manual"
PS C:\> (get-wmiobject win32_service -filter "DisplayName='Windows Audio'").StartMode
Manual
PS C:\> set-service -name "Audiosrv" -startup "Automatic"
PS C:\> (get-wmiobject win32_service -filter "DisplayName='Windows Audio'" ).StartMode
Auto
PS C:\> Start-service -name "Audiosrv"
```

This example displays how to change the start-up of a Windows service on a system. You first start by querying the system to see what the existing StartMode is. To do this, you need to leverage the get-wmiobject cmdlet referencing the win32_service class. You leverage the -filter parameter with the filter options of DisplayName='Windows Audio'. You then encapsulate that statement in parentheses and leverage the dot notation of .StartMode to print to the screen the start mode of a system. The command will print Auto to the screen designating that the service start-up type is set to Automatic. You then stop the service by calling the stop-service cmdlet with the -name parameter referencing the Audiosrv service name. You then configure the service start-up type to be Manual by calling the set-service cmdlet with the -name parameter referencing AudioSrv, and the -startup parameter referencing Manual. After running this command you verify the start-up change using the get-wmiobject cmdlet referencing the win32_service class. You leverage the -filter parameter with the filter options of DisplayName='Windows Audio'. You then encapsulate that statement in parentheses and leverage the dot notation of .StartMode to print to the screen the start mode of a system. The command will print Manual to the screen designating that the service start-up type is set to Manual.

You then set the service back to Automatic by calling the set-service cmdlet with the -name parameter referencing AudioSrv, and the -startup parameter referencing Automatic. After setting this command, you verify the start-up change using the get-wmiobject cmdlet referencing the win32_service class. You leverage the -filter parameter with the filter options of Displayname='Windows Audio'. You then encapsulate that statement in parenthesis and leverage the dot notation of .StartMode to print to the screen the start mode of a system. The command will print Auto to the screen designating that the service start-up type is set to Automatic. After the final configuration, you then start the service by calling the start-service cmdlet with the -name parameter referencing the Audiosrv service name.

In the instance where you want to modify a service's description, you first need to stop the service by leveraging the stop-service cmdlet. You then call set-service cmdlet with –name name of the service, and the –Description parameter with the description that you want to set for the particular service. The description property is unique as it is not made available to the get-service cmdlet. To get around this, you need to leverage the get-wmiobject cmdlet. To view the description, you can use the get-wmiobject cmdlet referencing the win32_service class, with the –filter parameter referencing DisplayName='Display Name'. After executing this script, the description will print to the screen. After setting the description, you can start the service using the start-service cmdlet.

To set the description for the Windows Audio Service, you can do the following:

```
$olddesc = (get-wmiobject win32_service -filter "DisplayName='Windows
Audio'").description

$olddesc

stop-service -DisplayName "Windows Audio"

Set-service -name "Audiosrv" -Description "My New Windows Audio
Description."

(get-wmiobject win32_service -filter "DisplayName='Windows Audio'").
description

Set-service -name "Audiosrv" -Description $olddesc

(get-wmiobject win32_service -filter "DisplayName='Windows Audio'").
description

start-service -DisplayName "Windows Audio"
```

The output of this is shown in the following screenshot:

This example displays how to change the description for a Windows service, and set it back to the original description. You first start by querying the system to see what the existing description is. To do this, you need to leverage the `get-wmiobject` cmdlet referencing the `win32_service` class. You leverage the `-filter` parameter with the filter options of `DisplayName='Windows Audio'`. You then encapsulate that statement in parenthesis and leverage the dot notation of `.description`. The output, which is the Windows service description, is then set to the variable `$olddesc`. To view the old description, you call the `$olddesc` variable, which displays: `Manages audio for Windows-based programs. If this service is stopped, audio devices and effects will not function properly. If this service is disabled, any services that explicitly depend on it will fail to start.` You then stop the service with the `stop-service` cmdlet and the `-DisplayName` parameter referencing `Windows Audio`. To set the description, you use the `set-service` cmdlet with the `-name` parameter set to `Audiosrv`, and the `-Description` parameter set to `My New Windows Audio Description`.

After setting the description, you query the system with the `get-wmiobject` cmdlet referencing the `win32_service` class, and the `-filter` parameter with the filter options of `DisplayName='Windows Audio'`. You then encapsulate that statement in parenthesis and leverage the dot notation of `.description`. The output from this will be the current description, which is `My New Windows Audio Description`. To set the description back to the original, you use the `set-service` cmdlet with the `-name` parameter set to `Audiosrv`, and the `-description` parameter referencing the `$olddesc` variable. After setting the description back to the original description, you query the system with the `get-wmiobject` cmdlet referencing the `win32_service` class, and the `-filter` parameter with the filter options of `DisplayName='Windows Audio'`. You then encapsulate that statement in parenthesis and leverage the dot notation of `.description`. The output from this will be the current description, which is `Manages audio for Windows-based programs. If this service is stopped, audio devices and effects will not function properly. If this service is disabled, any services that explicitly depend on it will fail to start.` You then complete this process by starting the Windows Audio Service. You use the `start-service` cmdlet with the `-DisplayName` parameter referencing `Windows Audio`.

There may be instances where you want to determine what user or service account is running a Windows Service. To do this, you can leverage the `get-wmiobject` cmdlet with the `-class` parameter and the `win32_service` argument. The WMI service object has multiple properties that enable you to view expanded information about the services running on the system. The `.DisplayName` property reveals the Windows Service display name, and the `.StartName` property displays the user delegated to start the Windows service.

To query Windows services requires a PowerShell window running with elevated privileges. You will need to open PowerShell with the `Run as administrator` parameter.

To query the Windows Audio Service for the user delegated to start the service, you can perform the following:

```
$service = get-wmiobject win32_service | where {$_.DisplayName -like
"Windows Audio"}

$servicedisplay = $service.DisplayName

$serviceAuthUser = $service.StartName

write-host "Service with $servicedisplay name is running with
$serviceAuthUser account."
```

The output of this is shown in the following screenshot:

```
PS C:\> $service = get-wmiobject win32_service  | where {$_.DisplayName -like "Windows Audio"}
PS C:\> $servicedisplay = $service.DisplayName
PS C:\> $serviceAuthUser = $service.StartName
PS C:\> write-host "Service with $servicedisplay name is running with $serviceAuthUser account."
Service with Windows Audio name is running with NT AUTHORITY\LocalService account.
```

This example displays how to determine the owner of services on a system. You first start by calling the `get-wmiobject` cmdlet with the `-class` parameter set to `win32_service`. This command is piped to `where {$_.DisplayName -like "Windows Audio"}`. The `Windows Audio` object is then placed into the `$service` variable. You gather the Windows service display name by calling the `$service.DisplayName` property and place the property into the `$servicedisplay` variable. You retrieve the Windows service start-up user by calling the `$service.StartName` property and place the property into the `$serviceAuthUser` variable. To display the collected data, you use the `write-host` cmdlet with `Service with $servicedisplay name is running with $serviceAuthUser account.`. On this particular system, `Service with Windows Audio name is running NT Authority\LocalService account.` is returned.

Managing Windows processes

There may be times in scripting where you need to check if there is a running process on a system. PowerShell offers the get-process cmdlet to search for available processes on a system. By running the get-process cmdlet alone, you will get a report of all the running services on the system. The default record set that is returned about running services includes:

- Handles: The number of thread handles that are being used by a particular process

- NPM (K): Non-Paged Memory is the memory that is solely in physical memory, and not allocated to the page file that is being used by a process

- PM (K): Pageable Memory is the memory that is being allocated to the page file that is used by a process

- WS(K): Working Set is the memory recently referenced by the process

- VM(M): Virtual Memory is the amount of virtual memory that is being used by a process

- CPU(s): This is the processor time, or the time the CPU takes to utilize the process

- ID: This is an assigned unique ID to the process

- ProcessName: This is the name of the process in memory

Typically, when you query the active running processes on a system, you will be looking for a particular process. To do this, you can leverage the get-process cmdlet with the -name parameter referencing a process name to view information about that particular process. You can also leverage the asterisk (*) as a wildcard to query processes that are like the partial word you specify. You may also directly reference the Process ID of a process if you invoke the -id parameter with an ID of a process. If you want more information about the process that is running, you can also leverage the -FileVersionInfo parameter to pull the ProductVersion, FileVersion, and FileName information from the process. In instances where you need to find all of the modules, or DLL references, that are loaded by a process, you may also leverage the -module parameter.

To search for a process using a wildcard and get a process by a process ID, you can do the following:

```
$process = get-process powersh*
$process
get-process -id $process.id
```

The output of this is shown in the following screenshot:

```
PS C:\> $process = get-process powersl*
PS C:\> $process
Handles  NPM(K)    PM(K)      WS(K)     CPU(s)     Id  SI ProcessName
-------  ------    -----      -----     ------     --  -- -----------
    620      29    61172      72524       0.75   2776   1 powershell
    757      52   119712     130984       1.45   4204   1 powershell_ise
PS C:\> get-process -id $process.id

Handles  NPM(K)    PM(K)      WS(K)     CPU(s)     Id  SI ProcessName
-------  ------    -----      -----     ------     --  -- -----------
    686      29    61400      73532       0.77   2776   1 powershell
    757      52   119712     130984       1.45   4204   1 powershell_ise
```

This script displays how to search for a process by a wildcard and obtain the process ID. You also view that same service by calling the process ID of that service. You first start by using the get-process cmdlet with the powersh* searching wildcard. The system returns the PowerShell process object into the $process variable. You then call the $process variable to view the information about the PowerShell process. You then leverage the get-process cmdlet with the -id parameter pointing to the $process variable referencing the dot notation of .id. This returns the same PowerShell process information, as the $process.id that is being referenced in the process ID of the first search result. After executing this script, you will see the Handles, NPM(K), PM(K), WS(K), VM, CPU(s), Id, and ProcessName information for the PowerShell process.

To get a process using a wildcard and get its FileVersionInfo information, you can do the following:

```
$process = get-process powersh*

get-process -id $process.id -FileVersionInfo | format-table -AutoSize
```

The output of this is shown in the following screenshot:

```
PS C:\> $process = get-process powersl*
PS C:\> get-process -id $process.id -FileVersionInfo

ProductVersion   FileVersion      FileName
--------------   -----------      --------
10.0.14393.0     10.0.14393.0 ... C:\Windows\System32\WindowsPowerShell\v1.0\powershell.exe
10.0.14393.103   10.0.14393.10... C:\Windows\System32\WindowsPowerShell\v1.0\powershell_ise.exe
```

This script displays how to search for a process by a wildcard and then use that information to view the file version information. You start by using the get-process cmdlet with the powersh* searching wildcard. The system returns the PowerShell process into the $process variable. You then call the get-process cmdlet and leverage the –id parameter pointing to the $process variable referencing the dot notation of .id. You also call the –FileVersionInfo parameter to display advanced information about the PowerShell process. You then pipe the result to the format-table cmdlet with the -AutoSize parameter, which formats the table so it does not truncate the results. After executing this script, you will see the ProductVersion, FileVersion, and FileName information about the PowerShell process.

There may be instances where you want to determine what user or service account is running a process. To do this, you can leverage the get-wmiobject cmdlet, with the -class parameter and the win32_process argument. The WMI process object has multiple properties and methods that enable you to view expanded information about the processes running on the system. The .Name property reveals the name, whereas the .GetOwner() method reveals information about the process owner. This method is a .User property, which displays the user running the service, and .Domain property, which provides the domain the user belongs to.

> To query a system process and the processes of other users requires a PowerShell window running with elevated privileges. You will need to open PowerShell with the Run as administrator parameter.

To get users running PowerShell.exe on a system, you can perform the following:

```
$processes = Get-WmiObject -class win32_process | where {$_.Name -like
"powersh*"}
foreach ($process in $processes) {
    $procname = $process.Name
    $procdom = $process.GetOwner().Domain
    $procuser = $process.GetOwner().User
    Write-host "$procname is running with the $procdom\$procuser
account."
}
```

The output of this is shown in the following screenshot:

```
PS C:\> $processes = Get-WmiObject -class win32_process   where {$_.Name -like "powersh*"}
PS C:\> foreach ($process in $processes) {
>>      $procname = $process.Name
>>      $procdom = $process.GetOwner().Domain
>>      $procuser = $process.GetOwner().User
>>      Write-host "$procname is running with the $procdom\$procuser account."
>> }
powershell_ise.exe is running with the POSHDEMO\Brenton account.
powershell.exe is running with the POSHDEMO\Brenton account.
```

This example displays how to determine the owner of processes on a system. You first start by calling the get-WmiObject cmdlet with the -class parameter set to win32_process. This command is piped to where {$_.Name -like "powersh*"}, which will retrieve all processes that have names that start with Powersh. These objects are then placed into the $processes variable. You then create a foreach statement to loop through each $process object in the $processes variable. You retrieve the process name using the $process.Name property and set it to the $procname variable. You gather the process owner domain name by leveraging the $process.GetOwner() method with the .Domain property. Finally, you retrieve the process owner name using the $procses.GetOwner() method with the .User property. To display the collected data, you use the write-host cmdlet with $procname is running with the $procdom\$procuser account. On this particular system, powershell_ise.exe is running with the POSHDEMO\Brenton account. and powershell.exe is running with the POSHDEMO\Brenton account are returned.

To start a new process, or invoke a program, you can leverage the start-process cmdlet. The proper syntax for using this cmdlet is calling the start-process cmdlet, providing the -FilePath parameter pointing to the location of the item you want to execute. You can then call the optional -argumentlist parameter referencing the parameters that are needed to execute the item, the optional -verb parameter to invoke any verbs associated with the file type (such as Edit, Open, Play, Print, and RunAs), the optional -NoNewWindow parameter to not spawn the command in a new PowerShell console, and the optional -wait parameter to wait for the process to complete before continuing with the script. If you do not execute the -wait parameter, the script will continue to the next step without waiting for the current step to be successful. After starting a process, the process will receive a process ID, which you can reference with the other process cmdlets.

To start a new Notepad process, you can do the following:

```
start-process -FilePath notepad.exe

$process = get-process notepad*
```

The output of this is shown in the following screenshot:

```
PS C:\> start-process –FilePath notepad.exe
PS C:\> $process = get-process notepad*
```

This script displays how to start a Notepad process and search for the notepad process by a wildcard. You first start by using the start-process cmdlet with the –FilePath parameter referencing the notepad.exe process. After execution, it will launch notepad.exe. You then use get-process cmdlet with the notepad* wildcard. The system returns the PowerShell process object into the $process variable. Storing the PowerShell process object in the $process variable enables you to interact with the properties of that object as needed.

To stop a process, or stop a program, you can leverage the stop-process cmdlet. The proper syntax for using this cmdlet is calling the stop-process cmdlet, providing the –FilePath parameter pointing to the location of the item you want to terminate. You may also leverage the –processname parameter to stop a service by its process name. You may also use wildcards with the –processname parameter to end processes that are like the partial word you specify. You can specify the –id parameter to terminate a process by its process ID as well. By default, if you kill a process, it will prompt for confirmation. Using the –force parameter will force the termination of the process without prompting the user.

To stop the running notepad process, you can do the following:

```
start-process -FilePath notepad.exe
$process = get-process notepad*
stop-process -ID $process.id
```

The output of this is shown in the following screenshot:

```
PS C:\> start-process –FilePath notepad.exe
PS C:\> $process = get-process notepad*
PS C:\> stop-process –ID $process.id
```

This script displays how to start a notepad process, search for the notepad process by a wildcard, and then use that information to stop the notepad process. You first start by using the start-process cmdlet with the –FilePath parameter referencing the notepad.exe process. After execution, it will launch notepad.exe. You then use get-process cmdlet with the notepad* wildcard. The system returns the PowerShell process into the $process variable. You then call the stop-process cmdlet and leverage the –id parameter pointing to the $process variable, referencing the dot notation of .id. After executing this script, you will see notepad open and close.

Identifying logged on users

There may be instances where you need to identify users that are logged in to your systems. When a user logs into your computer, they create an interactive session with your system. This spawns processes under that username as the process owner. Additionally, when you create a service account to start services on a system, the underlying processes run as that service account. Given that both methods invoke processes, the best method to determine currently logged on users is to evaluate the running processes.

In addition to identifying the logged in users, you will need to filter out the built-in Windows accounts. To perform this, you can create a `switch` statement to make multiple evaluations of the process owner. If the process owner username is NETWORK SERVICE, LOCAL SERVICE, $null, or SYSTEM, you can skip reporting the username. If it doesn't match any of these values, it will use the default `switch` and report the user to a list. Since multiple processes run under the same user, you can pipe the user results to the `Get-Unique` cmdlet, which will only select the unique values in the array.

 Depending on how many processes you have on your system, the following example will take up to 30 seconds to execute.

To evaluate the running processes to obtain a list of non-built-in logged on users, you can perform the following:

```
$users = @()
$processes = Get-WmiObject win32_process
foreach ($process in $processes) {
    $procuser = $process.GetOwner().User
    switch ($process.GetOwner().User) {
        "NETWORK SERVICE" { $continue = "Skip User" }
        "LOCAL SERVICE" { $continue = "Skip User" }
        "SYSTEM" { $continue = "Skip User"}
        "$null" { $continue = "Skip User" }
        default { $continue = "Report User" }
    }
    if ($continue -eq "Report User") {

        $users += $procuser

    }
}
$users | Get-Unique
```

The output of this is shown in the following screenshot:

```
PS C:\> $users = @()
PS C:\> $processes = Get-WmiObject win32_process
PS C:\> foreach ($process in $processes) {
>>       $procuser = $process.GetOwner().User
>>       switch ($process.GetOwner().User) {
>>           "NETWORK SERVICE" { $continue = "Skip User" }
>>           "LOCAL SERVICE" { $continue = "Skip User" }
>>           "SYSTEM" { $continue = "Skip User"}
>>           "$null" { $continue = "Skip User" }
>>           default { $continue = "Report User" }
>>       }
>>       if ($continue -eq "Report User") {
>>
>>           $users += $procuser
>>       }
>> }
>> $users | Get-Unique
>>
DWM-1
bblawat
LocalJoe
```

This example displays how to output the current non-built-in users on a system. You start by defining an array named $users. You then leverage the get-wmiobject with the argument of the win32_process class and place the result in $processes. You then create a foreach loop and loop through each $process in the $processes variable. You proceed to gather the iterative process owner using the $process. GetOwner() method and place the .User property in the $procuser variable. You then declare a switch statement evaluating the $process.GetOwner().User property. The first evaluations are for built-in accounts. If the accounts are NETWORK SERVICE, LOCAL SERVICE, SYSTEM, or $null, it will set $continue to "Skip User". If it doesn't match any of these built-in users, it will leverage the default value, which sets the $continue variable to "Report User".

After exiting the switch statement, you evaluate the $continue variable with an If statement, and proceed if the value is equal to "Report User". This step will add the $procuser variable to the $users array. After the foreach loop completes, you will have a large number of users listed for each non-built-in user. To trim the list to individual or unique users, you pipe the $users variable to Get-Unique cmdlet. The result is a list of the unique nonbuilt-in users on the system. The system the example was run on has three users: DWM-1, bblawat, and LocalJoe.

User profiles

User profiles are a common challenge in enterprises. Since they are autogenerated upon logon and there is no built-in automated functionality to remove local profiles, systems are plagued with old profile accounts. Old profiles not only consume data on systems, they also reveal information about other active accounts in the environment.

PowerShell offers the ability to retrieve user profile information. To retrieve user profiles from a system, you can leverage the `get-wmiobject` cmdlet calling the `win32_UserProfile` class. After you retrieve user profile objects, you have the ability to use multiple properties to gather information about the profiles. The `.SID` property is the security identifier of the user in the profile. While the SID is a unique user number, you can easily translate it with the `.NET System.Security.Principal` class. You first start by creating a new `.NET` object by calling the `New-Object` cmdlet with the `System.Security.Principal.SecurityIdentifier` class with the SID of the user as the argument. You then retrieve the value from the `.Translate()` method set to `[System.Security.Principal.NTAccount]` class. The `.NET` class will translate from the `SecurityIdentifier` to the `NTAccount`, which results in the output of the username.

To translate the security identifier of a user to a username, you can perform the following:

```
$sid = "S-1-5-18"

$usersid = New-Object System.Security.Principal.
SecurityIdentifier("$SID")

$usersid.Translate( [System.Security.Principal.NTAccount]).Value
```

The output of this is shown in the following screenshot:

```
PS C:\> $sid = "S-1-5-18"
PS C:\> $usersid = New-Object System.Security.Principal.SecurityIdentifier("$SID")
PS C:\> $usersid.Translate( [System.Security.Principal.NTAccount]).Value
NT AUTHORITY\SYSTEM
```

This example displays how to properly convert a SID to username. You first start by defining the security identifier of `"S-1-5-18"` and place it in the `$sid` variable. You then leverage the `New-Object` cmdlet to call the `System.Security.Principal.SecurityIdentifier` class with the `$sid` argument and set it equal to `$SID`. This places the SID object in the `$usersid` variable. You then call the `$userid.Translate()` method on the SID object, and specify the argument of `[System.Security.Principal.NTAccount]`. Finally, you call the `.Value` property on the translated data, and you get the value of the username. In this example, you learn that the SID of `S-1-5-18` is translated to `NT AUTHORITY\SYSTEM`.

Another common property you may use with the `win32_profile` class is the `LastUseTime` property. The `LastUseTime` provides insight as to the last time the profile was used. This timestamp is in the **Distributed Management Task Force (DMTF)** format, which is typically not a user-friendly format for reading. To simplify this value into a different time format, you can leverage the `[Management.ManagementDateTimeConverter]` class with the `ToDateTime()` method and the argument of the `LastUseTime`. After running this method, you will successfully convert the value into a user-friendly format.

To convert the `LastUseTime` into a user-friendly format, you can perform the following:

```
$profile = get-wmiobject Win32_UserProfile | Where {$_.SID -eq "S-1-5-18"}

$lastusetime = $profile.LastUseTime

$lastusetime

[Management.ManagementDateTimeConverter]::ToDateTime($lastusetime)
```

The output of this is shown in the following screenshot:

```
PS C:\> $profile = get-wmiobject Win32_UserProfile   Where {$_.SID -eq "S-1-5-18"}
PS C:\> $lastusetime = $profile.LastUseTime
PS C:\> $lastusetime
20170216051704.765000+000
PS C:\> [Management.ManagementDateTimeConverter]::ToDateTime($lastusetime)

Wednesday, February 15, 2017 11:17:04 PM
```

This example displays how to convert a DMTF-formatted value into a user-friendly format. You start by leveraging the `get-wmiobject` cmdlet and call the `win32_UserProfile` class. You then pipe this value to `Where {$_.SID -eq "S-1-5-18"}` and place this profile object into the `$profile` variable. You then retrieve the `.LastUseTime` property and place it in the `$lastusetime` variable. You then call the `$lastusetime` to display the DMTF-formatted time on the screen. In this example, the DMTF is `20170216051704.765000+000`. Finally, you call the `[Management.ManagementDateTimeConverter]` class and invoke the `ToDateTime()` method with the `$lastusetime` as the argument. The output from this command is the user-friendly value of `Wednesday, February 15, 2017 11:17:04 PM`.

To determine the `SID`, username, and age of user profiles, you can perform the following:

```
$profiles = get-wmiobject Win32_UserProfile
foreach ($profile in $profiles) {
    $currentdate = Get-Date
```

```
    $lastusetime = $profile.LastUseTime
    $lastusetime = [Management.ManagementDateTimeConverter]::ToDateTime($
lastusetime)
    $age = [math]::Round(($currentdate - $lastusetime).TotalDays)


    $sid = $profile.SID
    Try {
        $usersid = New-Object System.Security.Principal.
SecurityIdentifier("$SID")
        $username = $usersid.Translate( [System.Security.Principal.
NTAccount]).Value
    }
    Catch {
        Write-Host "There was an error translating SID value $sid to a
username. Account may not exist."
        $username = "(Deleted Account)"
    }
    Write-host "User with name $username and SID $sid last logged in
$lastusetime. ($age Days Old)"
}
```

The output of this is shown in the following screenshot:

This example displays how to retrieve the SID, username, and age of user profiles. You first start by leveraging the `get-wmiobject` cmdlet with the `win32_UserProfile` class argument and storing the `UserProfile` objects in the `$profiles` variable. You then leverage a `foreach` loop with the `$profile` as the iterator, and `$profiles` as the dataset. For the profile aging process, you call the `Get-Date` cmdlet and set the value in the `$currentdate` variable. You then take the current instance of the `$profile.LastUseTime` property, and place it in the `$lastusetime` variable.

To calculate the age, you first have to convert the `$lastusetime` to a friendly format. To do this, you leverage the `[Management.ManagementDateTimeConverter]::ToDateTime()` method with the `$lastusetime` variable as the argument and place the result in the `$lastusetime` variable. This overwrites the previous DMTF-formatted value with the standard time format value. You then calculate the age by subtracting the `$currentdate` variable from `$lastusetime`, and selecting the `.TotalDays` property. Since the returned value has decimals, you perform the .net rounding calculation using the `[math]::Round()` method on the `TotalDays` property result. This returns a single digit as a date age, which is set in the `$age` variable.

To calculate the username, you call the current instance `$profile.SID` property and set it equal to the `$sid` variable. You then perform a `Try{` statement to catch any .NET translate errors on the SID. Inside the `Try` statement, you obtain the SID object using the `New-Object` cmdlet with the `System.Security.Principal.SecurityIdentifier()` class and the `$SID` argument. The SID object is then returned to the `$usersid` variable. You then translate the SID to a `NTAccount` leveraging the `$usersid.Translate()` method set to the `[System.Security.Principal.NTAccount]` class object. After the value translates, you call the `.Value` property to place the result in the `$username` variable.

In the instance the SID or user doesn't exist, you perform a `Catch {` statement to catch the error. If this occurs, you write to the display using the `Write-Host` cmdlet `"There was an error translating SID value $sid to a username. Account may not exist"`. You then set the `$username` variable to `"(Deleted Account)"`.

As the last step, you write to the screen leveraging the `Write-Host` cmdlet `"User with the name $username and SID $sid last logged in $lastusetime. ($age Days old)"`. After processing this script, this example displays the built-in, local, and domain profiles that are on the system.

Summary

In this chapter, you learned about Windows services and how to stop, start, and set items in Windows Services. You went on to learn about Windows processes and how to get, stop, and start processes. You learned how to scan a system for logged in users through the running processes on a system. You ended the chapter by learning how to evaluate user profiles on a system using PowerShell.

In the next chapter, you will learn how to interact with scheduled tasks on a system.

6
Evaluating Scheduled Tasks

Enterprises leverage scheduled tasks for a multitude of purposes. Whether it is to process business transactions or to provide health checks, they have become the standard for running actions on a scheduled basis. Scheduled tasks are flexible, in that they can also be run on logon, after a certain event is triggered, or even manually. Scheduled tasks can run executables, or even start scripts to extend limitless possibilities for automation.

Due to the wide variety of uses for scheduled tasks, it's important to scan them with the Windows server scanning script. This will help you identify processes that only run on a triggered or scheduled basis, such as a quarterly report or a nightly process. It can also be used to identify alternate user accounts that are used to run these scheduled tasks. Since scheduled tasks are so flexible, it's essential to capture what the scheduled tasks are doing, how they are invoked, and what account is designated to run the task.

In this chapter, you will:

- Understand how to view scheduled tasks on a system
- Create scheduled task triggers, actions, and setting set objects
- Leverage the triggers, actions, and setting sets to create a scheduled task object
- Register and unregister scheduled tasks with a system
- Update an existing scheduled task with new actions
- Identify scheduled tasks running as alternate user accounts

Scheduled tasks

Scheduled tasks enable you to schedule automated actions on a system. Microsoft has a wide variety of built-in scheduled tasks, which include time synchronization, universal plug and play, Windows updates, and disk defragmentation. These task actions are invoked by different trigger criteria and automatically run on your system.

You can retrieve the list of scheduled tasks on a system by using the `get-scheduledtask` cmdlet. The `get-scheduledtask` cmdlet reveals a list of scheduled task names, their taskpath, and their current state. You may also return other properties such as author, date, description, version, and documentation.

To retrieve and count scheduled tasks on a system, you can leverage the following:

```
get-scheduledtask
(get-scheduledtask).count
```

The output of this command would look like this:

```
\Microso..\Windows\Storage Tiers Managemen..\  Storage Tiers Managemen.. ni.1...   Ready
\Microsoft\Windows\Storage Tiers Management\   Storage Tiers Optimization           Disabled
\Microsoft\Windows\Subscription\               EnableLicenseAcquisition             Ready
\Microsoft\Windows\Subscription\               LicenseAcquisition                   Disabled
\Microsoft\Windows\Sysmain\                    HybridDriveCachePrepopulate          Disabled
\Microsoft\Windows\Sysmain\                    HybridDriveCacheRebalance            Disabled
\Microsoft\Windows\Sysmain\                    ResPriStaticDbSync                   Ready
\Microsoft\Windows\Sysmain\                    WsSwapAssessmentTask                 Ready
\Microsoft\Windows\SystemRestore\              SR                                   Ready
\Microsoft\Windows\Task Manager\               Interactive                          Ready
\Microsoft\Windows\TextServicesFramework\      MsCtfMonitor                         Running
\Microsoft\Windows\Time Synchronization\       ForceSynchronizeTime                 Ready
\Microsoft\Windows\Time Synchronization\       SynchronizeTime                      Ready
\Microsoft\Windows\Time Zone\                  SynchronizeTimeZone                  Ready
\Microsoft\Windows\TPM\                        Tpm-HASCertRetr                      Ready
\Microsoft\Windows\TPM\                        Tpm-Maintenance                      Ready
\Microsoft\Windows\UpdateOrchestrator\         Maintenance Install                  Disabled
\Microsoft\Windows\UpdateOrchestrator\         Policy Install                       Disabled
\Microsoft\Windows\UpdateOrchestrator\         Reboot                               Ready
\Microsoft\Windows\UpdateOrchestrator\         Refresh Settings                     Ready
\Microsoft\Windows\UpdateOrchestrator\         Resume On Boot                       Disabled
\Microsoft\Windows\UpdateOrchestrator\         Schedule Scan                        Ready
\Microsoft\Windows\UpdateOrchestrator\         USO_UxBroker_Display                 Ready
\Microsoft\Windows\UpdateOrchestrator\         USO_UxBroker_ReadyToReboot           Ready
\Microsoft\Windows\UPnP\                        UPnPHostConfig                       Ready
\Microsoft\Windows\User Profile Service\       HiveUploadTask                       Disabled
\Microsoft\Windows\WCM\                        WiFiTask                             Ready
\Microsoft\Windows\WDI\                        ResolutionHost                       Ready
\Microsoft\Windows\Windows Error Reporting\    QueueReporting                       Ready
\Microsoft\Windows\Windows Filtering Platform\ BfeOnServiceStartTypeChange          Ready
\Microsoft\Windows\Windows Media Sharing\      UpdateLibrary                        Ready
\Microsoft\Windows\WindowsColorSystem\         Calibration Loader                   Disabled
\Microsoft\Windows\WindowsUpdate\              Automatic App Update                 Ready
\Microsoft\Windows\WindowsUpdate\              Scheduled Start                      Ready
\Microsoft\Windows\WindowsUpdate\              sih                                  Ready
\Microsoft\Windows\WindowsUpdate\              sihboot                              Ready
\Microsoft\Windows\Wininet\                    CacheTask                            Running
\Microsoft\Windows\WOF\                        WIM-Hash-Management                  Ready
\Microsoft\Windows\WOF\                        WIM-Hash-Validation                  Ready
\Microsoft\Windows\Work Folders\               Work Folders Logon Synchroniza...    Ready
\Microsoft\Windows\Work Folders\               Work Folders Maintenance Work        Ready
\Microsoft\Windows\Workplace Join\             Automatic-Device-Join                Disabled
\Microsoft\Windows Live\SOXE\                   Extractor Definitions Update Task   Ready
\Microsoft\XblGameSave\                        XblGameSaveTask                      Ready
\Microsoft\XblGameSave\                        XblGameSaveTaskLogon                 Ready

PS C:\> (get-scheduledtask).count
165
```

This example displays how to retrieve scheduled tasks on a system and how to count the total number of tasks:

1. You first start by calling the `get-scheduledtask` cmdlet. You will see a long list of scheduled tasks displayed on your system.

2. You then execute the `get-scheduledtask` cmdlet with the `.count` method. The system in this example returns 165 scheduled tasks.

The two components that are required to create a scheduled task are the task action and task trigger. Task triggers start the scheduled task. The most common triggers are on a schedule, at logon, at startup, on idle, on an event, and manual. In order to use a trigger, you must leverage the `New-ScheduledTaskTrigger` cmdlet to create a new task trigger object. You will then need to store the task trigger object in a variable for creating the scheduled task.

To create a scheduled task trigger on a schedule, you can perform the following:

```
$schTrigger = New-ScheduledTaskTrigger -Daily -DaysInterval 1 -At "23:00"
$schTrigger
```

The output of this command would look like this:

```
PS C:\> $schTrigger = New-ScheduledTaskTrigger -Daily -DaysInterval 1 -At "23:00"
PS C:\> $schTrigger

Id          Frequency      Time                        DaysOfWeek          Enabled
--          ---------      ----                        ----------          -------
0           Daily          2/18/2017 11:00:00 PM                           True
```

In this example, you learn how to create a scheduled task trigger:

1. You first start by calling the `New-ScheduledTaskTrigger` cmdlet with the `-Daily` parameter, the `-DaysInterval` parameter with the 1 attribute, and the `-At` parameter set to the `23:00` attribute.

2. You then store this scheduled task trigger object in the `$schTrigger` variable. When you call the `$schTrigger` variable, it returns the trigger `Id` of `0`, the `Frequency` of `Daily`, the `Time` of `2/18/2017 11:00:00 PM`, the `DaysofWeek` of `$null`, and `Enabled` set to `true`.

 For more information on scheduled task triggers and their syntax, you can browse to: `https://technet.microsoft.com/itpro/powershell/windows/scheduled-tasks/new-scheduledtasktrigger`.

Task actions define what the scheduled task is executing. Task actions can be as simple as running an executable, or can invoke a script to do a wide variety of actions. You use the `New-ScheduledTaskAction` cmdlet to create a new action object. Along with the cmdlet, you can leverage the `-Execute` parameter to start an executable. You also have the `-Argument` parameter, which enables you to pass in arguments to the executable being invoked. You will need to store the task action object in a variable to create the scheduled task.

To create a scheduled task action to open `calc.exe`, you can perform the following:

```
$schAction = New-ScheduledTaskAction -Execute "Calc.exe"
$schAction
```

The output of this command would look like this:

```
PS C:\> $schAction = New-ScheduledTaskAction -Execute "Calc.exe"
PS C:\> $schAction


Id                  :
Arguments           :
Execute             : Calc.exe
WorkingDirectory    :
PSComputerName      :
```

In this example, you learn how to create a scheduled task action:

1. You first start by calling the `New-ScheduledTaskAction` cmdlet with the `-Execute` parameter set to the `calc.exe` attribute.
2. You then save this scheduled task object in the `$schAction` variable.

When you call the `$schAction` variable, it returns the Id of `$null`, the `Arguments` of `$null`, the `Execute` of `Calc.exe`, the `WorkingDirectory` of `$null` and `PSComputerName` of `$null`. If there other parameters were passed into the `new-ScheduledTaskAction` cmdlet, the `$null` fields would be populated with data.

An optional component for configuration is task setting sets, which provide configurations for the scheduled task itself. If you want to include additional parameters, you can configure execution on batteries, execution duration, idle duration, restart count, and restart interval. You can use the `New-ScheduledTaskSettingsSet` cmdlet to define the scheduled task settings set, and you will need to store it in a variable to create the scheduled task.

To create a scheduled task setting set with the `-DisallowDemandStart`, `-Hidden`, and `-DisallowHardTerminate` parameters, you can perform the following actions:

```
$schSettingSet = New-ScheduledTaskSettingsSet -DisallowDemandStart
-Hidden -DisallowHardTerminate
```

```
$schSettingSet
```

The output of this command would look like the following:

```
PS C:\> $schSettingSet = New-ScheduledTaskSettingsSet -DisallowDemandStart -Hidden -DisallowHardTerminate
PS C:\> $schSettingSet

AllowDemandStart                : False
AllowHardTerminate              : False
Compatibility                   : Win7
DeleteExpiredTaskAfter          :
DisallowStartIfOnBatteries      : True
Enabled                         : True
ExecutionTimeLimit              : PT72H
Hidden                          : True
IdleSettings                    : MSFT_TaskIdleSettings
MultipleInstances               : IgnoreNew
NetworkSettings                 : MSFT_TaskNetworkSettings
Priority                        : 7
RestartCount                    : 0
RestartInterval                 :
RunOnlyIfIdle                   : False
RunOnlyIfNetworkAvailable       : False
StartWhenAvailable              : False
StopIfGoingOnBatteries          : True
WakeToRun                       : False
DisallowStartOnRemoteAppSession : False
UseUnifiedSchedulingEngine      : True
MaintenanceSettings             :
Volatile                        : False
PSComputerName                  :
```

In this example, you create a new scheduled task setting set:

1. You first start by declaring the `New-ScheduledTaskSettingSet`cmdlet with the `-DisallowDemandStart`, `-Hidden`, and `-DisallowHardTerminate` parameters.

2. You then set the scheduled task setting set object to the `$schSettingSet` variable.

When you call the `$schSettingSet` cmdlet, you reveal all of the parameters the scheduled task setting set has. In this setting set, you can see `AllowDemandStart` is set to `False`, `AllowHardTerminate` is set to `False`, and `Hidden` is set to `True`.

 For more information on scheduled task settings and their syntax, you can browse to: `https://technet.microsoft.com/itpro/powershell/windows/scheduled-tasks/new-scheduledtasksettingsset`.

After capturing the task action and task trigger in variables, you create the scheduled task object. You call the `New-ScheduledTask` cmdlet with the `-Action` parameter, referencing the task action object, and the `-Trigger` parameter referencing the task trigger object. You may also use the optional task settings set by the `-Settings` parameter, by referencing the task settings set object. You place all of these items into a variable that will contain the scheduled task object.

To create a scheduled task variable, you can perform the following actions:

```
$schAction = New-ScheduledTaskAction -Execute "Calc.exe"

$schTrigger = New-ScheduledTaskTrigger -Daily -DaysInterval 1 -At "23:00"

$schSettingSet = New-ScheduledTaskSettingsSet -DisallowDemandStart
-Hidden -DisallowHardTerminate

$schTask = New-ScheduledTask -Action $schAction -Trigger $schTrigger
-Settings $schSettingSet

$schTask

$schTask.Triggers
```

The output of this command would look like this:

This example displays how to take the scheduled task action, trigger, and setting set to create a scheduled task object:

1. You first start by calling the `New-ScheduledTaskAction` cmdlet with the `-Execute` parameter set to the `calc.exe` attribute.

2. You then save this scheduled task object in the `$schAction` variable.

3. You then use the `New-ScheduledTaskAction` cmdlet with the `-Execute` parameter set to the `calc.exe` attribute.

4. You then save this scheduled task object in the `$schAction` variable.

5. You continue to declare the `New-ScheduledTaskSettingSet` cmdlet with the `-DisallowDemandStart`, `-Hidden`, and `-DisallowHardTerminate` parameters.

6. You then set the scheduled task setting set object to the `$schSettingSet` variable.

7. Finally, you call the `New-scheduledTask` cmdlet with the `-Action` parameter set to `$schAction`, the `-Trigger` parameter set to `$schTrigger`, and the `-Settings` parameter set to `$schSettingSet`.

8. You then take the scheduled task object and place it in the `$schTask` variable.

   When you call the `$schTask` variable, however, it comes back with a blank `TaskPath`, `TaskName`, and `State`. This is because the task will need to be registered, as explained in the next step. Although `TaskPath`, `TaskName`, and `State` properties are blank, when you call properties such as `$schTask.Triggers`, you will see that those properties are populated properly. In this case, it returns the `11PM` trigger you set up in the earlier step.

9. The last step is to register the scheduled task on the system.

To register a scheduled task, you can leverage the `Register-ScheduledTask` cmdlet with the `-TaskName` parameter and the desired name as the argument. You will need to also include the `-InputObject` parameter, referencing the object you created with the `New-ScheduledTask` cmdlet. After execution, the scheduled task will be properly created on your system.

If you want to remove a scheduled task, you can leverage the `Unregister-ScheduledTask` cmdlet with the `-TaskName` parameter and the desired name for removal as the argument. After execution, the `Unregister-ScheduledTask` cmdlet will prompt you to confirm deleting the scheduled task. To suspend the confirm prompt, you can leverage `-Confirm:$false` as a parameter. This will remove the scheduled task from the system without prompting.

To register two scheduled tasks to start the calculator every day at 11:00 pm, and unregister one of the scheduled tasks, you perform the following actions:

```
$schAction = New-ScheduledTaskAction -Execute "Calc.exe"
$schTrigger = New-ScheduledTaskTrigger -Daily -DaysInterval 1 -At "23:00"
$schTask = New-ScheduledTask -Action $schAction -Trigger $schTrigger
Register-ScheduledTask -TaskName "Start Calc Daily at 11PM" -InputObject $schTask
```

```
Register-ScheduledTask -TaskName "Start Calc Daily at 11PM_DeleteMe"
-InputObject $schTask

Unregister-ScheduledTask -TaskName "Start Calc Daily at 11PM_DeleteMe"
-Confirm:$false

Get-ScheduledTask | where {$_.TaskName -like "Start Calc Daily at 11PM*"}
```

The output of this command would look like this:

```
PS C:\> $schAction = New-ScheduledTaskAction -Execute "Calc.exe"
PS C:\> $schTrigger = New-ScheduledTaskTrigger -Daily -DaysInterval 1 -At "23:00"
PS C:\> $schTask = New-ScheduledTask -Action $schAction -Trigger $schTrigger
PS C:\> Register-ScheduledTask -TaskName "Start Calc Daily at 11PM" -InputObject $schTask

TaskPath                              TaskName                    State
--------                              --------                    -----
\                                     Start Calc Daily at 11PM    Ready


PS C:\> Register-ScheduledTask -TaskName "Start Calc Daily at 11PM_DeleteMe" -InputObject $schTask

TaskPath                              TaskName                        State
--------                              --------                        -----
\                                     Start Calc Daily at 11PM_DeleteMe Ready


PS C:\> Unregister-ScheduledTask -TaskName "Start Calc Daily at 11PM_DeleteMe" -Confirm:$false
PS C:\> Get-ScheduledTask | where {$_.TaskName -like "Start Calc Daily at 11PM*"}

TaskPath                              TaskName                    State
--------                              --------                    -----
\                                     Start Calc Daily at 11PM    Ready
```

In this example, you learn how to create two scheduled tasks to launch calculator every day at 11:00 pm. You also learn how to remove one of the two scheduled tasks:

1. You first start by creating a scheduled task action leveraging the new-ScheduledTaskAction cmdlet with the -Execute parameter and the Calc.exe argument.

2. You place this object into the $schAction variable.

3. You continue to create the scheduled task trigger by leveraging the new-ScheduledTaskTrigger cmdlet with the -Daily parameter, the -DaysInterval parameter with the argument of 1, and the -At parameter with the argument of 23:00.

4. You place the scheduled task trigger object into the $schTrigger variable.

5. You then create the scheduled task object by leveraging the New-ScheduledTask cmdlet with the -Action parameter set to the argument of $schAction, and the -Trigger parameter set to the argument of $schTrigger.

6. You place this scheduled task object into the $schTask variable.

7. To register the scheduled task on the system with two different names, you leverage the `Register-ScheduledTask` cmdlet with the `-TaskName` parameter set to the `Start Calc Daily at 11pm` argument. You also include the `-InputObject` parameter set to the `$schTask` variable. After execution, a scheduled task is created with the name `Start Calc Daily at 11pm`.

8. To create a second scheduled task, you leverage the `RegisterScheduledTask` cmdlet with the `-TaskName` parameter set to the `Start Calc Daily at 11pm_DeleteMe` argument. You also include the `-inputobject` parameter set to the `$schTask` variable. After execution, a scheduled task is created with the name `Start Calc Daily at 11pm_DeleteMe`.

To unregister the scheduled task with the name ending in `_Deleteme`, you use the `Unregister-scheduledtask` cmdlet with the `-TaskName` parameter set to `Start Calc Daily at 11PM_DeleteMe`. You also use the `-Confirm:$false` parameter to designate that the cmdlet does not need to prompt for confirmation. After execution, the scheduled task named `Start Calc Daily at 11PM_DeleteMe` is deregistered from the system. You confirm this by running the `Get-ScheduledTask` cmdlet, piped to `where {$_.TaskName -like "Start Calc Daily at 11PM*"}`. After execution, the script returns a single instance of `Start Calc Daily at 11PM`.

There are two primary methods to modify a scheduled task:

1. You may choose to unregister and recreate a scheduled task.

2. You may choose to leverage the `set-scheduledtask` cmdlet. The `set-ScheduledTask` cmdlet allows you to call a specific scheduled task by the `-TaskName` parameter, and specify new or additional triggers, actions, and scheduled task settings.

Leveraging the previous example, to set two new scheduled task actions to open notepad and calc, you can do the following:

```
$schAction1 = New-ScheduledTaskAction -Execute "Calc.exe"

$schAction2 = New-ScheduledTaskAction -Execute "Notepad.exe"

Set-ScheduledTask -TaskName "Start Calc Daily at 11PM" -Action $schAction1,$schAction2
```

The output of this command would look like this:

```
PS C:\> $schAction1 = New-ScheduledTaskAction -Execute "Calc.exe"
PS C:\> $schAction2 = New-ScheduledTaskAction -Execute "Notepad.exe"
PS C:\> Set-ScheduledTask -TaskName "Start Calc Daily at 11PM" -Action $schAction1,$schAction2

TaskPath                                TaskName                      State
--------                                --------                      -----
\                                       Start Calc Daily at 11PM      Ready
```

This example displays how to update an existing scheduled task to have two new scheduled task actions:

1. You first start by calling the `New-ScheduledTaskAction` cmdlet with the `-Execute` parameter and the `calc.exe` argument.

2. You place this scheduled action task object in the `$schAction1` variable.

3. You then call the `New-ScheduledTaskAction` cmdlet with the `-Execute` parameter and the `notepad.exe` argument.

4. You place this scheduled action task object in the `$schAction2` variable.

5. Finally, you call the `Set-ScheduledTask` cmdlet with the `-TaskName` parameter set to `Start Calc Daily at 11PM`. You also call the `-Action` parameter and declare both actions: `$schAction1,$schAction2`. After execution, a scheduled task is set up for 11:00 pm and will launch both `calc.exe` and `notepad.exe`.

> At the time of writing, there is no native way to rename a scheduled task. In order to perform this, you need to export the scheduled task to XML, and register a new scheduled task with the XML file. More information on the export process can be found here: `https://technet.microsoft.com/itpro/powershell/windows/scheduled-tasks/export-scheduledtask`.

Identifying scheduled tasks running as alternate users

There may be instances where you need to identify scheduled tasks that are running with non-default credentials. If a user leverages their identity to run a scheduled task, or you are leveraging a service account, you will need to identify its usage on a system. The `Get-ScheduledTasks` cmdlet has the Principal property, which contains information about the user account running the scheduled task. The `UserID` reflects the username of the account that is designated to run the scheduled task.

In addition to identifying the Principal UserId, you will need to filter out built-in Windows accounts. To perform this, you can create a switch statement to make multiple evaluations of the Principal UserIds. If the process owner username is NETWORK SERVICE, LOCAL SERVICE, $null, or System, you can skip reporting the username. If it doesn't match any of those values, it will use the default switch and report the user to a list. Since multiple scheduled tasks run under the same user, you can pipe the user results to the `get-unique` cmdlet, which will only select the unique values in the array.

To evaluate scheduled tasks and obtain a list of accounts running scheduled tasks, you can perform the following actions:

```
$users = @()
$schtasks = Get-ScheduledTask
foreach ($Task in $schtasks) {
    $tskUser = $Task.Principal.UserId
    switch ($Task.Principal.UserId) {
"NETWORK SERVICE" { $continue = "Skip User" }
"LOCAL SERVICE" { $continue = "Skip User" }
"SYSTEM" { $continue = "Skip User"}
"$null" { $continue = "Skip User" }
        default { $continue = "Report User" }
    }
    if ($continue -eq "Report User") {

        $users += $tskUser

    }
}
$users | Get-Unique
```

The output of this is shown in the following screenshot:

```
PS C:\> $users = @()
PS C:\> $schtasks = Get-ScheduledTask
PS C:\> foreach ($Task in $schtasks) {
>>      $tskUser = $Task.Principal.UserId
>>      switch ($Task.Principal.UserId) {
>>          "NETWORK SERVICE" { $continue = "Skip User" }
>>          "LOCAL SERVICE" { $continue = "Skip User" }
>>          "SYSTEM" { $continue = "Skip User"}
>>          "$null" { $continue = "Skip User" }
>>          default { $continue = "Report User" }
>>      }
>>      if ($continue -eq "Report User") {
>>
>>          $users += $tskUser
>>      }
>> }
>> $users | Get-Unique
>>
POSHDEMO\bblawat
POSHDEMO\svcSchTasks
```

This example displays how to output non-built-in user accounts running scheduled tasks:

1. You start by defining an array named `$users`.

2. You then leverage the `Get-ScheduledTask` cmdlet, placing the result in the `$schtasks` variable.

3. You then create a `foreach` loop to loop through each `$Task` in the `$schtasks`variable.

4. You proceed to gather the iterative scheduled task's `Principal.UserID` by using the `$Task.Prinicipal.UserID` property and place it in the `$tskUser` variable.

5. You then declare a `switch` statement evaluating the `$Task.Principal. UserID` property. The first evaluations are for built-in accounts. If the accounts are `NETWORK SERVICE`, `LOCAL SERVICE`, `SYSTEM`, or `$null`, it will set `$continue` to `Skip User`. If it doesn't match any of these built-in users, it will leverage the `default` value, which sets the `$continue` variable to `Report User`.

6. After exiting the `switch` statement, you evaluate the `$continue` variable with an `If` statement, and proceed if the value is equal to `Report User`. This step will add the `$tskUser` variable to the `$users` array.

After the `foreach` loop completes, you will have a large number of users listed for each non-built-in user. To trim the list to individual or unique users, you pipe the `$users` variable to the `get-unique` cmdlet. The result is a list of unique non-built-in users on the system.

The system the example was run on has two non-default user accounts: `POSHDEMO\bblawat` and `POSHDEMO\svcSchTasks`.

Summary

In this chapter, you learned how to work with scheduled tasks in PowerShell. You started by learning how to get scheduled tasks on a system. You then learned how to set scheduled task triggers, scheduled task actions, and scheduled task setting sets. You continued by creating a scheduled task object and registering it with the system. You also learned how to unregister a scheduled task to remove it from the system. You then worked through updating an existing scheduled task. You completed the chapter by learning how to identify any users or service accounts whose permissions are being used to run the scheduled task.

In the next chapter, you will be learning how to query the system to determine disk statistics such as free space, disk utilization, and drive type determinations.

7
Determining Disk Statistics

Another important component to evaluate with the Windows server scanning script is disk statistics. Whether you are scanning to the identify configuration or scanning to replace a system, it's important to evaluate the full disk configuration. Through PowerShell, you have the ability to gather information about your physical disk layout, your logical disk layout, and even removable devices plugged into your system. This can be helpful to identify USB licensing key devices, or even external hard drives plugged in to back up the system.

The Windows server scanning script can also enable you to view the disk size and free space of all devices connected to the system. This information can be helpful in the event that the system is running low on disk space, or if the drive sizes don't conform to your corporate standards. This chapter will enable you to get detailed visibility into the disk configuration on your systems.

In this chapter, we discuss the following topics:

- Retrieving physical and logical disk information
- Determining the disk types connected to your system
- Converting from disk byte values into megabytes and gigabytes
- Dynamically determining disk unit of measure
- Creating a disk information script to query the disks on a system, convert disk size and freespace, calculate units of measure, and identify drive types

 For the best results with the examples in this chapter, it is recommended to use a system with multiple disks. You may also choose to plug in external hard disks or USB drives to emulate additional storage devices.

Disk statistics

Whether you are capacity-planning or planning for server replacements, there are many reasons why you may want to evaluate disk information. PowerShell offers several methods to retrieve disk information. If you want to learn more about the physical disks on your system, you can leverage the get-disk cmdlet. The get-disk cmdlet provides information such as Number, Friendly Name, Serial Number, HealthStatus, OperationalStatus,Total size, and Partition Style.

 To determine all of the properties available to the get-disk cmdlet, you can execute get-disk | get-member. This will display all of the available methods and properties for the physical disks.

Retrieving physical and logical disk information

To retrieve disk information about the physical disks on your system, you can perform the following command:

```
get-disk
```

The output of this is shown in the following screenshot:

This example displays how to get information about the physical disks on a system. When you execute the get-disk cmdlet, the cmdlet returns the disk Number, Friendly Name, Serial Number, HealthStatus, OperationalStatus, TotalSize, and Partition Style. The system this example was run on had five logical devices connected, which are reflected in the output from the cmdlet.

When you want to determine more information about the operating system usage of a disk, you can leverage **Windows Management Instrumentation (WMI)**. To read the logical disk information, you can use the get-wmiobject cmdlet with the -class parameter set to the win32_logicaldisk argument. When you query the win32_logicaldisk class, you can access the DeviceID, DriveType, ProviderName, FreeSpace, Size, and Volume name properties.

To query the `win32_logicaldisk` class for disk information, you can perform the following:

```
Get-WmiObject -class win32_logicaldisk
```

The output of this is shown in the following screenshot:

```
PS C:\> Get-WmiObject -class win32_logicaldisk

DeviceID     : C:
DriveType    : 3
ProviderName :
FreeSpace    : 866677022720
Size         : 999677751296
VolumeName   :

DeviceID     : D:
DriveType    : 3
ProviderName :
FreeSpace    : 281996746752
Size         : 1000202039296
VolumeName   : Data

DeviceID     : E:
DriveType    : 5
ProviderName :
FreeSpace    :
Size         :
VolumeName   :

DeviceID     : F:
DriveType    : 3
ProviderName :
FreeSpace    : 131263758336
Size         : 499983122432
VolumeName   : ADATA SH02

DeviceID     : G:
DriveType    : 3
ProviderName :
FreeSpace    : 99130903756 8
Size         : 1000169533440
VolumeName   : My Passport

DeviceID     : H:
DriveType    : 2
ProviderName :
FreeSpace    : 1910505472
Size         : 2003501056
VolumeName   : KINGSTON
```

The following example displays how to leverage `get-wmiobject` to query WMI to provide disk information:

1. You start by leveraging the `get-wmiobject` cmdlet with the `-class` parameter set to the `win32_logicaldisk` argument.

2. After execution, the cmdlet returns the `DeviceID`, `DriveType`, `ProviderName`, `FreeSpace`, `Size`, and `VolumeName` properties.

The system this example was run on had six devices connected, reflected in the output from the cmdlet. This differs from the get-disk cmdlet, and the WMI provider accounts for the empty CD-ROM/DVD drive.

The DriveType property

The DriveType property represents a numerical value that translates to a type of drive. This value ranges from 0 to 6, depending on the type of physical device connected. The DriveType correlation is as follows:

- **0**: Unknown device type
- **1**: Drive does not have a root directory
- **2**: Removable disk (USB key)
- **3**: Local disk (hard drive/USB hard drive/virtual drive mount)
- **4**: Network drive/mapped drive
- **5**: Compact disk (CD/DVD drive)
- **6**: RAM drive (memory mapped drive/PE OS drive)

To quickly determine the DriveType property correlation, you can perform the following switch command:

```
$disks = get-wmiobject win32_logicaldisk
Foreach ($disk in $disks) {
    $driveletter = $disk.DeviceID
    switch ($disk.DriveType) {
        0 { $type = "Type Unknown." }
        1 { $type = "Doesn't have a Root Directory." }
        2 { $type = "Removable Disk (e.g. USB Key)" }
        3 { $type = "Local Disk (e.g. Hard Drive / USB hard drive /
Virtual drive mount)" }
        4 { $type = "Network Drive (e.g. Mapped Drive)" }
        5 { $type = "Compact Disk (e.g. CD/DVD Drive)" }
        6 { $type = "RAM Disk (e.g. Memory Mapped Drive / PE OS Drive)" }
        default { $type = "Unable To Determine Drive Type!" }
    }
    Write-host "Drive: $driveletter | Disk Type: $type"
}
```

The output of this script is shown in the following screenshot:

```
PS C:\> $disks = get-wmiobject win32_logicaldis:
PS C:\> Foreach ($disk in $disks) {
>>      $driveletter = $disk.DeviceID
>>      switch ($disk.DriveType) {
>>          0 { $type = "Type Unknown." }
>>          1 { $type = "Doesn't have a Root Directory." }
>>          2 { $type = "Removable Disk (e.g. USB Key)" }
>>          3 { $type = "Local Disk (e.g. Hard Drive / USB hard drive / Virtual drive mount)" }
>>          4 { $type = "Network Drive (e.g. Mapped Drive)" }
>>          5 { $type = "Compact Disk (e.g. CD/DVD Drive)" }
>>          6 { $type = "RAM Disk (e.g. Memory Mapped Drive / PE OS Drive)" }
>>          default { $type = "Unable To Determine Drive Type!" }
>>      }
>>      Write-host "Drive: $driveletter | Disk Type: $type"
>> }
Drive: C: | Disk Type: Local Disk (e.g. Hard Drive / USB hard drive / Virtual drive mount)
Drive: D: | Disk Type: Local Disk (e.g. Hard Drive / USB hard drive / Virtual drive mount)
Drive: E: | Disk Type: Compact Disk (e.g. CD/DVD Drive)
Drive: F: | Disk Type: Local Disk (e.g. Hard Drive / USB hard drive / Virtual drive mount)
Drive: G: | Disk Type: Local Disk (e.g. Hard Drive / USB hard drive / Virtual drive mount)
Drive: H: | Disk Type: Removable Disk (e.g. USB Key)
```

In this example, you create a `switch` statement to correlate `DriveType` numbers with readable values:

1. You start by using `get-wmiobject` with the `win32_logicaldisk` argument and storing the drive information in the `$disks` variable.

2. You then create a `Foreach` statement to evaluate each `$disk` in the `$disks` variable.

3. You then gather the drive letter by calling the `$disk.DeviceID` property and setting the value in `$driveletter`.

4. You then start your `switch` statement and evaluate the `$disk.DriveType` value.

    The `switch` statement evaluates the number and correlates it to a readable value. If the `DriveType` is 0, it will set the `$type` variable to `Type Unknown`. If the `DriveType` is 1, it will set the `$type` variable to `Doesn't have a Root Directory`. If the `DriveType` is 2, it will set the `$type` variable to `Removable Disk (e.g. USB key)`. If the `DriveType` is 3, it will set the `$type` variable to `Local Disk (e.g. Hard Drive / USB hard drive / Virtual drive mount)`. If the `DriveType` is 4, it will set the `$type` variable to `Network Drive (e.g. Mapped Drive)`. If the `DriveType` is 5, it will set the `$type` variable to `Compact Disk (e.g. CD/DVD Drive)`. If the `DriveType` is 6, it will set the `$type` variable to `RAM Disk (e.g. Memory Mapped Drive / PE OS Drive)`.

5. After these evaluations, you then leverage the `write-host` cmdlet to print to the screen: `Drive: $driveletter | Disk Type: $type`.

The system this example was run on had five logical devices connected, with different drive types. The different drive types are reflected in the output from the cmdlet.

Converting disk space to MB and GB

When working with the `Size` and `FreeSpace` properties of the logical disks, the values are represented in bytes. PowerShell offers a quick method to convert bytes into multiple formats. You can take the `Size` or `FreeSpace` properties and divide them by 1MB for megabytes, 1GB for gigabytes, 1TB for terabytes, and 1PB for petabytes. After the conversion, however, you often need to round the numbers, leveraging the `[System.Math]::Round()` method. By default, this `.NET` `Round()` method rounds to the closest full number. To include decimal places, you can provide an additional numerical argument, such as `[System.Math]::Round($value,2)`, to round the `$value` to two decimal places.

To convert the disk `Size` property to megabytes and gigabytes, you can perform the following actions:

```
$disks = get-wmiobject win32_logicaldisk
Foreach ($disk in $disks) {
   $driveletter = $disk.DeviceID
   $sizeMB = [System.Math]::Round(($disk.size / 1MB),2)
   $sizeGB = [System.Math]::Round(($disk.size / 1GB),2)
   Write-host "$driveletter | Size (in MB): $sizeMB | Size (in GB):
$sizeGB"
}
```

The output of this script is shown in the following screenshot:

```
PS C:\> $disks = get-wmiobject win32_logicaldis:
PS C:\> Foreach ($disk in $disks) {
>>     $driveletter = $disk.DeviceID
>>     $sizeMB = [System.Math]::Round(($disk.size / 1MB),2)
>>     $sizeGB = [System.Math]::Round(($disk.size / 1GB),2)
>>     Write-host "$driveletter | Size (in MB): $sizeMB | Size (in GB): $sizeGB"
>> }
C: | Size (in MB): 953367 | Size (in GB): 931.02
D: | Size (in MB): 953867 | Size (in GB): 931.51
E: | Size (in MB): 0 | Size (in GB): 0
F: | Size (in MB): 476821.06 | Size (in GB): 465.65
G: | Size (in MB): 953836 | Size (in GB): 931.48
H: | Size (in MB): 1910.69 | Size (in GB): 1.87
```

This example displays how to format a hard drive `Size` property to megabytes and gigabytes:

1. You first start the script by leveraging the `get-wmiobject` cmdlet with the `win32_logicaldisk` argument and place the returned values in the `$disks` variable.

2. You then create a `Foreach` statement to evaluate each `$disk` in the `$disks` variable.

3. You evaluate the `$disk.DeviceID` property and set the drive letter value to the `$driveletter` variable.

4. You then leverage the `[System.Math]::Round()` method to round the value of the calculation from the `$disk.size` parameter, divided by 1MB.

5. You also pass the `,2` argument into the method to provide two decimal places in the calculation.

6. You store the output of this value in the `$sizeMB` variable.

7. You continue to leverage the `[System.Math]::Round()` method to round the value of the calculation from the `$disk.size` parameter, divided by 1GB.

8. You again pass the `,2` argument into the method to provide two decimal places in the calculation.

9. You store the output of this value in the `$sizeGB` variable.

10. Finally, you leverage the `write-host` cmdlet to print to the screen:`$driveletter | Size (in MB): $sizeMB | Size (in GB): $sizeGB`.

11. After executing this script on the system, you see that each drive letter is printed and the `Size` in MB and the size in GB are displayed.

You will also see that all of the values are rounded to two decimal places, unless they calculate to whole numbers. You will also see in the example that one drive evaluated to 0 for the drive size. From the previous example, you note that this drive is the CD-ROM/DVD drive on the system. Since there is no disk populated in this drive, the `Size` is `0`.

Free Space property

Another important property is the FreeSpace property. The FreeSpace property can range from the value of the disk's Size property to 0. When scripting to determine the free space, you have to consider that the remaining space may not be the same unit of measure you started with. For example, you may have a 2-terabyte drive, but you may only have 100 kilobytes left on the disk. If you were to convert the remaining 100 kilobytes to terabytes, the value would be many decimal places long. Instead, you need to build in logic to determine the appropriate unit of measure, based on the remaining space on the drive.

One of the easiest ways to accomplish this is to create a PowerShell function that evaluates the disk space on the system. This function will allow for a $diskspace argument. It will then leverage a switch statement to evaluate the $diskspace value. If it is greater than 1PB, 1TB, 1MB, or 1KB, in that order, it will perform the appropriate math calculation to convert the appropriate unit of measure. The value, rounded to two decimal places, would then be returned to the script, along with the unit of measure. The key to success with this methodology is leveraging a function for the evaluation. When the appropriate unit of measure is found, you use the Return command and the function exits after returning the values to the script.

To convert diskspace into the respective unit of measure, you can perform the following actions:

```
function measure-diskunit { param($diskspace)
    switch ($diskspace) {
        {$_ -gt 1PB} { return [System.Math]::Round(($_ / 1PB),2),"PB" }
        {$_ -gt 1TB} { return [System.Math]::Round(($_ / 1TB),2),"TB" }
        {$_ -gt 1GB} { return [System.Math]::Round(($_ / 1GB),2),"GB" }
        {$_ -gt 1MB} { return [System.Math]::Round(($_ / 1MB),2),"MB" }
        {$_ -gt 1KB} { return [System.Math]::Round(($_ / 1KB),2),"KB" }
        default { return [System.Math]::Round(($_ / 1MB),2),"MB" }
    }
}
measure-diskunit 868739194880123456
measure-diskunit 868739194880123
measure-diskunit 868739194880
measure-diskunit 868739194
measure-diskunit 868739
```

The output of this script is shown in the following screenshot:

```
PS C:\> function measure-diskunit { param($diskspace)
>>    switch ($diskspace) {
>>        {$_ -gt 1PB} { return [System.Math]::Round(($_ / 1PB),2),"PB" }
>>        {$_ -gt 1TB} { return [System.Math]::Round(($_ / 1TB),2),"TB" }
>>        {$_ -gt 1GB} { return [System.Math]::Round(($_ / 1GB),2),"GB" }
>>        {$_ -gt 1MB} { return [System.Math]::Round(($_ / 1MB),2),"MB" }
>>        {$_ -gt 1KB} { return [System.Math]::Round(($_ / 1KB),2),"KB" }
>>        default { return [System.Math]::Round(($_ / 1MB),2),"MB" }
>>    }
>> }
PS C:\> measure-diskunit 868739194880123456
771.6
PB
PS C:\> measure-diskunit 868739194880123
790.11
TB
PS C:\> measure-diskunit 868739194880
809.08
GB
PS C:\> measure-diskunit 868739194
828.49
MB
PS C:\> measure-diskunit 868739
848.38
KB
```

This example displays how to convert a byte value into multiple units of measure:

1. You first start by declaring a function named `measure-diskunit` with the `param` of (`$diskspace`).

2. You then create a `switch` statement with the argument `$diskspace`.

In the `switch` evaluations, you first evaluate the pipeline designated by `$_` and then determine whether the `$diskspace` value is greater than 1 petabyte (1PB):

- If the value is greater than 1PB, the script will use the pipeline value and divide it by 1PB. It will then round the resulting value leveraging the `[System.Math]::Round()` method with the argument 2, for two decimal places. As a second value for the return array, you provide a comma followed by the PB unit of measure. The converted value and the unit of measure are returned to the script, terminating further evaluations in the function.

- If the unit of measure is not greater than 1PB, it will continue to evaluate the statements in the `switch` statement.

- It will determine whether the `$diskspace` value is greater than 1TB, perform the rounding, and return the unit of measure to the script.

- If the $diskspace value is not greater than 1TB, it will continue in the switch statement to determine whether the value is greater than 1GB, 1MB, and 1KB in the same fashion, returning the converted value and unit of measure when matched.

- If no values match, the switch will by default return the value in MB.

In this example, you run the measure-diskunit function with five different $diskspace values. The first statement of measure-diskunit 868739194880123456 returns the array of 771.6 and PB. The next statement of measure-diskunit 868739194880123 returns the array of 790.11 and TB. The following statement of measure-diskunit 868739194880 returns the array of 809.08 and GB. The statement of measure-diskunit 868739194 returns the array of 828.49 and MB. The final statement of measure-diskunit 868739 returns the array of 848.38 and KB.

Disk information script

This chapter explains different methodologies for scanning the different aspects of the logical drives attached to your system. If you want to query the disks on a system, convert the disk size and free space, and identify the drive types, you can create the following script:

```
function measure-diskunit { param($diskspace)
    switch ($diskspace) {
        {$_ -gt 1PB} { return [System.Math]::Round(($_ / 1PB),2),"PB" }
        {$_ -gt 1TB} { return [System.Math]::Round(($_ / 1TB),2),"TB" }
        {$_ -gt 1GB} { return [System.Math]::Round(($_ / 1GB),2),"GB" }
        {$_ -gt 1MB} { return [System.Math]::Round(($_ / 1MB),2),"MB" }
        {$_ -gt 1KB} { return [System.Math]::Round(($_ / 1KB),2),"KB" }
        default { return [System.Math]::Round(($_ / 1MB),2),"MB" }
    }
}


$disks = get-wmiobject win32_logicaldisk
Foreach ($disk in $disks) {
    $driveletter = $disk.DeviceID
    $freespace = $disk.FreeSpace
    $size = $disk.Size
```

```
if ($freespace -lt 1) { $freespace = "0" }
if ($size -lt 1) { $size = "0" }


$freetype = measure-diskunit $freespace
$convFreeSpc = $freetype[0]
$funit = $freetype[1]


$sizetype = measure-diskunit $size
$convsize = $sizetype[0]
$sunit = $sizetype[1]


switch ($disk.DriveType) {
    0 { $type = "Type Unknown." }
    1 { $type = "Doesn't have a Root Directory." }
    2 { $type = "Removable Disk" }
    3 { $type = "Local Disk" }
    4 { $type = "Network Drive" }
    5 { $type = "Compact Disk" }
    6 { $type = "RAM Disk" }
    default { $type = "Unable To Determine Drive Type!" }
}


    write-host "Drive $driveletter | Drive Type: $type | Size: $convsize
$sunit   | Freespace: $convFreeSpc $funit"


}
```

The output of this script is shown in the following screenshot:

```
Drive C: | Drive Type: Local Disk | Size: 931.02 GB | Freespace: 809.07 GB
Drive D: | Drive Type: Local Disk | Size: 931.51 GB | Freespace: 262.63 GB
Drive E: | Drive Type: Compact Disk | Size: 0 MB | Freespace: 0 MB
Drive F: | Drive Type: Local Disk | Size: 465.65 GB | Freespace: 122.25 GB
Drive G: | Drive Type: Local Disk | Size: 931.48 GB | Freespace: 923.23 GB
Drive H: | Drive Type: Removable Disk | Size: 1.87 GB | Freespace: 1.78 GB
```

This example explains how to query the disks on a system, convert the disk size and freespace, and identify the drive types:

1. You first start by defining the measure-diskunit function.

   Earlier in the chapter, you learned that this function is used to determine the unit of measure, and calculate the converted value in that unit of measure. You learned that this function also leverages the [System.Math]::Round() method to round the values to two decimal places. You also learned that this function returns two values back to the script in an array. The first value is the converted value; the second value is the unit of measure.

2. You then proceed to query the local disks on a system, leveraging the get-wmiobject cmdlet with the win32_logicaldisk argument, and set the results in the $disks variable. You create a Foreach loop for each $disk in the $disksvariable.

3. You then proceed to obtain the drive letter by calling the $disk.DeviceID property and storing it in the $driveletter variable.

4. You retrieve the free space by calling the $disk.FreeSpace property and storing the result in the $freespace variable.

5. You finally call the $disk.Size property, and store the value in the $size variable.

6. The next step is to evaluate whether the disk freespace or the disk size is less than 1. This means that the drive is either full, or no media are loaded in the drive. To catch divide-by-zero errors, you set the $freespace value to 0 if the free space is 0. You set the $size to zero if the size is 0.

7. Next you evaluate the disk free space unit of measure by leveraging measure-diskunit with the $freespace argument. The result from the function is calculated, returned, and stored in the $freetype variable. Since the returned value from measure-diskunit is an array of two items, you set the first value, or $freetype[0], in the $convFreeSpc variable. You set the second value, or $freetype[1], in the $funit variable.

8. You continue to evaluate the disk size unit of measure by leveraging the measure-diskunit with the $size argument. The result from the function is calculated, returned, and stored in the $sizetype variable. Since the returned value from measure-diskunit is an array of two items, you set the first value, or $sizetype[0], in the $convSize variable. You set the second value, or $sizetype[1], in the $sunit variable.

9. Finally, you use the switch you created earlier to determine the drive type based on the drive type number.

The result of the drive type is then placed in the $type variable for use in the final output of the script. At the very end of the Foreach loop, you run the write-host cmdlet to output the result of Drive $driveletter | Drive Type: $type | Size: $convsize $sunit | Freespace: $convFreeSpc $funit for that disk iteration. After executing the script, all of the disk drive letters, drive types, sizes, free space, and appropriate units of measure are returned to the screen.

Summary

In this chapter, you learned about leveraging PowerShell to interact with disk drives. You started the chapter by learning about the get-disk cmdlet. You continued to leverage the get-wmiobject with the win32_logicaldrive class to query disk information. You then created a switch statement to determine the different disk types. You also learned how to convert bytes to megabytes and gigabytes. You created a function to dynamically convert to different units of measure and round the values to two decimal places. You ended the chapter by creating a disk information script that queries the disks on a system, converts the disk size and freespace, calculates the units of measure, and identifies the drive types.

In the next chapter, you will scan Windows features and the software installed on a system.

8
Windows Features and Installed Software Detection

Part of discovering a system's function is determining what Windows features and software titles are installed. In an enterprise environment, it is sometimes difficult to determine what is installed on individual systems. While you can manually log in to servers and evaluate the configurations, it can take a very long time to gather all of the server information.

The Windows server scanning script makes it easy to scan individual Windows features, roles, and software through a variety of cmdlets. You will learn how to scan the registry and individual executable files for information about installed software on your system. This enables you to detect both software that you'd find in add/remove programs, and software that does not add an installed entry in add/remove programs.

In this chapter, you will:

- Use the `get-windowsFeature` cmdlet to retrieve server features and roles
- Evaluate the `win32_serverfeature` class for feature and roles on legacy systems
- Correlate Windows features, role IDs, and parent IDs to user-friendly names
- Learn why you should not use the `win32_product` class for software discovery
- Leverage the registry to determine installed software
- Scan `Program Files` and `Program Files (x86)` for installed software information

To follow the examples in this chapter, it is recommended that you run the examples on a Windows Server 2012 system. Some of the cmdlets referenced in this chapter are not available in PowerShell 2.0, workstation operating systems, or in operating systems older than Server 2008 R2.

Windows features

When you are trying to determine the function of a Windows server, typically you start by evaluating the Windows features and roles. PowerShell has multiple methods to query server features and roles on a system. The get-WindowsFeature cmdlet, available in Server 2008 R2 and higher, provides a simple display of the features and roles installed on a system. The get-WindowsFeature cmdlet has multiple properties including the DisplayName property, Name property, Installed property, Parent property, and the InstallState property. The DisplayName property is the friendly name of the service. The Name property is the short version of DisplayName. The Installed property is a true or false property that reflects if the feature is installed. The InstallState property provides information as to whether the feature is installed, removed, or available for installation.

To query a server for the installed server features, you can perform the following:

```
get-WindowsFeature | where {$_.Installed -eq $true} | Select DisplayName,
InstallState, Parent
```

The output of this is shown in the following screenshot:

```
PS C:\> get-WindowsFeature  where {$_.Installed -eq $true}  Select DisplayName, InstallState, Parent

DisplayName                                       InstallState Parent
-----------                                       ------------ ------
File And Storage Services                         Installed
Storage Services                                  Installed FileAndStorage-Services
.NET Framework 4.5 Features                       Installed
.NET Framework 4.5                                Installed NET-Framework-45-Features
WCF Services                                      Installed NET-Framework-45-Features
TCP Port Sharing                                  Installed NET-WCF-Services45
User Interfaces and Infrastructure                Installed
Graphical Management Tools and Infrastructure     Installed User-Interfaces-Infra
Server Graphical Shell                            Installed User-Interfaces-Infra
Windows PowerShell                                Installed
Windows PowerShell 3.0                            Installed PowerShellRoot
Windows PowerShell ISE                            Installed PowerShellRoot
WoW64 Support                                     Installed
```

In this example, you display how to leverage the get-WindowsFeature cmdlet to report installed Windows features:

1. You start by calling the get-WindowsFeature cmdlet and piping it to where {$_.Installed -eq $true}. This selects all the Windows features installed on the system. You then pipe those results to the Select cmdlet to gather the DisplayName, InstallState, and Parent properties.

2. After execution, you see all of the Windows features installed on the server system, inclusive of their DisplayName, InstallState, and Parent properties.

On systems that are older than Windows Server 2008 R2, or that have PowerShell 2.0 installed on them, the get-WindowsFeature cmdlet is not available. Instead, you can leverage the **Windows Management Instrumentation (WMI)** to provide a list of installed server features. You first start by calling the get-wmiobject cmdlet with the win32_serverfeature class as the argument. After execution, you only receive the features installed on the system. The number of available properties is also limited to ID, Name, and ParentID.

To query a server for the installed server features on systems older than Windows Server 2008 R2, or that have PowerShell 2.0, you can perform the following:

```
get-wmiobject win32_serverfeature | select ID, Name, ParentID
```

The output of this is shown in the following screenshot:

```
PS C:\> get-wmiobject win32_serverfeature   select ID, Name, ParentID

  ID Name                                               ParentID
  -- ----                                               --------
 481 File And Storage Services                                 0
 418 .NET Framework 4.5                                      466
 466 .NET Framework 4.5 Features                               0
 420 WCF Services                                            466
 425 TCP Port Sharing                                        420
 412 Windows PowerShell 3.0                                  417
 351 Windows PowerShell ISE                                  417
 417 Windows PowerShell                                        0
 478 Graphical Management Tools and Infrastructure           477
  99 Server Graphical Shell                                  477
 482 Storage Services                                        481
 477 User Interfaces and Infrastructure                        0
 340 WoW64 Support                                             0
```

This example displays how to query Windows services by leveraging the `win32_serverfeature` class:

1. You first start by using the `get-wmiobject` cmdlet with the `win32_serverfeature` argument.

2. You then pipe the results to the `Select` cmdlet with the values of `ID`, `Name`, and `ParentID`.

3. After execution, the Windows features that are installed are displayed with their `ID`, `Name`, and `ParentID` properties.

> This section leverages a prepopulated XML file for Windows Feature ID searching. To obtain this file, you can download it from this book's resources page.

When you query the `win32_serverfeature` class, the feature and role parent information are returned as IDs. When you want to determine what the `ParentID` is for the feature or role, you have to come up with an alternative method to perform the correlation. In this chapter, you will leverage the pre-populated `ServerFeatureIDs.xml` file from the examples of this book to correlate the ID to their friendly names. The `ServerFeatureIDs.xml` file should be copied to the `c:\temp\POSHScript\` directory.

To call the `win32_serverfeature` class, query features and roles with `ParentIDs`, and correlate them by leveraging an XML file, you can do the following:

```
[xml] $frxml = Get-Content "C:\temp\POSHScript\ServerFeatureIDs.xml"

$featRoleTable = $frxml.GetElementsByTagName("feature")

$crntFeatures = Get-wmiobject win32_serverfeature

foreach ($feature in $crntFeatures) {

    $featurename = $feature.Name

    $featureparentID = $feature.ParentID

    if ($featureparentID) {

        $featureparentName = ($featRoleTable | where {$_.ID -eq
$featureparentID}).Name

        Write-host "The $featurename feature has the parentID of
$featureparentID. Parent Name: $featureparentName."

    }
}
```

The output of this is shown in the following screenshot:

```
PS C:\> [xml] $trxml = Get-Content "C:\temp\POSHScript\ServerFeatureIDs.xml"
PS C:\> $featRoleTable = $frxml.GetElementsByTagName("feature")
PS C:\>
PS C:\> $crntFeatures = Get-wmiobject win32_serverfeature
PS C:\> foreach ($feature in $crntFeatures) {
>>      $featurename = $feature.Name
>>      $featureparentID = $feature.ParentID
>>      if ($featureparentID) {
>>          $featureparentName = ($featRoleTable | where {$_.ID -eq $featureparentID}).Name
>>          Write-host "The $featurename has the parentID of $featureparentID. Parent Name: $featureparentName."
>>      }
>> }
>>
The .NET Framework 4.5 has the parentID of 466. Parent Name: .NET Framework 4.5 Features.
The WCF Services has the parentID of 466. Parent Name: .NET Framework 4.5 Features.
The TCP Port Sharing has the parentID of 420. Parent Name: WCF Services.
The Windows PowerShell 3.0 has the parentID of 417. Parent Name: Windows PowerShell - Features (417) Windows PowerShell.

The Windows PowerShell ISE has the parentID of 417. Parent Name: Windows PowerShell - Features (417) Windows PowerShell.

The Graphical Management Tools and Infrastructure has the parentID of 477. Parent Name: User Interfaces and Infrastructu
re.
The Server Graphical Shell has the parentID of 477. Parent Name: User Interfaces and Infrastructure.
The Storage Services has the parentID of 481. Parent Name: File and Storage Services - Role (481) File and Storage Servi
ces.
```

This example displays how to query Windows features and roles leveraging the win32_serverfeature class, and correlate their ParentIDs to friendly names:

1. You first start by getting the XML content from the ServerFeatureIDs. xml file. This is done by using the Get-Content cmdlet with the c:\temp\ POSHScritp\ServerFeatureIDS.xml argument.

2. You save the result in the $frxml variable, forcing the [XML] data type.

3. You then create a table of the correlation data from the ServerFeatureIDs.xml. To do this, you call the $frxml variable with the .GetElementsByTagName() method, and use the feature argument. The array of correlation data is then stored in the $featRoleTable variable.

4. You then continue to query all of the installed features on the system.

5. You leverage the get-wmiobject cmdlet with the win32_serverfeature class as the argument, and store the result in the $crntFeatures variable.

6. You then use the foreach loop to evaluate each $feature in $crntFeatures.

7. You gather the $feature.Name property to place it in the $featurename variable and the $feature.parentid property to place it in the $featureparentid variable.

8. To ensure that only features with parent IDs are displayed, you leverage an if ($featureparentID) statement, which will only continue if the $featureparentID is populated with data. If a parent ID exists, you then search the $featRoleTable array by using the pipeline. You query | where {$_.ID -eq $featureParentID}, which matches $featureparentID to the IDs in the correlation data.

9. You then embrace the entire statement in parentheses and select the `.Name` property of the result from the query.

10. Finally, you write to the screen leveraging the `write-host` cmdlet. The `$featurename feature has the parentID of $featureparentID. Parent Name: $featureparentName`. After execution, the script returns the active features on the system, the feature or role name , the `parentID` of the feature, and the correlation from the `parentID` to the feature's parent-friendly name.

 Server features and role names are constantly evolving with different versions of Window Servers. For an up-to-date list of Windows Feature and Role IDs and names, you can refer to the following MSDN link: `https://msdn.microsoft.com/en-us/library/cc280268(v=vs.85).aspx`.

Installed software detection

Detecting software on your system can be a difficult task. While the WMI `win32_product` class has a record of each **Microsoft Installer** (**MSI**)-installed software on your system, it is strongly recommended you do NOT use this class. When you query the `win32_product` class, it reconfigures each MSI software installed on your system. This can create unintended service disruptions due to applications being reinstalled, configurations being overwritten, and MSI repairs not completing successfully:

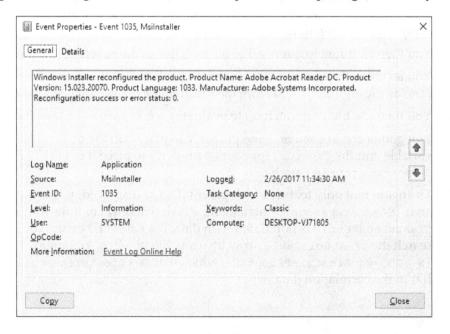

The preceding screenshot displays one of the multiple messages generated when the win32_product class is invoked. You will see that the Windows installer forces a reconfiguration of the installed software product. You will also see a reconfiguration status and error status message. If you accidently use the win32_product class, you can scan the event log for status messages and properly reinstall the application upon error.

 Avoid using the win32_product class in your scripts. Since the MSI performs a repair/reconfiguration of the installed software, this will create instabilities in your environment. Use the other methods in this chapter to identify software installed on the system.

Due to the limitations with the win32_product class, you will need to access multiple areas of the operating system to identify installed applications. The first place to start is the registry. Since MSIs, and other software installers, place the logic for uninstalling the application in the registry, you can identify installed software in the HKLM:\Software\Microsoft\Windows\CurrentVersion\Uninstall\ and HKLM:\Software\Wow6432Node\Microsoft\Windows\CurrentVersion\Uninstall\ registry key locations. To identify those software titles, you have to loop through each sub-key and search for the property: DisplayName. If the key does not have a DisplayName property, it is highly likely that you need to discover the installed software by leveraging alternative methods.

To identify installed software by using the registry, you can perform the following:

```
$RegLocations = "HKLM:\Software\Microsoft\Windows\CurrentVersion\
Uninstall\*","HKLM:\Software\Wow6432Node\Microsoft\Windows\
CurrentVersion\Uninstall\*"
foreach ($reg in $RegLocations) {
    $softwareKeys = get-ItemProperty $Reg | Select DisplayName | Sort
DisplayName
    foreach ($software in $softwareKeys) {
        if ($software.DisplayName -ne $null) { Write-host "Software
Found: " $software.DisplayName }
    }
}
```

The output of this is shown in the following screenshot:

```
Software Found:  Microsoft Expression Design 4
Software Found:  Microsoft SQL Server 2005 Compact Edition [ENU]
Software Found:  Microsoft Visual C++ 2010  x86 Redistributable - 10.0.40219
Software Found:  Microsoft Visual C++ 2012 Redistributable (x64) - 11.0.50727
Software Found:  Microsoft Visual C++ 2012 Redistributable (x86) - 11.0.50727
Software Found:  Microsoft Visual C++ 2012 x86 Additional Runtime - 11.0.50727
Software Found:  Microsoft Visual C++ 2012 x86 Minimum Runtime - 11.0.50727
Software Found:  Microsoft Visual C++ 2013 Redistributable (x64) - 12.0.30501
Software Found:  Microsoft Visual C++ 2013 Redistributable (x86) - 12.0.30501
Software Found:  Microsoft Visual C++ 2013 x86 Additional Runtime - 12.0.21005
Software Found:  Microsoft Visual C++ 2013 x86 Minimum Runtime - 12.0.21005
Software Found:  Movie Maker
Software Found:  Movie Maker
Software Found:  MSVCRT
Software Found:  MSVCRT110
Software Found:  Office 16 Click-to-Run Extensibility Component
Software Found:  Office 16 Click-to-Run Localization Component
Software Found:  Photo Common
Software Found:  Photo Gallery
Software Found:  Photo Gallery
Software Found:  Steam
Software Found:  Windows Live Communications Platform
Software Found:  Windows Live Essentials
Software Found:  Windows Live Essentials
Software Found:  Windows Live Installer
Software Found:  Windows Live Photo Common
Software Found:  Windows Live PIMT Platform
Software Found:  Windows Live SOXE
Software Found:  Windows Live SOXE Definitions
Software Found:  Windows Live UX Platform
Software Found:  Windows Live UX Platform Language Pack
```

This example displays how to identify installed software by leveraging the Uninstall registry keys:

1. You first start by declaring both the standard registry location of `HKLM:\Software\Microsoft\Windows\CurrentVersion\Uninstall\*` and the `WOW6432Node` location of `HKLM:\Software\Wow6432Node\Microsoft\Windows\CurrentVersion\Uninstall\*`, and placing it into the `$regLocations` array.

2. You continue to create a `foreach` loop to evaluate each `$reg` key in `$RegLocations`.

3. To get the sub-keys of both registry locations, you leverage the `get-ItemProperty` cmdlet with the current `$reg` key.

4. You pipe that value to select the `DisplayName` property, and pipe those results to sort by `DisplayName`.

5. You then place the result of this in the `$softwarekeys` variable.

6. After gathering all of the sub-keys, you leverage a `foreach` loop to examine each $software in `$softwarekeys`.

7. You create an If statement to ensure that the `$software.DisplayName` is not equal to blank or `$null`.

8. You then use the `write-host` cmdlet with `Software Found: $software.Displayname`. When you execute this command, the script will look at both registry locations, gather the sub-keys, select `DisplayName` properties that are not blank, and output the values on the screen.

Scanning executables in \Program Files

When you are scripting, there will be additional applications that do not place Uninstall data in the registry. For these applications, you may be able to find them by evaluating the executables in the `Program Files` and `Program Files (X86)` directories. To create a dynamic script, you will need to evaluate all of the logical drives for the Program Files directories, and scan the subdirectories for files ending in .exe. You can then evaluate the individual files, leveraging the `get-itemproperty` cmdlet, and reveal the `ProductName` and `ProductVersion` executables' properties. You may also pipe the results from the `get-itemproperty` cmdlet to get-member to access extended properties about the executable.

 Scanning `Program Files` requires a PowerShell window running with elevated privileges. You will need to open PowerShell with the **Run as Administrator** parameter.

To evaluate the `Program Files` and `Program File (x86)` directories for .exe files, and retrieve their extended properties, you can do the following:

```
$progpaths = "\Program Files\","\Program Files (x86)\"
$disks = (Get-WmiObject win32_logicaldisk | where {$_.DriveType -eq
"3"}).DeviceID
foreach ($disk in $disks) {
    foreach ($progpath in $progpaths) {
        $progfile = $disk + $progpath
        $test = test-path $progfile
        if ($test) {
            $files = Get-ChildItem -file $progfile -Recurse | where {$_.
FullName -like "*.exe"} | Select Fullname
            foreach ($file in $files) {
                $productName = (get-itemproperty $file.FullName).
VersionInfo.ProductName
                if (!$productName) { $productName = "Product Name n/a" }
```

```
            $productVersion = (get-itemproperty $file.FullName).
VersionInfo.ProductVersion

            if (!$productVersion) { $productVersion = "Product
Version n/a"}

            Write-host $file.Fullname " | Name: $productName |
Version: $productVersion"

          }

       }

    }

}
```

The output of this is shown in the following screenshot:

```
C:\Program Files\Common Files\microsoft shared\MSInfo\msinfo32.exe  | Name: Microsoft® Windows® Operating System | Versi
on: 6.2.9200.16384
C:\Program Files\Internet Explorer\iediagcmd.exe  | Name: Windows® Internet Explorer | Version: 10.00.9200.16384
C:\Program Files\Internet Explorer\ieinstal.exe  | Name: Windows® Internet Explorer | Version: 10.00.9200.16384
C:\Program Files\Internet Explorer\ielowutil.exe  | Name: Windows® Internet Explorer | Version: 10.00.9200.16384
C:\Program Files\Internet Explorer\iexplore.exe  | Name: Windows® Internet Explorer | Version: 10.00.9200.16384
C:\Program Files\Oracle\VirtualBox Guest Additions\uninst.exe  | Name: Oracle VM VirtualBox Guest Additions | Version: 5
.1.14.0
C:\Program Files\Oracle\VirtualBox Guest Additions\VBoxControl.exe  | Name: Oracle VM VirtualBox Guest Additions | Versi
on: 5.1.14.112924
C:\Program Files\Oracle\VirtualBox Guest Additions\VBoxDrvInst.exe  | Name: Oracle VM VirtualBox Guest Additions | Versi
on: 5.1.14.112924
C:\Program Files\Oracle\VirtualBox Guest Additions\VBoxTray.exe  | Name: Oracle VM VirtualBox Guest Additions | Version:
5.1.14.112924
C:\Program Files\Oracle\VirtualBox Guest Additions\VBoxWHQLFake.exe  | Name: Product Name n/a | Version: Product Version
n/a
C:\Program Files\Windows Mail\wab.exe  | Name: Microsoft® Windows® Operating System | Version: 6.2.9200.16384
C:\Program Files\Windows Mail\wabmig.exe  | Name: Microsoft® Windows® Operating System | Version: 6.2.9200.16384
C:\Program Files\Windows NT\Accessories\wordpad.exe  | Name: Microsoft® Windows® Operating System | Version: 6.2.9200.16
384
C:\Program Files (x86)\Common Files\Microsoft Shared\ink\pipanel.exe  | Name: Microsoft® Windows® Operating System | Ver
sion: 6.2.9200.16384
C:\Program Files (x86)\Common Files\Microsoft Shared\MSInfo\msinfo32.exe  | Name: Microsoft® Windows® Operating System |
Version: 6.2.9200.16384
C:\Program Files (x86)\Internet Explorer\ExtExport.exe  | Name: Windows® Internet Explorer | Version: 10.00.9200.16384
C:\Program Files (x86)\Internet Explorer\ieinstal.exe  | Name: Windows® Internet Explorer | Version: 10.00.9200.16384
C:\Program Files (x86)\Internet Explorer\ielowutil.exe  | Name: Windows® Internet Explorer | Version: 10.00.9200.16384
C:\Program Files (x86)\Internet Explorer\iexplore.exe  | Name: Windows® Internet Explorer | Version: 10.00.9200.16384
C:\Program Files (x86)\Windows Mail\wab.exe  | Name: Microsoft® Windows® Operating System | Version: 6.2.9200.16384
C:\Program Files (x86)\Windows Mail\wabmig.exe  | Name: Microsoft® Windows® Operating System | Version: 6.2.9200.16384
C:\Program Files (x86)\Windows NT\Accessories\wordpad.exe  | Name: Microsoft® Windows® Operating System | Version: 6.2.9
200.16384
```

In this example, you learned how to evaluate the Program Files directories for .exe files, and retrieve their extended properties:

1. To start the script, you begin by declaring the \Program Files\ and \Program Files (x86)\ strings in the $progpaths array. These strings are used to build dynamic paths for all of the local drives on the system.

2. Next, you gather the local drive letters by using the get-wmiobject cmdlet with the win32_logicaldisk class.

3. You filter the data by piping the result to where {$_.DriveType -eq "3"}, or where the drive is equal to a local disk.

4. You then set the entire statement in parentheses and set the DeviceID property of each disk in the $disks variable. The $disks variable will now contain all of the drive letters of the local disks on the system.

5. You then create a `foreach` loop to query each $disk drive letter in the $disks variable.

6. You create a second `foreach` loop to dynamically build the \Program Files\ and \Program Files (x86)\ directories for each drive letter. Within the second `foreach` loop, you build the drive letter by combining the current $disk and the current $progpath and set the result to the $progfile variable.

To verify that the directory exists, you leverage the `test-path` cmdlet with the $progfile argument. If the directory exists, the script continues to gather all of the executable files in that directory. This is done by leveraging the `get-childitem` cmdlet with the `-file` parameter, the $progfile argument, and the `-recurse` parameter:

1. You then filter the returned list by piping the result to where {$_.Fullname -like "*.exe"}.

2. You finally pipe this result to select `FullName`, to only return the `FullName` property of each file, and set the individual files in the $files variable.

3. To dig deeper into the individual file for extended attributes, you create a third `foreach` loop to query each $file in the $files variable.

4. You gather the `ProductName` attribute by leveraging the `get-itemproperty` cmdlet with the $file.Fullname argument.

5. You embrace the statement in parentheses and leverage dot notation to access the extended attributes of .VersionInfo.ProductName for that file.

6. You then set the `ProductName` property result in the $productName variable. In the instance that the `ProductName` property is not defined for an executable, you create an `If` statement of !$productname, where $productname is not TRUE. The script will set the $productname variable to Product Name n/a.

7. You then gather the `ProductVersion` attribute by leveraging the `get-itemproperty` cmdlet with the $file.Fullname argument.

8. You embrace the statement in parentheses and leverage dot notation to access the extended attributes of .VersionInfo.ProductVersion for that file.

9. You then set the `ProductVersion` property result in the $productVersion variable. In the instance that the `ProductVersion` property is not defined for an executable, you create an If statement of !$productVersion, where $productVersion is not TRUE. The script will set the $productVersion variable to Product Version n/a.

10. Finally, you print the result to the screen by leveraging the `write-host` cmdlet with $file.Fullname | Name: $productName | Version: $productVersion.

After executing this script, PowerShell will scan the system for drive letters; for each drive on the system it will look for the `Program Files` and `Program Files (x86)` directories. If a drive contains one or both of those folders, it will evaluate the individual files in those directories whose extension matches `.exe`. It will continue to dig into the extended properties for those executables to retrieve their `ProductNames`, and `ProductVersions`. It will print all of the file information to the screen, successfully scanning all of the Program Files directories for installed software.

Summary

In this chapter, you learned how to get Windows features with the `get-windowsFeature` cmdlet. You then learned how to use the `win32_serverfeature` to retrieve Windows features on legacy systems. You also leveraged an XML file to correlate feature, role, and parent IDs from the `win32_serverfeature` class to user-friendly names. You proceeded to evaluate why `win32_product` should not be used in scripts. You then leveraged the registry to discover installed software. Finally, you learned how to scan the `Program Files` and `Program Files (x86)` directories for executables and extended properties for software identification.

In the next chapter, you will learn a method for scanning a folder structure for files that contain specific strings.

9
File Scanning

When you are evaluating systems in your environment, there may be a time where you need to scan files for specific content. The Window server scanning script enables you to search directories for files with specific strings. Common strings may include error messages, clear text passwords, or even specific server information such as hostnames and IP addresses. The ability to scan systems for specific content is an immensely powerful tool that can reveal a plethora of information about your systems.

It is common, when scanning a system, to have a lot of results that are not what you are looking for, also known as false positives. This chapter will explore how to reduce the number of false positives by narrowing the search to specific file types. It will also explain how to exclude files from your search to help you get the data you need.

In this chapter, you will:

- Understand how to obtain subdirectories and their contents
- Limit the file discovery process to specific file types
- Efficiently search files for strings and identify their location in a file
- Learn how to handle errors from long paths that exceed 248 characters and permission issues
- Exclude files that are false positives in your search

File scanning

File scanning is an important activity in enterprise environments. Whether it is to identify where credentials are being used, the use of sensitive information, or server configuration information, you will need a technique to quickly and efficiently scan file data. PowerShell natively has the ability to gather data from clear text files and parse information. Some of the most common clear text files include, but are not limited to, text files, log files, XML files, configuration files, and scripting files.

When you are developing a `scanning` function, you will have to scan the directories for specific file types and the contents of the file itself. To scan for specific file types, you can leverage the `Get-ChildItem` cmdlet with a folder path as an argument. You also use the `-Include` parameter with the wildcard file extension that you want to search for. For log and text files, wildcard file extensions would look like `*.log` and `*.txt` respectively. If you want to scan multiple extensions, you can place a comma between each file extension you want to search for. If you want to scan subdirectories for file types, you can include the `-recurse` parameter to recursively go through the subdirectories.

To scan the `Program Files` directory and subdirectories for `*.log` and `*.txt` files, you can perform the following:

```
Get-ChildItem "c:\Program Files\" -Include *.log,*.txt -recurse
```

The output of this is shown in the following screenshot:

```
PS C:\> Get-ChildItem "c:\Program Files\" -Include *.log,*.txt -recurse


    Directory: C:\Program Files\ESET

Mode                LastWriteTime     Length Name
----                -------------     ------ ----
-a----        3/5/2017   8:43 PM          0 eset_install.log


    Directory: C:\Program Files\Windows Defender

Mode                LastWriteTime     Length Name
----                -------------     ------ ----
-a----        7/16/2016   6:43 AM       1091 ThirdPartyNotices.txt


    Directory: C:\Program Files\Windows NT\TableTextService

Mode                LastWriteTime     Length Name
----                -------------     ------ ----
-a----        7/16/2016   6:42 AM      14186 TableTextServiceAmharic.txt
-a----        7/16/2016   6:42 AM    1272944 TableTextServiceArray.txt
-a----        7/16/2016   6:42 AM     980224 TableTextServiceDaYi.txt
-a----        7/16/2016   6:43 AM      14198 TableTextServiceTigrinya.txt
-a----        7/16/2016   6:42 AM      45170 TableTextServiceYi.txt


    Directory: C:\Program Files\WindowsPowerShell\Modules\Pester\3.4.0\en-US

Mode                LastWriteTime     Length Name
----                -------------     ------ ----
-a----        7/16/2016   6:43 AM       3110 about_BeforeEach_AfterEach.help.txt
-a----        7/16/2016   6:43 AM       6396 about_Mocking.help.txt
-a----        7/16/2016   6:43 AM       5056 about_Pester.help.txt
-a----        7/16/2016   6:43 AM       5945 about_should.help.txt
-a----        7/16/2016   6:43 AM       1156 about_TestDrive.help.txt
```

This example displays how to scan the Program Files directory for .config and .txt file types. You start by calling the Get-ChildItem cmdlet with the C:\Program Files\ argument. You also leverage the -Include parameter with the *.log,*.txt argument to scan for .log and .txt files. Finally, you leverage the -recurse parameter to scan the subdirectories of C:\Program Files\. After execution, the PowerShell script displays all of the .log files and .txt files in the C:\Program Files\directory.

To scan for specific content inside a file, you need to obtain the contents of the file and place them in memory. To do this, you can leverage the get-content cmdlet with the path to the file you want to scan as the argument. You then place the result into a variable for evaluation. To scan the contents of the file, you can leverage the select-string cmdlet, which allows you to match content strings to regular expressions. You start by defining the select-string cmdlet followed by the -path parameter with a file argument. You then call the -pattern parameter with a regular expression as an argument. To search for a literal string, you can use the -pattern parameter with a string as the argument and leverage the -SimpleMatch parameter to match to a specific string.

You may also choose to leverage the select-string cmdlet after a pipe. To scan for specific content inside a file, you have the ability to pipe the filename result of the Get-ChildItem cmdlet to the select-string cmdlet. The select-string cmdlet will then evaluate the individual files for string patterns. This avoids the need to leverage a foreach loop to query the individual files, and each file will be evaluated as it is returned by the Get-ChildItem cmdlet.

Another unique feature of the select-string cmdlet is that it also returns the line number in the file, and the whole line of the matched content as it finds the individual results. You can call the Line property to return the whole line, and the LineNumber property, to return the line number. You can also call the FileName property to return the specific file that the criteria were found in.

To search Program Files for .log and .txt files and scan them for a string, you can do the following:

```
$matches = Get-ChildItem"c:\Program Files\" -Include *.log,*.txt -recurse
| select-string -pattern "Complete" -SimpleMatch
foreach ($match in $matches) {
    Write-Host "Filename: " $match.FileName
    Write-Host "Line Number: " $match.LineNumber
    Write-Host "Line Contents: " $match.Line
}
```

The output of this is shown in the following screenshot:

```
PS C:\> $matches = Get-ChildItem "c:\Program Files\" -Include *.log,*.txt -recurse  select-string -pattern "Complete"
SimpleMatch
PS C:\> foreach ($match in $matches) {
>>      Write-Host "Filename:    "$match.FileName
>>      Write-Host "Line Number: "$match.LineNumber
>>      Write-Host "Line Contents: "$match.Line
>> }
Filename:    about_TestDrive.help.txt
Line Number:  14
Line Contents:            completes. You may use this drive to isolate the file operations of your
Filename:    about_TestDrive.help.txt
Line Number:  33
Line Contents:            When this test completes, the contents of the TestDrive PSDrive will
```

This example displays how to scan the `Program Files` directory for `.log` and `.txt` files, and search the files for the string `"Complete"`. You first start by calling the `Get-ChildItem` cmdlet with the `c:\Program Files\` argument. You also leverage the `-Include` parameter set to the `*.log,*.txt` argument and the `-recurse` parameter to search subdirectories. You then pipe the result to the `select-string` cmdlet with the `-pattern` parameter set to the string of `"Complete"` as the argument. You then issue the `-SimpleMatch` parameter to perform simple searching for that string. The outputs from these commands are then stored in the `$matches` variable.

You then continue to leverage the `foreach` loop to evaluate each `$match` in `$matches`. You then leverage the `Write-Host` cmdlet to display `"FileName:"` with the `.FileName` property of the `$match` variable. You also use the `Write-Host` cmdlet to display `"Line Number:"` with the `.LineNumber` property of the `$match` variable. Finally, you use the `Write-Host` cmdlet to display `"Line Contents:"` with the `.Line` property of the `$match`variable.

After execution, the script will have scanned the `c:\Program Files\` directory for `.log` and `.txt` files. When a file with the correct file type is identified, the script will evaluate the file for the string of `"Complete"`. If the string is found, the script will proceed to provide the `Filename`, `Line Number`, and contents of the line in the individual files.

Excluding long paths

With enterprise file servers, you may run into situations where the folder structures and file character count are over 248 characters. Windows, by default, restricts the use of long file paths to 248 characters in length. It is not uncommon to have Linux-based file servers, or mapped network drives with long file paths that go over the 248-character limit.

PowerShell has the same file path limitations as the Windows operating systems. All of the PowerShell cmdlets will have issues querying file systems that have folder paths longer than 248 characters. There are several programs such as `robocopy.exe` that can be leveraged to display the full paths of files and folders longer than 248 characters. While you have the ability to return long paths, you still would not be able to interact with any of the files in that directory using PowerShell cmdlets. Additionally, `robocopy.exe` is very slow in comparison to the `Get-ChildItem` cmdlet, and requires administrative backup privileges to the systems it is being run on.

This leaves you with limited options for interacting with long file and folder paths. As a result, it's recommended that you work through handling the file path, and access error messages in your script. Handling errors with the `Get-ChildItem` cmdlet is done by using the `-ErrorAction` and `-ErrorVariable` parameters. Instead of creating a single variable for errors, however, you will need to place the errors in an array. This is because the `Get-ChildItem` cmdlet obtains all files and directories in a specified path, even if it has access issues or cannot access the path due to path length. If you only use a variable, the only error that would be in the error variable is the last one to occur. Instead, to work around this, you can define an array leveraging `$errors = @()` and use `+errors` as the argument to `-ErrorVariable`. This tells PowerShell to add an additional item to the `$errors` array when an error occurs.

 To execute the following example, you will need to create a local user on your system named `"Brenton"`. Alternatively, you can update the line that reflects `"$env:computername\Brenton"` to whatever username you would like.

To create a shared directory structure that exceeds 248 characters, gather the file and directory information, and catch the errors, you can perform the following actions:

```
# Create Folder Structure to Scan

$userdrive = "c:\Temp\POSHScript\Chapter9Examples\CompanyXYZ\Milwaukee\
InformationTechnologyDepartment\UserHomeDrives\UserLoginID\"

new-item $userdrive -ItemType Directory -Force

$domainuser = "$env:computername\Brenton"

New-SmbShare -name "UserData" -Path $userdrive -FullAccess $domainuser

New-PSDrive -Name H -root "\\$env:computername\Userdata" -Persist
-PSProviderFileSystem

cd H:

$userFolder = "Information Technology Department\All Company Software\
ISO\Microsoft\Microsoft SQL Server 2012 R2\SQL Server Update Patches\
Service Pack 3\Cumulative Update 7\AutomatedWindowsInstaller\"
```

```
new-item $userFolder -ItemType Directory -Force

#Scan Folder Struture
$directory = "c:\Temp\POSHScript\Chapter9Examples\CompanyXYZ\"
$errors = @()
get-childitem $directory -recurse -ErrorActionSilentlyContinue
-ErrorVariable +errors
if ($errors) {
foreach ($err in $errors) {
if ($err.Exception -like "*Could not find a part of the path*") {
        $filepath = ($err.Exception).ToString().split("'")[1]
        Write-Host "Error Accessing Path: `"$filepath`" may be over
248 Characters."
    }
if ($err.Exception -like "*is denied.*") {
        $filepath = ($err.Exception).ToString().split("'")[1]
        Write-Host "Error Accessing Path: `"$filepath`" Access Is
Denied."
    }
  }
}
# Remove Mapped Drive and Share
cd c:
Remove-PSDrive -Name H -Force
Remove-SmbShare -name "UserData" -Force
```

The output of this is shown in the following screenshot:

```
Error Accessing Path: "C:\Temp\POSHScript\Chapter9Examples\CompanyXYZ\Milwaukee\InformationTechnologyDepartment\UserHome
Drives\UserLoginID\Information Technology Department\All Company Software\ISO\Microsoft\Microsoft SQL Server 2012 R2\SQL
Server Update Patches\Service Pack 3\Cumulative Update 7" may be over 248 Characters.
```

This example displays how to properly query a system for file and folder information, while catching access denied and long file path errors:

1. You first start by creating the required folder structure. Since you cannot create a folder structure that is more than 248 characters long, you create a smaller set of directories, share those directories, map a drive to that directory path, and create additional folders with the mapped drive location. The output of this is a directory structure in excess of 248 characters.

2. To create the first directory structure, you define the string of `"C:\Temp\POSHScript\Chapter9Examples\CompanyXYZ\Milwaukee\ InformationTechnologyDepartment\UserHomeDrives\UserLoginID\"` and set it to the `$userdrive` variable.

3. You then leverage the `new-item` cmdlet with the `$userdrive` variable as the argument, the `-ItemType` parameter with the `Directory` argument, and the `-Force`parameter. This creates the first directory structure.

4. To create the directory share, you have to specify a credential that the share will be shared with. You specify `$env:computername` to denote the computer name, a backslash, the user of `Brenton`, and place the value in the `$domainuser` variable.

5. You share this directory structure by leveraging the `New-SmbShare` cmdlet with the `-name` parameter set to the `"UserData"`. You also include the `-Path` parameter and specify the `$userdrive` argument, and the `-FullAccess` parameter with the `$domainuser` argument.

   After execution, `"c:\Temp\POSHScript\Chapter9Examples\CompanyXYZ\ Milwaukee\InformationTechnologyDepartment\UserHomeDrives\ UserLoginID\"` is shared on the system and can be accessed with the UNC path of `\\computername\Userdata`.

6. You then continue to map the `H` drive by leveraging the `New-PSDrive` cmdlet with the `-Name` parameter and `H` as the argument. You then specify the `-root` parameter and specify `\\$env:computername\Userdata` as the argument. You also include the `-Persist` parameter to make the mapping persistent, and the `-PSProvider` parameter set to `FileSystem`. After execution, you have the `H:\`drive mapped to `\\computername\Userdata`.

7. You then issue a change of directory to the `H:` drive with `cd H:` and continue building the directory structure.

8. You build the string `"Information Technology Department\All Company Software\ISO\Microsoft\Microsoft SQL Server 2012 R2\ SQL Server Update Patches\Service Pack 3\Cumulative Update 7\ AutomatedWindowsInstaller\"` and place it in the `$userFolder` variable.

9. You then leverage the `new-item` cmdlet with `$userFolder` as the argument, the`-ItemType` parameter with the `Directory` argument, and the `-Force` parameter.

   This creates the second set of directories in the `H:`drive. You then move on to scanning the folder structure.

10. You first start by defining the directory you want to scan in `C:\Temp\POSHScript\Chapter9Examples\CompanyXYZ\` and setting it to the `$directory` variable.

11. You then define the `$errors` array by setting it to the value of `@()`.

12. You leverage the `Get-ChildItem` cmdlet with the `$directory` argument and the `-recurse` parameter to scan the `C:\Temp\POSHScript\Chapter9Examples\CompanyXYZ\` directory and its subdirectories. You leverage the `-ErrorAction` parameter with the `SilentlyContinue` argument and the `-ErrorVariable` with the `+errors` argument. This enables the additive operation for a series of error messages, as they happen to the `$errors` array.

13. After the `Get-ChildItem` cmdlet completes, you evaluate the `$errors` variable to determine whether there are any values in it.

14. Since you created a folder structure longer than 248 characters, the `$errors` variable will have data in it, causing the `if` statement to evaluate to `$true`.

15. The script then continues to perform a `foreach` loop to evaluate each `$err` in the `$errors` array.

16. The script then performs an `if` statement to determine whether the `$err.Exception` property is like `"*Could not find a part of the path*"`. This particular error message is specified if `Get-ChildItem` knows the path exists but cannot traverse the directories any further. This indicates that the file path is longer than 248 characters.

17. If this evaluates to true, the script will take the `$err.Exception` property, and convert the `Exception` to a string.

18. You evaluate the string to split it by the apostrophe character.

19. You specify `[1]` to select the second value, which is the filename, and set it to the `$filepath` variable.

20. You leverage the `Write-Host` cmdlet with the string `"Error Accessing Path:`"$filepath`" may be over 248 Characters"`.

21. If this particular `$err` in the `$errors` variable matches, it will display the appropriate message on the screen.

    You proceed to your second evaluation of the `$errors` variable.

22. During this evaluation, you determine whether the `$err.Exception` property is like `"*is denied.*"`. This catches access denied error messages that may be occurring in the system.

23. If this evaluates to true, the script will take the `$err.Exception` property and convert the `Exception` to a string.

24. You evaluate the string to split it by the apostrophe character.

25. You specify `[1]` to select the second value, which is the `Filename`, and set it to the `$filepath` variable.

26. You leverage the `Write-Host` cmdlet with the string `"Error Accessing Path: `"$filepath`"" Access Is Denied."`.

27. If this particular `$err` in the `$errors` variable matches, it will display the appropriate message on the screen.

    The final step is the cleanup portion of the script.

28. To clean up the script, you execute `cd c:` to change the directory back to the `c:` drive.

29. You disconnect the `H` drive by leveraging the `Remove-PSDrive` cmdlet with the `-name` parameter set to `H` and the `-Force` parameter.

30. You close the SMB share, leveraging the `Remove-SmbShare` cmdlet with the `-name` parameter set to `"UserData"` and the `-Force` parameter.

If this script was executed on a server file share, the `Get-Childitem` cmdlet would report all of the files and directories in the `$directory` variable. It would also print out to screen if there were any directories longer than 248 characters, and if there were any access denied error messages generated on the folder structure.

Excluding files

As you perform scanning in your environment, you will eventually want to filter out some of the false positives. This is especially true if you leverage a template to build your systems, as a multitude of commonalities might be detected. You may also want to filter out very large files that are known to be safe to optimize the scanning duration.

The `Get-ChildItem` cmdlet includes the `-exclude` parameter, which enables you to specify a string of objects that you want to exclude. The `-exclude` parameter also supports multiple values separated by commas and wildcards with the asterisk character. To start, you specify the `Get-ChildItem` cmdlet with a directory to scan as the argument. You then provide the `-exclude` parameter with a file specified as its argument. When the `Get-ChildItem` cmdlet executes, it will filter out those items specified as the arguments to the `-exclude` parameter.

To create a function to scan a system for the word `"Complete"` in `.xml` and `.txt` files without exclusions, then again with exclusions, you can perform the following actions:

```
function scan-directory { param($directory)

    $errors = @()

    $content = get-childitem $directory -Include $include -Exclude
$exclude -recurse -ErrorActionSilentlyContinue -ErrorVariable
+errors | select-string -Pattern $findword -SimpleMatch
-ErrorActionSilentlyContinue


if ($errors) {
foreach ($err in $errors) {
if ($err.Exception -like "*Could not find a part of the path*") {
                $filepath = ($err.Exception).ToString().split("'")[1]
                Write-Host "Error Accessing Path: `"$filepath`" may be
over 248 Characters."
            }
if ($err.Exception -like "*is denied.*") {
                $filepath = ($err.Exception).ToString().split("'")[1]
                Write-Host "Error Accessing Path: `"$filepath`" Access Is
Denied."
            }
        }
    }
foreach ($match in $content) {
        Write-Host "Filename: " ($match.FileName).Trim()
        Write-Host "Line Number: " $match.LineNumber
        Write-Host "Line Contents: " ($match.Line).Trim()
    }
}


$include = "*.xml","*.txt"
$exclude = ""
$findword = "Complete"
scan-directory"c:\Windows\System32\"


$include = "*.xml","*.txt"
```

```
$exclude = "*hppcl3-pipelineconfig.xml*","Cleanup.xml"

$findword = "Complete"

scan-directory "c:\Windows\System32\"
```

The output of this is shown in the following screenshot:

```
PS C:\>
PS C:\> $include = "*.xml","*.txt"
PS C:\> $exclude = ""
PS C:\> $findword = "Complete"
PS C:\> scan-directory "c:\Windows\System32\"
Error Accessing Path: "C:\Windows\System32\LogFiles\WMI\RtBackup" Access Is Denied.
Filename:  hppcl3-pipelineconfig.xml
Line Number:  30
Line Contents:  Pipeline manager will not complete filter initialization if a FilterServiceProvider is
Filename:  Cleanup.xml
Line Number:  2
Line Contents:  <deleteValue name="HashingCompleted" path="HKEY_LOCAL_MACHINE\SOFTWARE\Microsoft\Windows NT\CurrentVersi
on\Schedule"></deleteValue>
Filename:  Cleanup.xml
Line Number:  3
Line Contents:  <deleteValue name="MigrationCleanupCompleted" path="HKEY_LOCAL_MACHINE\SOFTWARE\Microsoft\Windows NT\Cur
rentVersion\Schedule"></deleteValue>
Filename:  Cleanup.xml
Line Number:  8
Line Contents:  <deleteValue name="HashingCompleted" path="HKEY_LOCAL_MACHINE\SOFTWARE\Microsoft\Windows NT\CurrentVersi
on\Schedule"></deleteValue>
Filename:  Cleanup.xml
Line Number:  9
Line Contents:  <deleteValue name="MigrationCleanupCompleted" path="HKEY_LOCAL_MACHINE\SOFTWARE\Microsoft\Windows NT\Cur
rentVersion\Schedule"></deleteValue>
PS C:\>
PS C:\> $include = "*.xml","*.txt"
PS C:\> $exclude = "*hppcl3-pipelineconfig.xml*","Cleanup.xml"
PS C:\> $findword = "Complete"
PS C:\> scan-directory "c:\Windows\System32\"
Error Accessing Path: "C:\Windows\System32\LogFiles\WMI\RtBackup" Access Is Denied.
PS C:\>
```

This example displays how to scan a directory structure for `.xml` and `.txt` files for the word `"Complete"`. It also displays how to successfully exclude results returned from the scanning function:

1. You first start by creating a function named `scan-directory`.

2. You create a parameter block setting the first argument as `$directory`.

3. To start the function you declare the `$errors` array by setting `$errors` equal to `@()`.

4. You call the `Get-ChildItem` cmdlet with the `$directory` argument, the `-Include` parameter with the `$include` argument, and the `-exclude` parameter with the `$exclude` argument.

5. You continue to include the `-recurse` parameter for subdirectory scanning, the `-ErrorAction` parameter set to the `SilentlyContinue` argument, and the `-ErrorVariable` set to the `+errors` additive operator.

6. The `Get-ChildItem` cmdlet statement is then piped to the `select-string` cmdlet with the `$findword` argument, the `-SimpleMatch` parameter, and the `-ErrorAction` of `SilentlyContinue`.

7. This section will query the $directory location, and its subdirectories, for the files types specified in $include, excluding the files in $exclude, and select the strings that has -Simplematch$findword.

8. The -ErrorAction is applied to the select-string cmdlet to suppress the errors on files and folders that cannot be accessed, or are greater than 248 characters.

9. Those errors are already added to the $errors variable via the Get-ChildItem cmdlet.

10. The result from this command is then stored in the $content variable.

11. After the Get-ChildItem cmdlet completes, you evaluate the $errors variable to determine whether there are any values in it.

12. Since you created a folder structure longer than 248 characters, the $errors variable will have data in it, causing the if statement to evaluate to $true. The script then continues to perform a foreach loop to evaluate each $err in the $errors array.

13. The script then performs an if statement to determine whether the $err. Exception property is like "*Could not find a part of the path*".

14. If this evaluates to true, the script will take the $err.Exception property and convert the Exception to a string.

15. You evaluate the string to split it by the apostrophe character.

16. You specify [1] to select the second value, which is the filename, and set it to the $filepath variable.

17. You leverage the Write-Host cmdlet with the string "Error Accessing Path:`"$filepath`" may be over 248 Characters". If this particular $err in the $errors variable matches, it will display the appropriate message on the screen.

    You proceed to your second evaluation of the $errors variable.

18. During this evaluation, you determine if the $err.Exception property is like "*is denied.*". This catches access denied error messages that may be occurring on the system.

19. If this evaluates to true, the script will take the $err.Exception property and convert the Exception to a string.

20. You then evaluate the string to split it by the apostrophe character.

21. You specify [1] to select the second value, which is the filename, and set it to the $filepath variable.

22. You leverage the `Write-Host` cmdlet with the string `"Error Accessing Path: ` `"$filepath`" Access Is Denied."`

    If this particular `$err` in the `$errors` variable matches, it will display the appropriate message on the screen.

23. After the error handling section, you continue to evaluate each `$match` in the `$content` variable.

24. You leverage the `Write-Host` cmdlet to display `"Filename: "` and the `$match.FileName` property.

25. You use the `.Trim()` method on this result to remove the leading and trailing spaces in the result. This displays the file name the match is found in.

26. You then use the `Write-Host` cmdlet to display `"Line Number: "` and the `$match.LineNumber` property. This displays the line number the match is found on.

27. Last, you leverage the `Write-Host` cmdlet to display `"Line Contents: "` and the `$match.line`property.

28. You use the `.Trim()` method on this result to remove the leading and trailing spaces in the result. This displays the contents of the line where the match is found.

This completes the creation of the function. After creating the function, you continue to set up the function call with the following steps:

1. Since you want to search for `*.xml` files and `*.txt` files, you define `"*.xml","*.txt"` and place it in the `$include` variable.

2. You define the `$exclude` variable, but set it to blank or `""`. This is because you don't want to exclude any items.

3. You then define the search word `"Complete"` and place the value in the `$findword` variable. Finally, you invoke the `scan-directory` function with the argument `"c:\windows\system32"`.

4. After the function is invoked, `scan-directory` will leverage the `Get-ChildItem` cmdlet to determine whether the files with the `$include` file extension exist in the `$directory`.

5. Since the `$exclude` variable is blank, the script doesn't exclude any values. It is then passed through the pipeline to the `select-string` cmdlet to determine whether there is a `-SimpleMatch` that includes the `$findword` of `"Complete"`.

6. The function reports any "access or paths exceeding 248 character" messages.

7. The function prints to the screen the files that meet the criteria you are searching for.

In this example, the `scan-function` cmdlet reports an access denied message on the `C:\Windows\System32\LogFiles\WMI\Rtbackup` directory. It also reports that it found the word `"Complete"` once in the `hppc13-pipelineconfig.xml` file and multiple times in the `Cleanup.xml` file.

You then proceed to the second set of files you want to scan for:

1. For the second attempt, you still search for `*.xml` files and `*.txt` files, and you define `"*.xml","*.txt"` for the `$include` variable.

2. You define the `$exclude` variable, and set it as `"*hppc13-pipelineconfig.xml*","Cleanup.xml"`, to exclude both the `hppc13-pipelineconfig.xml` and `Cleanup.xml` files.

3. You define the search word `"Complete"` and place the value in the `$findword` variable.

4. Finally, you invoke the `scan-directory` function with the argument `"C:\windows\system32\"`.

In the second run of the `scan-directory` function, you receive the access denied message on the `C:\Windows\System32\LogFiles\WMI\Rtbackup directory`. You don't, however, receive any messages about the `hppc13-pipelineconfig.xml` and `Cleanup.xml` files as they are defined in the exclude list. You have successfully excluded files from the search.

It is important to note that the `-Include` and `-Exclude` parameters accept arrays of objects, not comma-separated strings. If you define the exclusions as `"*.xml,*.txt"`, the cmdlet will not return the proper results. You need to have two separate array items, separated by a comma, like `"*.xml","*.txt"` for the `-Include` or `-Exclude` to work properly.

Summary

In this chapter, you learned how to efficiently scan files and folders on a system. You started by exploring how to list folders, subfolders, and files by using the `Get-ChildItem` cmdlet. You then learned how to narrow your search by including only certain file extensions through using the `-Include` parameter. You proceeded to scan the contents of files by leveraging the `select-string` cmdlet. You then explored how to handle long file paths and access denied messages. You continued by learning how to narrow your search results by excluding specific files. Finally, you created a function to scan directories, including specific extensions, excluding specific files, and handling long file path and access denied errors.

In the next chapter, you will learn different scripting techniques to optimize your script execution speed.

10
Optimizing Script Execution Speed

When you execute the Windows server scanning script, you most likely will be processing a large number of objects. Small efficiencies in your coding practices can equate to exponentially faster execution times for large sets of data. Due to PowerShell being so flexible, it is possible to write two different sets of code that perform the exact same activity. However, you will find that certain coding techniques are much more efficient than others. In some cases, you can increase your script performance by over 200 percent.

This chapter focuses on the quick changes that you can make to your scripts to optimize efficiency. You will also learn about cmdlets and methods that you should avoid to ensure that you are not impacting your script's performance. By following the recommendations in this chapter, you can significantly reduce the amount of time that the Window server scanning script takes to scan systems.

In this chapter, you will:

- Learn how to measure the duration of commands in scripts
- Determine the overhead of writing all actions to the screen
- Create a logging function that allows you to turn on and off verbose logging
- Evaluate the write-progress function's impact on script performance
- Determine the speed differences between multiple `if` and `switch` statements

Script execution speed

When PowerShell scripts are executing, they consume both memory and CPU resources on a system. With larger scanning scripts, this may spike system resources for a noticeable duration of time. As a result, it's important to optimize your scripts to quickly execute the task at hand. One of the cmdlets that you can use to measure script execution time is the measure-command cmdlet. To measure the execution time, you call the measure-command cmdlet and place the code you want to execute in curly brackets. The output of the measure-command cmdlet will display the Days, Hours, Seconds, Milliseconds, Ticks, TotalDays, TotalHours, TotalMinutes, TotalSeconds, and TotalMilliseconds of the operation. This represents the duration of time the code took to execute the section of code.

To measure a command by leveraging the measure-command cmdlet, you can perform the following:

```
measure-command { ping localhost }
```

The output of this is shown in the following screenshot:

```
PS C:\> measure-command { ping localhost }

Days              : 0
Hours             : 0
Minutes           : 0
Seconds           : 3
Milliseconds      : 137
Ticks             : 31377194
TotalDays         : 3.63161967592593E-05
TotalHours        : 0.000871588722222222
TotalMinutes      : 0.0522953233333333
TotalSeconds      : 3.1377194
TotalMilliseconds : 3137.7194
```

In this example, you measure the duration it takes to ping the localhost on a system. You first start by declaring the measure-command cmdlet. In curly brackets, you specify ping localhost. After execution, the measure-command returns the Days, Hours, Seconds, Milliseconds, Ticks, TotalDays, TotalHours, TotalMinutes, TotalSeconds, and TotalMilliseconds of the operation. You will see that the duration for ping localhost in this example is 3.13 seconds.

Speed considerations for the write-host cmdlet

Displaying progress information is helpful in determining what actions are being performed in a script, or during the script troubleshooting process. When you start writing a large volume of information to the PowerShell window, however, you will start seeing slower performance with the script's execution. When you keep PowerShell operations in memory, the system interacts with the operation in memory. When you display content to the screen, you have to wait for the kernel to write the operation to the screen before it can continue to the next operation. This is inherently much slower than keeping operations in memory.

 The following examples will take approximately four minutes to execute. Execution times will vary depending on system hardware and available resources.

To display operations being printed to screen versus operations in memory, you can execute the following:

```
$time1 = measure-command {
    1..10000 | % {
                write-host "Number $_"
                # Get the contents of C:\Windows\
                $contents = Get-ChildItem c:\windows\
                }
}

$time2 = measure-command {
    1..10000 | % {
                # Get the contents of C:\Windows\
                $contents = Get-ChildItem c:\windows\
                }
}
$time1
$time2
$timediff = ($time2 - $time1).TotalSeconds
Write-host "Total Difference in Speed: $timediff Total Seconds"
```

The output of this is shown in the following screenshot:

```
Number 9998
Number 9999
Number 10000
PS C:\>
PS C:\> $time2 = measure-command {
>>      1..10000 | % {
>>              # Get the contents of C:\Windows\system32\
>>              $contents = Get-ChildItem c:\windows\
>>              }
>> }
PS C:\> $time1


Days             : 0
Hours            : 0
Minutes          : 0
Seconds          : 52
Milliseconds     : 385
Ticks            : 523859039
TotalDays        : 0.000606318332175926
TotalHours       : 0.0145516399722222
TotalMinutes     : 0.873098398333333
TotalSeconds     : 52.3859039
TotalMilliseconds : 52385.9039


PS C:\> $time2


Days             : 0
Hours            : 0
Minutes          : 0
Seconds          : 44
Milliseconds     : 34
Ticks            : 440344620
TotalDays        : 0.000509658125
TotalHours       : 0.012231795
TotalMinutes     : 0.7339077
TotalSeconds     : 44.034462
TotalMilliseconds : 44034.462


PS C:\> $timediff = ($time1 - $time2).TotalSeconds
PS C:\> Write-host "Total Difference in Speed: $timediff Total Seconds"
Total Difference in Speed: 8.3514419 Total Seconds
```

In this example, you time the difference between writing data to the screen and keeping operations in memory:

1. You first start by declaring the measure-command cmdlet.

2. You declare the range from 1 to 10000 and pipe that to the %, which is the alias for foreach.

3. You then leverage the `write-host` cmdlet with `"Number $_"` to display the number of the current step.

4. You also leverage the `Get-ChildItem` cmdlet with the `c:\Windows\` argument and set those results to `$contents`.

    This action will repeat 10,000 times. The execution duration will be captured by the `measure-command` cmdlet and stored in the `$time1` variable.

5. You then set up a second measuring command.

6. You declare the `measure-command` cmdlet.

7. You also declare the range from `1` to `10000` and pipe that to the `%`.

8. You leverage the `Get-ChildItem` cmdlet with the `c:\Windows\` argument and set those results to `$contents`.

    This action will repeat 10,000 times. The execution duration will be captured by the `measure-command` cmdlet and stored in the `$time2` variable.

    After execution of the second command, you display the duration in `$time1` and `$time2` by calling the variables.

9. You then calculate the difference in execution time by calling `$time1 - $time2` and referencing the `TotalSeconds` property.

10. You set this value in the `$timediff` variable.

11. Finally, you print the time value to the display by using the `write-host` cmdlet with `"Total Difference in Speed: $timediff Total Seconds"`.

You will see that, in this example, keeping operations in memory is about 15 times as fast as displaying it on the screen.

This example demonstrates that writing individual item progress to the screen is slower than keeping calculations in memory. While it is recommended to provide progress information in your script, it's equally important to know the right locations in which to use the script progress information. When you want to designate the starting or stopping of different script actions, it's appropriate to write to screen. If you are scanning a file system, however, you don't want to display every file being scanned on the screen. This would significantly impact the execution of the script due to the volume of data printed to the screen.

There are two strategies to improving displaying information on the screen. The first strategy is to leverage a function to write information to the screen that you can turn on and off with a variable. In this, you have the ability to display verbose information on screen during the testing phase. When you are done testing, you can turn off all writing to the screen for production use.

The second strategy is to write only high-level script status information. Instead of writing each operation to the screen, designate the start with `Running Operation...` and complete it with `Operation Complete`. This will reduce the volume of text that is being placed on the screen; however, it will still display progress on the screen. Creating a function that allows you to enable and disable printing to the screen can allow you to disable verbose output in certain sections of your code, while enabling it in others for testing purposes. This combination provides great flexibility in your ability to manage screen writing performance.

To create a `write-host` function that can be enabled and disabled, disable verbose logging half-way through an operation, and time the difference, you can do the following:

```
$verbose = $true
function log { if ($verbose) { write-host $_ } }

$time1 = measure-command {
    1..10000 | % {
                log "Number $_"
                # Get the contents of C:\Windows\
                $contents = Get-ChildItem c:\windows\
                }
}

$time2 = measure-command {
    1..5000 | % {
                log "Log $_"
                # Get the contents of C:\Windows\
                $contents = Get-ChildItem c:\windows\
                }
                $verbose = $false
                Write-host "Running Folder Scanning Operation..."

    1..5000 | % {
                log "Number $_"
                # Get the contents of C:\Windows\
```

```
            $contents = Get-ChildItem c:\windows\
        }
        Write-host "Folder Scanning Operation Complete."
}


$time1
$time2
$timediff = ($time1 - $time2).TotalSeconds
Write-host "Total Difference in Speed: $timediff Total Seconds"
```

The output of this is shown in the following screenshot:

```
4994
4995
4996
4997
4998
4999
5000
Running Folder Scanning Operation...
Folder Scanning Operation Complete.
PS C:\>
PS C:\> $time1


Days              : 0
Hours             : 0
Minutes           : 0
Seconds           : 51
Milliseconds      : 291
Ticks             : 512911818
TotalDays         : 0.0005936479375
TotalHours        : 0.0142475505
TotalMinutes      : 0.85485303
TotalSeconds      : 51.2911818
TotalMilliseconds : 51291.1818



PS C:\> $time2


Days              : 0
Hours             : 0
Minutes           : 0
Seconds           : 46
Milliseconds      : 743
Ticks             : 467435808
TotalDays         : 0.000541013666666667
TotalHours        : 0.012984328
TotalMinutes      : 0.77905968
TotalSeconds      : 46.7435808
TotalMilliseconds : 46743.5808



PS C:\> $timediff = ($time1 - $time2).TotalSeconds
PS C:\> Write-host "Total Difference in Speed: $timediff Total Seconds"
Total Difference in Speed: 4.547601 Total Seconds
```

In this example, you create a `write-host` function that can be enabled and disabled, disable verbose logging half-way through an operation, and time the difference:

1. You first start by declaring the `$verbose` variable and setting the value to `$true`.

2. You then create the `log` function, which has an `if` statement to verify if `$verbose` is set to `$true`. If `$verbose` is set to `$true`, the `write-host` cmdlet prints the pipeline, or `$_`, to the screen.

3. You declare the `measure-command` cmdlet to measure the time.

4. You create a range from `1` to `10000` and pipe that to the `%`, which is the alias for `foreach`.

5. You leverage the `log` function with the `"Number $_"` to display the number of the current step.

6. You then use the `Get-ChildItem` cmdlet with the `"c:\Windows\"` argument and set those results to `$contents`.

   This action will repeated 10,000 times. The execution duration will be captured by the `measure-command` cmdlet and stored in the `$time1` variable.

7. For the second operation, you call the `measure-command` cmdlet.

8. You create the range from 1 to 5000 and pipe that to the `%`.

9. You issue the `log` function with `"Number $_"` as the pipeline.

10. You then leverage the `Get-ChildItem` cmdlet with the `"c:\Windows\"` argument and set those results to `$contents`.

11. After the action repeats 5,000 times, you disable verbose logging by setting `$verbose` to `$false`.

12. You also write high-level information to the screen with the `write-host` cmdlet set to `"Running Folder Scanning Operation..."`.

13. You continue to create a second range from 1 to 5000, or the second half of the operation. You pipe the range to the `%`.

14. You issue the `log` function with `"Number $_"` as the pipeline.

15. You leverage the `Get-ChildItem` cmdlet with the `"c:\Windows\"` argument and set those results to `$contents`.

    After the action repeats 5,000 additional times, the execution duration will be captured by the `measure-command` cmdlet and stored in the `$time2` variable. To view the measured times, you display the duration in `$time1` and `$time2` by calling the variables.

16. You then calculate the difference in execution time by calling `$time1` - `$time2` and referencing the `TotalSeconds` property.

17. You set this value in the `$timediff` variable.

18. Finally, you print the time value to the display by using the `Write-host` cmdlet with the `"Total Difference in Speed: $timediff Total Seconds"`.

You will see that, in this example, while both operations call the same `logging` function, disabling `$verbose` improves performance by roughly 10%.

Speed considerations for the write-progress cmdlet

The `write-progress` cmdlet is an excellent way to display progress on the screen for operations. It doesn't flood the screen with information, and provides a clear measure of the current progress. The `write-progress` cmdlet, however, has similar issues to the `write-host` cmdlet. Since you are providing visual feedback in a loop, it slows the overall performance of the script.

To display the speed difference between using the `write-progress` loop and keeping operations in memory, you can do the following:

```
$time1 = measure-command {
    1..10000 | % {
                $attempt = $_
                $perComplete = [math]::truncate(($attempt/10000)*100)
                write-progress -Activity "Looping Retrieval of Contents
of c:\Windows" -Status "$attempt of 10000." -PercentComplete $perComplete
                # Get the contents of C:\Windows\
                $contents = Get-ChildItem c:\windows\
                }
}
$time2 = measure-command {
    1..10000 | % {
                # Get the contents of C:\Windows\
                $contents = Get-ChildItem c:\windows\
                }
}
$time1
$time2
$timediff = ($time1 - $time2).TotalSeconds
Write-host "Total Difference in Speed: $timediff Total Seconds"
```

The output of this is shown in the following screenshot:

```
Days              : 0
Hours             : 0
Minutes           : 1
Seconds           : 33
Milliseconds      : 544
Ticks             : 935448318
TotalDays         : 0.0010826948125
TotalHours        : 0.0259846755
TotalMinutes      : 1.55908053
TotalSeconds      : 93.5448318
TotalMilliseconds : 93544.8318


PS C:\> $time2

Days              : 0
Hours             : 0
Minutes           : 0
Seconds           : 42
Milliseconds      : 549
Ticks             : 425496020
TotalDays         : 0.000492472245370037
TotalHours        : 0.0118193338888889
TotalMinutes      : 0.709160033333333
TotalSeconds      : 42.549602
TotalMilliseconds : 42549.602


PS C:\> $timediff = ($time1 - $time2).TotalSeconds
PS C:\> Write-host "Total Difference in Speed: $timediff Total Seconds"
Total Difference in Speed: 50.9952298 Total Seconds
```

This example displays the difference between using the `write-progress` cmdlet and keeping operations in memory:

1. You first start by declaring the `measure-command` cmdlet.

2. You then declare the range from `1` to `10000` and pipe that to `%`, which is the alias for `foreach`.

3. Next, you create the `$attempt` variable and set it to the pipeline `$_`, which is the current iteration of the script.

4. Since the `write-progress` cmdlet doesn't auto-round the percent complete, you have to leverage the `[math]`.Net assembly to truncate the percent complete to a whole number.

5. To calculate the percent complete, you take the current attempt, divided by the total number of iterations (10,000), and obtain the percentage by multiplying the value by 100. This rounded value is then stored in the `$perComplete` variable.

6. You continue to use the `write-progress` cmdlet with the `-Activity` parameter set to `"Looping Retrieval of Contents of c:\Windows:"`, the `-status` parameter set to `"$attempt of 10000."`, and the `-PercentComplete` parameter set to `$perComplete`.

7. Finally, you call the `Get-ChildItem` cmdlet with the `c:\windows\` argument. This action will repeat 10,000 times.

   The execution duration will be captured by the `measure-command` cmdlet and stored in the `$time1` variable.

8. You then set up a second measuring command.

9. You declare the `measure-command` cmdlet.

10. You declare the range from `1` to `10000` and pipe that to the `%`.

11. You leverage the `Get-ChildItem` cmdlet with the `"c:\Windows\"` argument and set those results to `$contents`.

12. This action will repeat 10,000 times. The execution duration will be captured by the `measure-command` cmdlet and stored in the `$time2` variable.

    After execution of the second command, you display the duration in `$time1` and `$time2` by calling the variables.

13. You then calculate the difference in execution time by calling `$time1 - $time2` and referencing the `TotalSeconds` property.

14. You set this value in the `$timediff` variable.

15. Finally, you print the time value to the display by using the `write-host` cmdlet with `"Total Difference in Speed: $timediff Total Seconds"`.

You will see that, in this example, keeping operations in memory is about 219% times as fast than using the `write-progress` cmdlet.

Speed consideration - switches versus if statements

There may be times where you need to evaluate a string for multiple values. It's common to start by creating multiple `if` statements to evaluate those strings. While this may work well in small datasets, you can get a gain in performance by leveraging a `switch` statement. This is due to the way that `switch` statements evaluate data as it passes through. `Switch` statements stop evaluating down the list of statements after a match is found. Conversely, multiple `if` statements will evaluate every time even if a match is found. This also means that, if you are sorting a large amount of data, you will want to place your most common data near the top of the `switch` statement, and the less likely data at the bottom. This will allow you to quickly match the most common denominator and move on to the next value being passed through the loop.

The next example will emulate a large folder structure of `.exe`, `.dll`, and `.xml` files. Part one of this example sets up the dataset for evaluation, whereas part two will sort the data counts of file types into different variables. You will leverage both `if` statements and switches to determine the efficiency of switches.

> Part 1 and Part 2 require that a PowerShell Window is **Run as administrator**. When testing this code, you will want to right-click the **PowerShell** icon and select **Run as administrator**. If you are remotely executing this code, you will want to ensure that the user credentials you are using have administrative rights to the system.

Part 1 – To create a dataset of `.dll`, `.exe`, and `.xml` files, you can perform the following:

```
# Gather all the File Extensions c:\windows\System32
$dlls = 0
$exes = 0
$xmls = 0
$extensions = @()
$contents += ((Get-ChildItem"c:\windows\System32\" -include "*.xml","*.
dll","*.exe" -Recurse -ErrorActionSilentlyContinue) | Select Name)
foreach ($item in ($contents.Name)) {
    $sline = $item.split(".").length
    $extensions += '.' + $item.split(".")[$sline-1]
}
1..13 | % { $extensions += $extensions }
Write-host "Total number of Extensions: " $extensions.count
```

The output of this is shown in the following screenshot:

```
PS C:\> $dlls = 0
PS C:\> $exes = 0
PS C:\> $xmls = 0
PS C:\> $extensions = @()
PS C:\> $contents += ((Get-ChildItem "c:\windows\System32\" -include "*.xml","*.dll","*.exe" -Recurse -ErrorAction SilentlyContinue) | Select Name
)
PS C:\> foreach ($item in ($contents.Name)) {
>>>     $sline = $item.split(".").length
>>>     $extensions += "," + $item.split(".")[$sline-1]
>>> }
PS C:\> 1..13 | % { $extensions += $extensions }
PS C:\> Write-host "Total number of Extensions: " $extensions.count
Total number of Extensions:  42713088
```

In this example, you create a dataset to sort for Part 2:

1. You first start by setting the variables $dlls, $exes, and $xmls to the value of zero.

2. You declare the $extensions array by setting it equal to @().

3. Next, you leverage the Get-ChildItem cmdlet with the "c:\Windows\ System32" argument, the -include parameter with the "*.xml","*. dll","*.exe" argument, and the -Recurse parameter, and the -ErrorAction parameter set to the argument of SilentlyContinue.

4. You then pipe that value to Select Name, to select the name property of each file.

5. You then add each value to the $contents variable by using the add+= assignment operator.

    You then continue to obtain the file extension for each file.

6. You first start by using the foreach loop to evaluate each $item in the $contents using the Name property.

7. Since filenames can contain multiple periods, you have to determine what the extension is by the last period in the filename. You continue to split the current $item by the period character and count the number of periods in the filename.

8. You set the number of counted periods in the $sline variable.

9. To select the last value in the filename, you set the $item and use the .split(".") method.

10. You then select the last split value by the $sline number minus one, and arrays are zero base.

11. You add to the $extensions array a "," plus the final extension of the file.

The final section of Part 1 is to compound the extensions located by a factor of 13. This will emulate a large volume of information to pass through scripts in Part 2. You then leverage the `write-host` cmdlet to display `"Total number of extensions: "` with the number of extensions using `$extensions.count`. This example returns `42,713,088` extensions to be sorted.

Part 2 – To measure the difference in duration between sorting the data using `if` statements and switch statements, you can perform the following:

```
$time1 = measure-command {
foreach ($extension in $extensions) {
        # Determine the file types
        if ($extension -like "*.xml") { $xmls += 1 }
        if ($extension -like "*.exe") { $exes += 1 }
        if ($extension -like "*.dll") { $dlls += 1 }
    }
}
# Reset Count
$dlls = 0
$exes = 0
$xmls = 0
$time2 = measure-command {
foreach ($extension in $extensions) {
        # Determine the file types
        switch($extension) {
".dll" { $dlls += 1 }
".exe" { $exes += 1 }
".xml" { $xmls += 1 }
            default { } #do nothing
        }
    }
}

$time1
$time2
$timediff = ($time1 - $time2).TotalSeconds
Write-Host "Total Number of Counted DLL files $dlls"
Write-host "Total Number of Counted EXE files $exes"
Write-host "Total Number of Counted XML files $xmls"
Write-host "Total Difference in Speed: $timediff Total Seconds"
```

The output of this is shown in the following screenshot:

```
TotalMinutes       : 4.00791666333333
TotalSeconds       : 240.4749998
TotalMilliseconds  : 240474.9998


PS C:\> $time2


Days               : 0
Hours              : 0
Minutes            : 3
Seconds            : 7
Milliseconds       : 725
Ticks              : 1877250665
TotalDays          : 0.00217274382523148
TotalHours         : 0.0521458518055556
TotalMinutes       : 3.12875110833333
TotalSeconds       : 187.7250665
TotalMilliseconds  : 187725.0665


PS C:\> $timediff = ($time1 - $time2).TotalSeconds
PS C:\> Write-Host "Total Number of Counted DLL files $dlls"
Total Number of Counted DLL files 34996224
PS C:\> Write-host "Total Number of Counted EXE files $exes"
Total Number of Counted EXE files 5627904
PS C:\> Write-host "Total Number of Counted XML files $xmls"
Total Number of Counted XML files 1966080
PS C:\> Write-host "Total Difference in Speed: $timediff Total Seconds"
Total Difference in S eed: 52.7499333 Total Seconds
```

In this example, you measure the difference between sorting data using `if`
statements and `switch` statements:

1. You first start by leveraging the `measure-command` cmdlet to measure the
   duration of sorting using `if` statements.

2. You continue to use the `foreach` loop to evaluate each `$extension` in the
   `$extensions` array.

3. You declare the statement of `if` the `$extension` is `-like "*.xml"`. If this
   evaluates to true, it will add one value to the `$xmls` variable leveraging the
   `+=` assignment operator.

4. You then evaluate the statement of `if` the `$extension` is `-like"*.exe"`. If
   this evaluates to true, it will add one value to the `$exes` variable leveraging
   the `+=` assignment operator.

5. Finally, you evaluate the statement of if the $extension is -like "*.dll". If this evaluates to true, it will add one value to the $dlls variable leveraging the += assignment operator. After the data sort is complete, the script adds the measured time in the $time1 variable.

   To prepare the script for the second data sort, you reset the $dlls, $exes, and $xmls variables by setting them to 0.

6. You proceed to leverage the measure-command cmdlet to measure the duration of sorting using switch statements.

7. You call the foreach loop to evaluate each $extension in the $extension array.

8. You call the switch statement with the $extension as the argument.

9. You declare ".dll"; if matched, the script will add one value to the $dlls variable.

10. You then declare ".exe"; if matched, the script will add one value to the $exes variable.

11. You also declare ".xml"; if matched, the script will add one value to the $xmls variable.

12. Finally, you use the default statement and set it to { }, to do nothing.

13. After the data sort is complete, the script adds the measured time in the $time2 variable.

    After the time measurements, you then display the duration in $time1 and $time2 by calling the variables.

14. You call the write-host cmdlet and display "Total Number of Counted DLL files $dlls".

15. You call the write-host cmdlet again, and display "Total Number of Counted EXE files $exes".

16. You call the write-host cmdlet a final time, and display "Total Number of Counted XML files $xmls".

17. You calculate the difference in execution time by calling $time1 - $time2 and referencing the TotalSeconds property. You set this value in the $timediff variable.

18. Finally, you print the time value to the display by using the write-host cmdlet with "Total Difference in Speed: $timediff Total Seconds".

You will see that, in this example, switches for data sorting are about 128 times as fast than using `if` statements.

You will notice that the order of evaluation in the `switch` statement is set as `.dll` first, `.exe` second, and `.xml` last. These are evaluated based on commonality on the system. Since switches stop evaluation after a match is found, the script is written to have the most popular items evaluated first, optimizing the switches' function.

Summary

In this chapter, you learned different scripting techniques that can optimize execution speed. You first learned how to measure script execution duration by leveraging the `measure-command` cmdlet. You then compared the time difference between writing data to the screen and keeping operations in memory. You then learned a technique to turn on and off writing data on the screen to optimize script execution during runtime. You proceeded to evaluate the `write-progress` cmdlet and how it affects performance. You completed the chapter by evaluating the performance differences between `if` statements and `switch` statements.

In the next chapter, you will learn how to leverage regular expressions for string matching, to significantly improve scripting performance.

11
Improving Performance by Using Regular Expressions

As you are evaluating systems with the Windows Server scanning script, there may be instances where you need to find sensitive data that doesn't match specific values. Credit card numbers, social security numbers, and even tax identification numbers are great examples of data that you need to identify, but would be impossible to search for using strings alone.

Regular expressions, however, provide pattern matching to identify data that you normally wouldn't be able to find with string searching. Regular expressions are very dynamic and can be used to detect any pattern that you need in your script. In fact, regular expressions can be so granular that they can search parts of words. This means that you can find the word `Password` in the `MyPasswordIsString` string.

Regular expressions are also very quick. In comparison to using multiple arrays and `if` statements, regular expressions often outperform other techniques by over 50%! This is why developers choose to leverage regular expressions to optimize their code, and provide a robust searching platform.

In this chapter, you will:

- Learn the common regular expression used in organizations
- Leverage comparison operators to utilize regular expressions
- Dynamically build regular expressions for use in scripts
- Evaluate the performance gains of using regular expressions over multiple `foreach` loops

This chapter does not go in-depth into how to create and read regular expressions. A good guide to help you break down individual regular expressions can be found here: `https://msdn.microsoft.com/en-us/library/az24scfc(v=vs.110).aspx`.

Using regular expressions

One of the best ways to increase your script performance is by leveraging regular expressions. Regular expressions provide robust pattern matching to provide quick evaluation of large amounts of data. The two common methods for using regular expressions are comparison operators and cmdlets that support the use of regular expressions. The `-match` comparison operator, for example, allows you to match a string or an array to an expression. If the pattern matches, the regular expression evaluates the statement to be `true`, that is, a match was found.

You may also use cmdlets such as the `select-string` cmdlet, which natively supports regular expression patterns. While the `select-string` cmdlet provides the `-SimpleMatch` parameter for simplicity of searching, you can also use the same cmdlet to match regular expression patterns. This adds to the versatility of pre-existing cmdlets, as they can now support regular expressions to search for patterns in addition to strings.

The following table represents some of the more popular regular expressions:

Expression type	Regular expression
IP address	`\b\d{1,3}\.\d{1,3}\.\d{1,3}\.\d{1,3}\b`
MAC address	`^([0-9a-f]{2}:){5}[0-9a-f]{2}$`
E-mail address	`^.+@[^\.].*\.[a-z]{2,}$`
Visa credit card number	`^\d{4}-\d{4}-\d{4}-\d{4}$`
Social security number	`^\d{3}-\d{2}-\d{4}$`

To leverage the `-match` operator to validate different patterns, you can perform the following:

```
"192.168.12.24" -match "\b\d{1,3}\.\d{1,3}\.\d{1,3}\.\d{1,3}\b"
```

```
"00:A0:F8:12:34:56" -match "^([0-9a-f]{2}:){5}[0-9a-f]{2}$"
```

```
"brent@testingdomain.com" -match "^.+@[^\.].*\.[a-z]{2,}$"


"4000-4000-4000-4000" -match "^\d{4}-\d{4}-\d{4}-\d{4}$"


"123-45-6789" -match "^\d{3}-\d{2}-\d{4}$"
```

The output of this is shown in the following screenshot:

```
PS C:\> "192.168.12.24" -match "\b\d{1,3}\.\d{1,3}\.\d{1,3}\.\d{1,3}\b"
True
PS C:\> "00:A0:F8:12:34:56" -match "^([0-9a-f]{2}:){5}[0-9a-f]{2}$"
True
PS C:\> "brent@testingdomain.com" -match "^.+@[^\.].*\.[a-z]{2,}$"
True
PS C:\> "4000-4000-4000-4000" -match "^\d{4}-\d{4}-\d{4}-\d{4}$"
True
PS C:\> "123-45-6789" -match "^\d{3}-\d{2}-\d{4}$"
True
```

In this example, you evaluate multiple strings against regular expressions. You first start by evaluating the IP address 192.168.12.24 with the -match operator:

1. You define the \b whole word boundary followed by the expression \d to only accept digits.

2. You specify the range of {1,3} to accept 1-3 digits.

3. You then specify \.\ to allow for a period between the octet, and continue to repeat the statement \d{1,3} an additional three times.

4. This allows for four octets in the IP address. Finally, you close the expression with \b to close the word boundary.

5. When the -match comparison operator evaluates the string 192.168.12.24, it will return True.

You then evaluate the MAC address of 00:A0:F8:12:34:56 with the -match operator:

1. You start by using the anchor of ^ to start evaluating from the beginning.

2. The expression then uses the grouping construct of ( ) to group the expression of [0-9a-f]{2}:

3. This expression is validating to see if each character has valid hexadecimal [0-9a-f] values and uses a quantifier to specify only two characters per sequence.

4. The expression ends with :, which is the separator between each set of values.

5. Moving on, you then use another quantifier of {5} to repeat the two hexadecimal characters with a colon at the end five times.

6. The final part of the expression is matched from the ending anchor of $.

7. The ending anchor is validating to see if each character has valid hexadecimal [0-9a-f] values and uses a quantifier to specify only two characters as the ending of the string.

8. When the -match operator evaluates the string 00:a0:f8:12:34:56, it will return True.

You continue to evaluate the e-mail address of brent@testingdomain.com with the -match operator:

1. You start by using the anchor of ^ to start evaluating from the beginning.

2. You specify the . character to denote that anything can be contained as the beginning of the email address.

3. You use the +@ to evaluate the literal character of @.

4. You then specify the range of [^\.], which specifies that the first character after the @ must not be a period.

5. It then continues to evaluate .*, which designates that any characters can be specified.

6. The expression then specifies \. to allow for a single period after the top-level domain is specified.

7. Finally, you specify the character set range of [a-z] with a minimum of two characters, specified by {2,}.

8. The final part of the expression is matched from the ending anchor of $.

9. When the -match operator evaluates the brent@testingdomain.com string, it will return True.

You then evaluate the visa credit card of 4000-4000-4000-4000 with the -match operator:

1. You start by using the anchor of ^ to start evaluating from the beginning.

2. You specify \d to designate all digits.

3. You then provide the range of {4} to allow for exactly four digits.

4. You use the - character as the number separator followed by \d{4} to provide an additional four digits.

5. You repeat the - character as the number separator followed by \d{4} an additional two times.

6. The final part of the expression is matched from the ending anchor of $.

7. When the -match operator evaluates the string 4000-4000-4000-4000, it will return True.

Finally, you evaluate the social security number of 123-45-6789 with the -match operator:

1. You start by using the anchor of ^ to start evaluating from the beginning.

2. You specify \d to designate all digits.

3. You then provide the range of {3} to allow for exactly three digits.

4. You provide the - character as the number separator followed by \d{2} to allow for exactly two digits.

5. You then specify the \d{4} to allow for exactly four digits.

6. The final part of the expression is matched from the ending anchor of $.

7. When the -match operator evaluates the string 123-45-6789, it will return True.

Dynamically building expressions

When you are creating a script to search for strings with regular expressions, the search pattern may need to change with each execution. Instead of updating your regular expressions each time you run the script, PowerShell offers the ability to dynamically build regular expressions. For example, if you needed to search files for members of an Active Directory group that frequently changed, you would need to update the expression each time you ran the script. Instead you could query the Active Directory group during runtime, and dynamically build the regular expression for searching. This provides the flexibility to change search terms on-the-fly, and doesn't require you to edit your script for each execution.

To start, you will need to declare an array of objects to feed into the regular expression. In this case, we will define "administrator", "password", and "username" and set them in the $myarray variable. You then continue to build the regular expression string by declaring the (?i)^.*(string. This declares case insensitivity with (?i) to allow for both upper- and lower-case within the following strings and uses the anchor of ^ to start evaluating from the beginning. You continue to use .*(to accept any characters before the strings defined in the next sequence. Inside the parentheses, you call $myarray and pipe it to %, which is the alias for foreach.

Inside the `foreach` loop, you take the current value and leverage the `[regex]` .NET class to `::escape` any characters that may interfere with the regular expression. This will dynamically interpret those characters as literal characters instead of regular expression instructions. You then leverage the `-join` operator to add a `|` between each of the words in the `$myarray` array. The `|` character in the search string designates the OR operation. The `foreach` loop continues to add the remaining words to the regular expression string. This creates the search pattern of `administrator | password | username`.

You continue to add the `).*$` to the end of the pattern to close the parenthetical statement, and match any characters from the end of the pattern. Finally, you place the string you built into a variable named `$searchregex`. You can then use this regular expression to search by leveraging the `-match` operator, or a cmdlet that supports regular expressions.

> By default, regular expressions in PowerShell are case-insensitive. When you leverage the `[regex]` .NET class, however, the class casts the expression with case sensitivity, overriding the default setting. This requires you to force the expression to evaluate with case insensitivity by calling `(?i)`.

To create an array and search using a dynamically built regular expression, you can do the following:

```
$myarray = "administrator","password","username"
$searchRegex = '(?i)^.*(' + (($myarray| % {[regex]::escape($_)}) -join
"|") + ').*$'
"This String has Administrators in it." -match $searchRegex
"This PASSWORD is not secure." -match $searchRegex
"TheUsernames are not written." -match $searchRegex
$searchRegex.tostring()
```

The output of this is shown in the following screenshot:

```
PS C:\> $myarray = "administrator","password","username"
PS C:\> $searchRegex = '(?i)^.*(' + (($myarray| % {[regex]::escape($_)}) -join "|") + ').*$'
PS C:\> "This String has Administrators in it." -match $searchRegex
True
PS C:\> "This PASSWORD is not secure." -match $searchRegex
True
PS C:\> "TheUsernames are not written." -match $searchRegex
True
PS C:\> $searchRegex.tostring()
(?i)^.*(administrator|password|username).*$
```

In this example, you will learn how to build a dynamic string searching regular expression from an array:

1. You first start by building an array of `"administrator"`, `"password"`, `"username"`, and set it in the `$myarray` variable.

2. You then continue to build the regular expression string by declaring the `(?i)^.*(` string.

3. This declares case insensitivity with `(?i)` to allow for both upper- and lower-case within the following strings and uses the anchor of `^` to start evaluating from the beginning.

4. You continue to use `.*(` to accept any characters before the strings defined in the next sequence.

5. Inside the parentheses, you call `$myarray` and pipe it to `%`, which is the alias for `foreach`.

6. Inside the `foreach` loop, you take the value current value and leverage the `[regex]` .NET class to `::escape` any characters that may interfere with the regular expression.

7. You then leverage the `-join` operator to add a `|` between each of the words in the `$myarray` array.

8. You add the `).*$` to the end of the pattern to close the parenthetical statement, and match any characters from the end of the pattern.

9. Finally, you place the string you built into a variable named `$searchRegex`.

After you create the regular expression, you start to evaluate for the values of `administrator`, `password`, or `username`.

1. You declare `"This string has Administrators in it."` and use the `-match` comparison operator with the `$searchRegex` regular expression.

2. The result of this returns the value of `True`.

3. This is due to the regular expression matching the string `"administrator"` in the `"administrators"`.

4. Since you declared that the administrator can appear with any characters before or after the string, the expression is returned as `True`.

You then continue to evaluate the next string.

1. You declare `"This PASSWORD is not secure."` and use the `-match` comparison operator with the `$searchRegex` regular expression.

2. The result of this returns the value of `True`.

3. This is due to the regular expression matching the string of `"password"`, ignoring the case of the string.

4. Since you declared `(?i)` for case insensitivity, the string is matched and the expression is returned as `true`.

5. You then declare `"TheUsernames are not written."` and use the `-match` comparison operator with the `$searchRegex` regular expression.

6. The result of this returns the value of `True`.

7. This is due to the regular expression matching the string `"username"` in the string `"TheUsernames"`.

8. Since you declared that username can appear with any characters before or after the string, the expression is returned as `True`.

9. Finally, you call the `$searchRegex` expression with the `.toString()` method.

10. This displays the text of the regular expression as it was dynamically built.

11. The regular expression of `(?i)^.*(administrator|password|userna me).*$` is then displayed on the screen.

Implementating regular expression performance

Regular expressions are very versatile when implemented in PowerShell scripts. Not only are they used for pattern validation, they are much faster at analyzing large sets of data. When you compare regular expressions and `foreach` array loops side-by-side, the former will consistently outperform the latter.

> Part 1 and Part 2 require that a PowerShell Window is **Run as administrator**. When testing this code, you will want to right-click the **PowerShell** icon and select **Run as administrator**. If you are remotely executing this code, you will want to ensure that the user credentials you are using have administrative rights to the system.
>
> The total number of files in the `$files` array may be slightly different than what's displayed in this example.

Part 1 — To create a large dataset of filenames in `c:\Window\System32`, you can perform the following:

```
$files = (Get-ChildItem c:\Windows\System32 -Recurse -ErrorAction
SilentlyContinue).Name
1..8 | % { $files += $files }
Write-host "Total Number of Files to Analyze: " $files.count
```

The output of this is shown in the following screenshot:

```
PS C:\>
PS C:\> $files = (Get-ChildItem c:\Windows\System32 -Recurse -ErrorAction SilentlyContinue).Name
PS C:\> 1..8 | % { $files += $files }
PS C:\> Write-host "Total Number of Files to Analyze: " $files.count
Total Number of Files to Analyze:  4700928
```

In this example, you create a large dataset of filenames in `c:\Windows\System32`:

1. You first start by leveraging the `Get-ChildItem` cmdlet with the `c:\Windows\System32` argument.

2. You leverage the `-Recurse` parameter to scan the subdirectories and the `-ErrorAction` parameter set to the `SilentlyContinue` argument.

3. You place that statement in parentheses and select the `.Name` property to return the filenames.

4. The filenames are placed in the `$files` variable.

5. You then declare the `1..8` range to compound the filenames in the `$files` variables eight times.

6. You do this by piping the range to `%`, the alias for `foreach`.

7. You then declare the assignment operator of `$files += $files`. This takes the current values in `$files` and adds them to the `$files` variable. Essentially, it is duplicating the contents contained in `$files` each time it is called.

8. Finally, you use the `write-host` cmdlet and specify `"Total Number of Files to Analyze:"` referencing the `$files` variable and the `.count` method.

9. This displays:`"Total Number of Files to Analyze: 4700928"`.

Part 2—To measure the difference in duration between identifying strings using `foreach` loops and regular expressions, you can perform the following:

```
$types = ".xml",".exe",".dll"

$filefound = 0

$time1 = Measure-Command {

    foreach ($type in $types) {

        foreach ($file in $files) {

            if ($file -like "*$type*") { $filefound += 1 }

        }

    }

}

Write-host "Total Number of Found Files $filefound"

$filefound = 0
```

```
$searchRegex = '^.*(' + (($types | foreach {[regex]::escape($_)}) -join
"|") + ').*$'

$time2 = Measure-Command {
        foreach ($file in $files) {
            if ($file -match $searchRegex) { $filefound += 1 }
        }
}

Write-host "Total Number of Found Files $filefound"

$time1

$time2

$timediff = ($time1 - $time2).TotalSeconds

Write-host "Total Difference in Speed: $timediff Total Seconds"
```

The output of this is shown in the following screenshot:

```
Total Number of Found Files 1288960
PS C:\> $time1


Days              : 0
Hours             : 0
Minutes           : 0
Seconds           : 50
Milliseconds      : 270
Ticks             : 502707197
TotalDays         : 0.000581837033564815
TotalHours        : 0.0139640888055556
TotalMinutes      : 0.837845328333333
TotalSeconds      : 50.2707197
TotalMilliseconds : 50270.7197




PS C:\> $time2


Days              : 0
Hours             : 0
Minutes           : 0
Seconds           : 36
Milliseconds      : 985
Ticks             : 369856105
TotalDays         : 0.000428074195601852
TotalHours        : 0.0102737806944444
TotalMinutes      : 0.616426841666667
TotalSeconds      : 36.9856105
TotalMilliseconds : 36985.6105




PS C:\> $timediff = ($time1 - $time2).TotalSeconds
PS C:\> Write-host "Total Difference in Speed: $timediff Total Seconds"
Total Difference in Speed: 13.2851092 Total Seconds
```

In this example, you will measure the difference in duration between identifying strings using `foreach` loops and regular expressions:

1. You first start by declaring the strings that you want to search for in the filenames.

2. The strings of `".xml"`, `".exe"`, and `".dll"` are added to the `$types` array.

3. You then set the `$filecount` variable to `0`.

4. You leverage the `measure-command` cmdlet to measure the duration of sorting using multiple `foreach` loops.

5. You continue to use the `foreach` loop to evaluate each `$type` in the `$types` variable.

6. You nest a second `foreach` loop inside that `foreach` loop to evaluate each `$file` in the `$files` variable.

7. Finally, you leverage an `if` statement to evaluate if the `$file` variable is `-like *$type`. This is a wildcard search that allows any characters prior to the current file `$type`.

8. If the filename matches the type, it will add one value to the `$filefound` variable.

9. After both loops complete, you then capture the execution duration in the `$time1` variable.

10. You also use the `write-host` cmdlet with the `"Total Number of Found Files $filefound"` argument.

11. This displays `Total Number of Found Files 1288960`.

12. You then proceed to reset the file counter by setting the `$filefound` variable to `0`.

13. You start creating the regular expression by declaring `(?i)` for case insensitivity and `^` to start evaluating from the beginning.

14. You continue to use `.*(` to accept any characters before the strings defined in the next sequence.

15. Inside the parentheses, you call `$myarray` and pipe it to `%`, which is the alias for `foreach`.

16. Inside the `foreach` loop, you take the value current value and leverage the `[regex]`.NET class to `::escape` any characters that may interfere with the regular expression.

17. You then leverage the `-join` operator to add a `|` between each of the words in the `$myarray` array.

18. You add the $ ending anchor at the end to ensure that it only evaluates the file type, not the file extension as part of a word.

19. You store this regular expression in the $searchRegex variable.

20. You proceed to leverage the measure-command cmdlet to measure the evaluation of the foreach loop and regular expressions.

21. You start by using foreach to evaluate each $file in $files.

22. You then declare an if statement using the -match comparison operator to determine if the $file matches the regular expression set in $searchRegex.

23. If the regular expression returns True, the $filefound variable will be increased by 1.

24. After the foreach loop is done evaluating every file, you then capture the execution duration in the $time2 variable.

25. You also use the write-host cmdlet with the "Total Number of Found Files $filefound" argument.

26. This displays Total Number of Found Files 1288960.

27. Finally, you display the duration in $time1 and $time2 by calling the variables.

28. You then calculate the difference in execution time by calling $time1 - $time2 and referencing the TotalSeconds property.

29. You set this value in the $timediff variable.

30. Finally, you print the time value to the display by using the write-host cmdlet with the "Total Difference in Speed: $timediff Total Seconds".

31. You will see that, in this example, leveraging regular expressions is 13.285 seconds faster than processing data using foreach loops.

Summary

In this chapter, you learned about regular expressions. You explored different common regular expressions and learned that you can use them with the -match comparison operator. You also learned that that there are cmdlets that support the use of regular expressions. You then created a dynamic regular expression using values from an array and identified strings that matched those expressions. Finally, you evaluated the performance difference between using regular expressions and multiple arrays for string searching. In the next chapter, you will be combining all of the concepts that you've learned in this book to create a Windows server scanning script.

12
Overall Script Workflow, Termination Files, and Merging Data Results

As you are preparing to create the Windows server scanning script, there are multiple components that you will want to create prior to executing the script itself. For example, if you are intending on using encrypted strings, you will need to develop a script to create the randomized password, salt, and init. You will also need another script to perform the encryption of the strings. Due to the multiple scripts that you may need to create, this chapter outlines a recommended script workflow to ensure you have all the components you need to run the scanning script in your environment.

After exploring the workflow, you will proceed to develop a script to create randomized strings. These randomized strings are direct inputs into the encryption script, and are stored in the `answer` file. You will also learn about how to develop an encryption script to encrypt multiple strings on a loop.

When you are done encrypting strings, you will proceed to learn about `answer` files. You will learn about the different components that you can include in your answer file to enable a multitude of features in your scripts.

You will explore methods that leverage termination files to locally and remotely stop the execution of the scanning script. You will also learn how to remove the `termination` file to enable running of the Windows server scanning script again.

The last component you will learn about in this chapter is how to merge the results from the server scanning script. If you ran the script on multiple systems, you'll need a method to merge the CSV files together. This will allow you to view all of the collected data in one location, and discover similarities in the systems in your environment.

In this chapter, you will:

- Obtain an overview of the Windows server scanning script
- Create a script to generate randomized strings for use in the encryption script
- Develop an encryption script that will enable encrypting of multiple strings
- Learn the `answer` file's structure
- Understand the purpose of creating and deleting `termination` files locally and remotely on a system
- Merge multiple CSVs into a single CSV file

Windows server scanning script overview

The Windows server scanning script is an enterprise-ready tool that you can use to inspect systems in your environment. This script can be used as a starting point to enable the creation of your own scripts. When implementing the Windows server scanning script, you need to follow a general workflow to ensure that the script is secure and reliable.

The workflow steps include:

1. **Security key generation**: You will create a string generation script that can randomly create your encryption password, salt, and init. You will also leverage encoding to strengthen the password, salt, and init. The output of this script will be used by the `encryption` function, `decryption` function, and `answer` file.

2. **Encryption script**: You will then leverage the values that are generated in the security key generation to create an encryption script. This will enable you to encrypt strings for use in your `answer` File.

3. **Answer file**: You will learn the different answers that you will need to store in your `answer` file. You will also learn that you need to download the `Scan_Answers.xml` answer file from the book's code files for this chapter.

4. **Termination script**: To ensure that you can terminate the Windows server scanning script remotely, you will create a termination script. This script will create a termination file on the system that, if present, will make the Windows server scanning script stop.

5. **Windows server scanning script**: In the next chapter, you will be combining concepts from all of the examples in this book to create a complete scanning script. All of the other workflow steps in this section create scripts and data that complement the Windows server scanning script.

6. **Merging files**: The final script in the workflow is the merging script. If the Windows sever scanning script is run on multiple systems, you can merge the results into one easy to read file.

Pre-script security

When you want to create an enterprise-ready script, you need to start with your security components. In *Chapter 4, String Encryption and Decryption*, you learned the importance of leveraging encoding and encryption to provide added security to your scripts. You can follow several enterprise strategies to ensure that you properly implement encoding and encryption. One of the popular strategies is to create an encryption and decryption salt, init, and password that are shared by all of your scripts. While this is a simpler method from a script management perspective, you provide all departments access to the same encrypted data. Alternatively, you can have the departments create their own encoded salt, init, and passwords for scripts. In this, the encrypted data is different than what your department generates. This provides an additional layer of obscurity to the encrypted data as it's implemented in `answer` files. While this is more secure, it is a bit more difficult to coordinate a shared script. You will need to ensure that each team implements their own encoded salt, init, and password in the script and `answer` file.

Script 1 - randomized password and string generator

Whatever strategy you choose for your environment, you will need to start the scripting process by creating a randomized password. You then encode this password to split into the **Script Side Decryptor (SSD)**, or `$SSD`, the **Answer File Decryptor (AFD)**, or `$AFD`, and the **Runtime Decryptor (RTD)**, or `$RTD`. Finally, you specify an salt string, and encode it in a `$salt` variable, and specify an init string, and encode it in a `$init` variable. You now have all of the prerequisites to start encrypting data by leveraging an `encryption` function.

You will not want to include the encoding and encryption section of code in any of your scripts that you intend on deploying to your environment. Since you are generating secured values, you will want to place this script in a secure place with limited access.

To create a randomized password, salt, and init, you can perform the following:

```
Function create-password {
    $password = ""
    For ($a=33;$a -le 126;$a++) {
        $ascii += ,[char][byte]$a
    }
    1..30 | % { $password += $ascii | get-random }
    return $password
}
$pass = create-password
$salt = create-password
$init = create-password
```

The output of this is shown in the following screenshot:

```
PS C:\> Function create-password {
>>       $password = ""
>>       For ($a=33;$a -le 126;$a++) {
>>           $ascii += ,[char][byte]$a
>>       }
>>       1..30 | % { $password += $ascii | get-random }
>>       return $password
>> }
PS C:\> $pass = create-password
PS C:\> $salt = create-password
PS C:\> $init = create-password
```

In this example, you create a randomized password, salt, and init for the encryption functions:

1. You first start by defining a `create-password` function.

2. Inside the function, you define a blank `$password` variable to build the password string.

3. You continue to create a for loop starting with the `$a` value equal to `33`, while `$a` is less than or equal to `126`, and through each iteration add one value to `$a`.

4. Inside the loop, you create an $ascii variable to which you add each character [char] byte [byte] value between 33 and 126.

5. The results inside the $ascii variable are all characters for randomization.

6. After, you call the 1..30 range piped to %, which is the alias for foreach.

7. You then pipe the $ascii variable to get-random and add the value to the $password variable.

8. After adding 30 characters, you leverage return with the $password variable to return the value to the line where the function was called. This generates random values for $pass, $salt, and $init.

> The values that you generate in this example will be used in the following encryption script example. Take note of the values you generate for the SSD, AFD, RTD, salt, and init. These will be direct inputs to the encryption function.

To create encoded values of $salt, $init, and $pass, split the $pass variable into three values for the Script Side Decryptor, Answer File Decryptor, and Runtime Decryptor; you can do it as follows:

```
$encodedpass = [System.Text.Encoding]::Unicode.GetBytes($pass)
$encodedvalue = [Convert]::ToBase64String($encodedpass)
$SSD = $encodedvalue.substring(0,27)
$AFD = $encodedvalue.substring(27,27)
$RTD = $encodedvalue.substring(54,26)
$encSalt = [System.Text.Encoding]::Unicode.GetBytes($salt)
$encSalt = [Convert]::ToBase64String($encSalt)
$encInit = [System.Text.Encoding]::Unicode.GetBytes($init)
$encInit = [Convert]::ToBase64String($encInit)
Write-host "The SSD is: $SSD"
Write-host "The AFD is: $AFD"
Write-host "The RTD is: $RTD"
Write-host "The Salt is: $encSalt"
Write-host "The Init is: $encInit"
```

The output of this is shown in the following screenshot:

```
PS C:\> $encodedpass = [System.Text.Encoding]::Unicode.GetBytes($pass)
PS C:\> $encodedvalue = [Convert]::ToBase64String($encodedpass)
PS C:\> # Since the returned encoding is 80 characters in length, you split into 27, 27, 26
PS C:\> $SSD = $encodedvalue.substring(0,27)
PS C:\> $AFD = $encodedvalue.substring(27,27)
PS C:\> $RTD = $encodedvalue.substring(54,26)
PS C:\>
PS C:\> $encSalt = [System.Text.Encoding]::Unicode.GetBytes($salt)
PS C:\> $encSalt = [Convert]::ToBase64String($encSalt)
PS C:\>
PS C:\> $encInit = [System.Text.Encoding]::Unicode.GetBytes($init)
PS C:\> $encInit = [Convert]::ToBase64String($encInit)
PS C:\>
PS C:\> Write-host "The SSD is: $SSD"
The SSD is: LAAyAGwAdQBRAG8AZABMAEwAJgA
PS C:\> Write-host "The AFD is: $AFD"
The AFD is: 5AFIAQgBYACYAXgBRAC4AUgASAF
PS C:\> Write-host "The RTD is: $RTD"
The RTD is: AAZwAmAE4AMgAoAFEAVAAhAFAA
PS C:\> Write-host "The Salt is: $encSalt"
The Salt is: NABFAEIASgAzADsAOgBnAHEAagBxAGgAJgBcAH4AZgBRADOARAAzACEAZwAiACYATQBuAGwAWABzAHkA
PS C:\> Write-host "The Init is: $encInit"
The Init is: ZgA/ADoAbQBGAFMAewAjAHcAMgBYAGQALwBYACEAVgB4AHEARABVAHAANwBgACQAeAAqADOAbgBnADEA
```

In this example, you take the encoded password stored in $pass from the previous example. You will then split the $pass variable into three segments for the AFD, the SSD, and the RTD. Finally, you proceed to create encoded values of $salt and $init for use in the encryption script:

1. You first start by encoding the password by leveraging the [System.Text. Encoding]::Unicode.GetBytes($pass) method and storing the value in the $encodedpass variable.

2. You then convert the encoded value into a string by leveraging the [Conver t]::ToBase64String($encodedpass) method and storing the value in the $encodedvalue variable.

3. To derive the SSD, you take a substring of the $encodedvalue variable starting at the 0-text position and obtain 27 characters after that position. You set this value to the $SSD variable.

4. To derive the AFD, you take a substring of the $encodedvalue variable starting at the 27th text position and obtain 27 characters after that position. You set this value to the $AFD variable.

5. To derive the RTD, you take a substring of the $encodedvalue variable starting at the 54th text position and obtain 26 characters after that position.

In total, you will have taken all 80 characters in the `$encodedvalue` variable and split them into three variables for use in your script:

1. You then continue to encode the salt by leveraging the `[System.Text. Encoding]::Unicode.GetBytes($salt)` method and storing the value in the `$encSalt` variable. You then convert the encoded value into a string by leveraging the `[Convert]::ToBase64String($encSalt)` method and storing the value in the `$encSalt` variable.

2. Finally, you encode the init by leveraging the `[System.Text. Encoding]::Unicode.GetBytes($init)` method and storing the value in the `$encInit` variable. You then convert the encoded value into a string by leveraging the `[Convert]::ToBase64String($encInit)` method and storing the value in the `$encInit` variable.

Script 2 - string encryption script

In the instance that you want to have encrypted strings in your `answer` files, you will be required to develop an encryption script. Using the password (AFD, SSD, and RTD), salt, and init values that you generated with script 1, you can create an `encryption` function. You can also create a loop for that function, which will enable you to encrypt multiple strings in one session. After you generate the encrypted strings, you can place them securely in the `answer` file.

 To obtain a detailed explanation of encoding, encryption, and decryption, you can refer to *Chapter 4, String Encryption and Decryption*.

To create an `encryption` function to leverage the encoded salt, init, and `answer` file decryptor, you can do the following:

```
Add-Type -AssemblyName System.Security
function Encrypt-String { param($String)
    try{
        $r = new-Object System.Security.Cryptography.RijndaelManaged
        $pass = [Text.Encoding]::UTF8.GetBytes($pass)
        $salt = [Text.Encoding]::UTF8.GetBytes($salt)
        $init = [Text.Encoding]::UTF8.GetBytes($init)


        $r.Key = (new-Object Security.Cryptography.PasswordDeriveBytes
$pass, $salt, "SHA1", 50000).GetBytes(32)
        $r.IV = (new-Object Security.Cryptography.SHA1Managed).
```

```
ComputeHash($init)[0..15]


        $c = $r.CreateEncryptor()

        $ms = new-Object IO.MemoryStream

        $cs = new-Object Security.Cryptography.CryptoStream
$ms,$c,"Write"

        $sw = new-Object IO.StreamWriter $cs

        $sw.Write($String)

        $sw.Close()

        $cs.Close()

        $ms.Close()

        $r.Clear()

        [byte[]]$result = $ms.ToArray()

    }

    catch {

        $err = "Error Occurred Encrypting String: $_"

    }

    if($err) {

        # Report Back Error

        return $err

    }

    else {

        return [Convert]::ToBase64String($result)

    }

}

# All of the encoded values from YOUR execution of Script 1 example.

$rtd = "AAZwAmAE4AMgAoAFEAVAAhAFAA"

$ssd = "LAAyAGwAdQBRAG8AZABMAEwAJgA"

$afd = "5AFIAQgBYACYAXgBRAC4AUgA5AF"

$encSalt =

ABFAEIASgAzADsAOgBnAHEAagBxAGgAJgBcAH4AZgBRAD0ARAAzACEAZwAiACYATQBuAG
wAWABzAHkA"

$encInit ="ZgA/ADoAbQBGAFMAewAjAHcAMgBYAGQALwBYACEAVgB4AHEARABVAHAANwBg
ACQAeAAqAD0AbgBnADEA"


# Decode the Password

$encpass = $ssd + $afd + $rtd
```

```
$encbytes = [System.Convert]::FromBase64String($encpass)
$pass = [System.Text.Encoding]::Unicode.GetString($encbytes)


# Decode the Salt
$encbytes = [System.Convert]::FromBase64String($encSalt)
$salt = [System.Text.Encoding]::Unicode.GetString($encbytes)


# Decode the Init
$encbytes = [System.Convert]::FromBase64String($encInit)
$Init = [System.Text.Encoding]::Unicode.GetString($encbytes)


cls
write-host "To End This Application, Close the Window"
Write-host ""


do
    {
        $string = read-host "Please Enter a String to Encrypt"
        $encrypted = Encrypt-String $string
        write-host "Encrypted String is: $encrypted"
    }
While ($good -ne "True")
```

The output of this is shown in the following screenshot:

```
PS C:\> write-host "To End This Application, Close the Window"
To End This Application, Close the Window
PS C:\> Write-host ""

PS C:\>
PS C:\> do
>>     {
>> $string = read-host "Please Enter a String to Encrypt"
>> $encrypted = Encrypt-String $string
>> write-host "Encrypted String is: $encrypted"
>>     }
>> While ($good -ne "True")
Please Enter a String to Encrypt: TestingEncryptedValue
Encrypted String is: D4IQO6Lp5DyAsKuKX2+25YaMa9PpNXiHJhYWurAlF5g=
Please Enter a String to Encrypt:
```

In this example, you leverage the encoded salt, init, and password and an `encryption` function to generate encrypted values:

1. You first start by adding in the `System.Security` class by using the `Add-Type` cmdlet.

2. You then declare the `Encrypt-String` function with a parameter of `$string`.

3. Since `$pass`, `$init`, and `$salt` are generated outside the function, they are not included in the parameter block.

4. You then create a `System.Security.Cryptography.RijndaelManaged` object and place it in the `$r` variable.

5. You get the bytes of `$pass` and place it in the `$pass` variable, the bytes of `$salt` and place it in the `$salt` variable, and the bytes of `$init` and place it in the `$init` variable.

6. You continue to generate a key with the `$pass` and `$salt` variables and place this value in the `$r.Key` property.

7. You generate an IV with `$init` and place the value in the `$r.IV` property.

8. You continue to create an encryptor with `$r.CreateEncryptor()` and place it in the `$c` variable.

9. You open a memory stream with `IO.MemoryStream` and place it in the `$ms` variable.

10. You open a crypto stream with the `$ms` and `$c` variables and place it in the `$cs` variable.

11. You open a stream writer with the `$cs` and place it in the `$sw` variable.

12. Finally, you write the `$string` value into the stream writer.

13. You close the `$sw`, `$cs`, and `$ms` variables and clear the `$r` variable.

14. You take the value in `$ms` and convert it to an array and place it in the `$result` variable.

15. You convert the `$result` to a string and return the encrypted value.

16. You then declare all of the encoded values of `$rtd`, `$ssd`, `$afd`, `$encSalt`, and `$encInit`.

17. You combine `$ssd`, `$afd`, and `$rtd` to generate the password and place it in the `$encpass` variable.

18. You decode the encoded `$encpass` value and place it in the `$pass` variable.

19. You decode the `$encSalt` value and place it in the `$salt` variable.

20. Finally, you decode the `$encInit` value and place it in the `$init` variable.

At this point, you have everything you need to encrypt strings. You create a looping function to encrypt multiple strings:

1. You clear the screen with the `cls` command, and leverage the `write-host` cmdlet to display `"To End This Application, Close the Window."`.

2. You leverage the `write-host` cmdlet to create a new line.

3. You create a `do...while` loop with a condition of `$good -ne "True"`. This is to infinitely loop for generating multiple encrypted values.

4. Inside the loop, you use the `read-host` cmdlet with the argument of `"Please Enter a String to Encrypt"`. The entered value will be stored in the `$string` variable.

5. You then encrypt that string by calling the `Encrypt-String` function with the `$string` variable.

6. The `encryption` function will return an encrypted value and you store this value in the `$encrypted` variable.

7. You then leverage the `write-host` cmdlet to display this value by using the `"Encrypted String is: $encrypted"` argument.

In this example, `TestingEncryptedValue` was typed into the `read-host` cmdlet. The value of `"Encrypted String is: D4IQO6Lp5DyAsKuKX2+25YaMa9PpNXiHJhYW urAlF5g="` is displayed. You also see that the `do...while` loop then prompts for an additional value to encrypt. You can continue to use the script to encrypt multiple values for use in your script.

XML answer file creation

`Answer` files are essential to creating flexible PowerShell scripts. They provide the ability to change a script's function without actually modifying the code of the script itself. For the Windows server scanning script, there are several key items that you will want to include in your `answer` file.

The core components to include in the scanning script `answer` file are:

- **Security information**: This will include the AFD, salt, init, and other important encoded or encrypted data for the script.

- **Logging**: This will provide the ability to enable and disable writing to the event log, writing on the screen, and writing to a `log` file.

- **Features**: This will include the full list of scanning features of the script, and the ability to turn them on or off.

- **Search data**: This will include encrypted search information for identifying sensitive data on systems.

- **Kill file location**: This will provide the location of where the script termination file is located.

- **Directory scan list**: This will list the directories you want to scan for sensitive data. This will also include the file types that you want to scan.

- **File ignore list**: This will list the files that you want the script to ignore during the file scan portion of the script.

- **Search ignore list**: This will be the negative search terms, or false positives, that you want the script to ignore.

- **Built-in users list**: This is the list of the built-in users and accounts to be ignored while scanning a system.

 The Scan_Answers.xml answer file used in this chapter can be found in the code files for this chapter. This will be required to execute the examples in this chapter.

The answer file for a Windows server scanning script is designed to be a one-time use file. This is to prevent sensitive data sitting on a remote system, which could eventually be compromised. Additionally, since the answer file has an AFD, it makes brute forcing the encoding and encryption exponentially more difficult. The best time to delete the answer file is directly after placing contents into memory. PowerShell will only need to interact with the in-memory version of the answer file after the initial read, making it the perfect time to delete the file.

PowerShell script 3 - the termination files

There may come a time where you will need to terminate the execution of the Windows server scanning script. This could be due to the script consuming too many resources, or the script taking too long to execute. One of the most efficient ways to quickly and gracefully terminate a script is leveraging a termination file. When a termination file is placed on the system, the script will stop its current action, and gracefully exit the script.

The two methods to deploy the termination file in an environment are either locally on the server, or by leveraging remote commands. When you leverage deployment tools, you may have to create a script that runs locally on the system. If you want to create the termination file locally on a system, you can leverage the new-item cmdlet with the -path parameter set to "c:\temp\KILL_SERVER_SCAN.NOW". You then specify the -ItemType parameter with the argument of File. After execution, the termination file will be created.

To create a `termination` file locally on a system, you can perform the following:

```
new-item -path "c:\temp\KILL_SERVER_SCAN.NOW" -ItemType File
```

The output of this is shown in the following screenshot:

```
PS C:\> new-item -path "c:\temp\KILL_SERVER_SCAN.NOW" -ItemType File


    Directory: C:\temp


Mode                LastWriteTime         Length Name
----                -------------         ------ ----
-a----         3/22/2017    9:38 PM             0 KILL_SERVER_SCAN.NOW
```

In this example, you create the `termination` file locally on a system:

1. You start by leveraging the `new-item` cmdlet with the `-path` parameter set to `"c:\temp\KILL_SERVER_SCAN.NOW"`.

2. You then specify the `-ItemType` parameter with the argument of `File`.

3. After execution, the `KILL_SERVER_SCAN.NOW` file will be created on the system, and the `new-item` cmdlet will display the file creation.

To create a `termination` file remotely on a system, you can leverage a `PSSession` to enable a remote PowerShell session on a system. You can open a `PSSession` by leveraging the `Enter-PSSession` cmdlet with the `-ComputerName` parameter set to a server name. You can then create the `termination` file by leveraging the `new-item` cmdlet as you did locally. After running the command, you can leverage the `Exit-PSSession` cmdlet to close the PowerShell session. If you need to leverage different credentials to access a server, you can leverage the `get-credentials` cmdlet to obtain or declare new credentials, and store it in a variable. You then can leverage the `Enter-PSSession` cmdlet, the `-credential` parameter, and the variable containing the credentials to authenticate to a PowerShell session with a different user account.

> PSSession is meant to be manually typed in a PowerShell console. If you execute the commands in the script, you will want to build in a delay to ensure you are in the PSSession. If you don't, the commands after the `Enter-PSSession` cmdlet may run locally, versus in the session itself.

To leverage `Enter-PSSession` to remotely create a `termination` file, you can perform the following:

```
Enter-PSSession -ComputerName POSHDEMO-SQL01
new-item -path "c:\temp\KILL_SERVER_SCAN.NOW" -ItemType File
Exit-PSSession
```

The output of this is shown in the following screenshot:

```
PS C:\> Enter-PSSession -ComputerName POSHDEMO-SQL01
[POSHDEMO-SQL01]: PS C:\Users\bblawat\Documents> new-item -path "c:\temp\KILL_SERVER_SCAN.NOW" -ItemType File


    Directory: C:\temp


Mode                LastWriteTime         Length Name
----                -------------         ------ ----
-a----         3/22/2017   9:56 PM              0 KILL_SERVER_SCAN.NOW


[POSHDEMO-SQL01]: PS C:\Users\bblawat\Documents> Exit-PSSession
```

In this example, you create a `termination` file remotely by leveraging the `Enter-PSSession` cmdlet:

1. You first start by leveraging the `Enter-PSSession` cmdlet with the `-ComputerName` parameter set to the `POSHDEMO-SQL01` argument.
2. You then leverage the `new-item` cmdlet with the `-path` parameter set to `c:\temp\KILL_SERVER_SCAN.NOW`.
3. You also leverage the `-ItemType` parameter with the `File` argument.
4. After execution, the `KILL_SERVER_SCAN.NOW` file will be created on the system, and the `new-item` cmdlet will display the file creation.
5. To close the remote session, you leverage the `Exit-PSSession` cmdlet.
6. This will terminate the connection to the remote server.

After terminating the script, it is best practice to remove the `termination` file. This would be required if you wanted to run the Windows server scanning script again. If you want to remove the `termination` file locally on a system, you can leverage the `remove-item` cmdlet with the `-path` parameter set to `"c:\temp\KILL_SERVER_SCAN.NOW"`. You then specify the `-Force` parameter to force the deletion of the file. After execution, the `termination` file will be removed from the system.

To remove a `termination` file locally on a system, you can perform the following:

```
Remove-Item -Path "c:\temp\KILL_SERVER_SCAN.NOW" -Force
```

There is no output from executing this command.

In this example, you remove a `termination` file from a local system. You first start by declaring the `Remove-Item` cmdlet with the `-Path` parameter set to the `c:\temp\KILL_SERVER_SCAN.NOW` argument. You then leverage the `-Force` command. After execution, the file will be removed from the system; however, the cmdlet does not provide any visual feedback of the removal.

To remove a `termination` file remotely on a system, you can leverage a `PSSession` to enable a remote PowerShell session on a system. You can open a `PSSession` by leveraging the `Enter-PSSession` cmdlet with the `-ComputerName` parameter set to a server name. You can then remove the `termination` file by leveraging the `remove-item` cmdlet as you did locally. After running the command, you can leverage the `Exit-PSSession` cmdlet to close the PowerShell session.

To leverage `Enter-PSSession` to remotely remove a `termination` file, you can perform the following:

```
Enter-PSSession -ComputerName POSHDEMO-SQL01

Remove-Item -Path "c:\temp\KILL_SERVER_SCAN.NOW" -Force

Exit-PSSession
```

The output of this is shown in the following screenshot:

```
PS C:\> Enter-PSSession -ComputerName POSHDEMO-SQL01
[POSHDEMO-SQL01]: PS C:\Users\bblawat\Documents> Remove-Item -Path "c:\temp\KILL_SERVER_SCAN.NOW" -Force
[POSHDEMO-SQL01]: PS C:\Users\bblawat\Documents> Exit-PSSession
```

In this example, you remove a `termination` file, remotely leveraging the `Enter-PSSession` cmdlet:

1. You first start by leveraging the `Enter-PSSession` cmdlet with the `-ComputerName` parameter set to the `POSHDEMO-SQL01` argument.

2. You then leverage the `Remove-Item` cmdlet with the `-Path` parameter set to `c:\temp\KILL_SERVER_SCAN.NOW`.

3. You also leverage the `-Force` parameter.

4. After execution, the `KILL_SERVER_SCAN.NOW` file will be removed from the system.

5. To close the remote session, you leverage the `Exit-PSSession` cmdlet. This will terminate the connection to the remote server.

PowerShell script 4 - merging the scanning script result data

As you run the Windows server scanning script on multiple systems in your environment, you will have a need to merge multiple CSV files into a single CSV file. This will allow for better searching of the scan results, and help you identify trends in your server infrastructure. PowerShell offers the `Import-csv` and `Export-csv` cmdlets, which provide the ability to manipulate CSV data. A common technique is to use the `Import-csv` and `Export-csv` cmdlets with a pipeline to import, manipulate, and export the data to a new CSV file.

To get started, you will need to create several CSV files to merge together. To create multiple CSVs that are similar to the Windows server scanning script output, you can perform the following:

```
$logloc = "C:\temp\POSHScript\CSVDEMO\"

$date = (Get-Date -format "yyyyMMddmmss")

Function create-testcsv { param($servername)

    $csvfile = "$logloc\$servername" + "_" + $date + "_ScanResults.csv"

    new-item $csvfile -ItemType File -Force | Out-Null


    $csvheader = "ServerName, Classification, Other Data"

    Add-content $csvfile -Value $csvheader


    $csvcontent = "$servername, CSVTestData, This is CSV Test Data for
$servername."

    Add-content $csvfile -Value $csvcontent

}

create-testcsv POSHDEMO-Server1

create-testcsv POSHDEMO-Server2

create-testcsv POSHDEMO-Server3

create-testcsv POSHDEMO-Server4

create-testcsv POSHDEMO-Server5

get-childitem $logloc
```

The output of this is shown in the following screenshot:

```
PS C:\> $logloc = "C:\temp\POSHScript\CSVDEMO\"
PS C:\> $date = (Get-Date -format "yyyyMMddmmss")
PS C:\> Function create-testcsv { param($servername)
>>     $csvfile = "$logloc\$servername" + "_" + $date + "_ScanResults.csv"
>>     new-item $csvfile -ItemType File -Force | Out-Null
>>
>>     $csvheader = "ServerName, Classification, Other Data"
>>     Add-content $csvfile -Value $csvheader
>>
>>     $csvcontent = "$servername, CSVTestData, This is CSV Test Data for $servername."
>>     Add-content $csvfile -Value $csvcontent
>> }
PS C:\> create-testcsv POSHDEMO-Server1
PS C:\> create-testcsv POSHDEMO-Server2
PS C:\> create-testcsv POSHDEMO-Server3
PS C:\> create-testcsv POSHDEMO-Server4
PS C:\> create-testcsv POSHDEMO-Server5
PS C:\> get-childitem $logloc


    Directory: C:\temp\POSHScript\CSVDEMO


Mode              LastWriteTime        Length Name
----              -------------        ------ ----
-a----       3/21/2017  10:04 PM          116 POSHDEMO-Server1_201703210429_ScanResults.csv
-a----       3/21/2017  10:04 PM          116 POSHDEMO-Server2_201703210429_ScanResults.csv
-a----       3/21/2017  10:04 PM          116 POSHDEMO-Server3_201703210429_ScanResults.csv
-a----       3/21/2017  10:04 PM          116 POSHDEMO-Server4_201703210429_ScanResults.csv
-a----       3/21/2017  10:04 PM          116 POSHDEMO-Server5_201703210429_ScanResults.csv
```

In this example, you create multiple CSV files to emulate data from the server scanning script:

1. You start by defining the log location by declaring "C:\temp\POSHScript\CSVDEMO\" and storing it in the $logloc variable.

2. You then continue to generate the date timestamp by using the get-date cmdlet with the -format parameter set to the "yyyyMMddmmss" argument.

3. You store this value in the $date variable.

4. You then proceed to declare the create-testcsv function with the parameter block set to $servername.

5. You continue to build the string for the log location by declaring "$logloc\$servername" + "_" + $date + "_ScanResults.csv and setting it in the $csvfile variable.

6. You then leverage the new-item cmdlet with the $csvfile argument, the parameter of -ItemType set to the File argument, and the -Force parameter.

7. You pipe this to Out-Null to suppress notification of the file creation.

8. You then define the script header of "ServerName, Classification, Other Data" and set it to the $csvheader variable.

9. You continue to add the header to the newly created CSV file by leveraging the `Add-Content` cmdlet with the `$csvfile` argument and the `-Value` parameter set to the `$csvheader` variable.

10. You then create the content for the CSV file by defining the `"$servername, CSVTestData, This is CSV Test Data for $servername."` value and placing the `$csvcontent` variable.

11. You complete the function by adding the CSV content to the CSV file by calling the `Add-Content` cmdlet with the `$csvfile` argument and the `-Value` parameter set to `$csvcontent`.

12. Finally, you leverage the `create-testcsv` function multiple times to create CSV files for the servers named `POSHDEMO-Server1`, `POSHDEMO-Server2`, `POSHDEMO-Server3`, `POSHDEMO-Server4`, and `POSHDEMO-Server5`.

13. You verify the file creation by leveraging the `Get-ChildItem` cmdlet with the `$logloc` variable.

You will see that the function created five files in the `C:\temp\POSHScript\CSVDEMO\` directory.

After generating the CSV files, you will be able to merge all of the results into a single CSV file. To do this, you leverage the `Get-ChildItem` cmdlet, calling the directory where the CSV files are stored. You leverage the `-filter` parameter with the `"*.csv"` argument to only select the CSV files in that directory. You place the results in a parenthetical statement calling the `.FullName` property, which returns the full pathname to all of the CSV files. You use the pipeline to import all of the CSV files in memory using the `Import-csv` cmdlet, and you use another pipeline to export all of the CSV files in memory to a file. To remove all type information from the CSV export, you can leverage the `-NoTypeInformation` parameter with the `Export-csv` cmdlet.

To merge the CSV files into a single CSV file, you can perform the following:

```
$logloc = "C:\temp\POSHScript\CSVDEMO\"
$date = (Get-Date -format "yyyyMMddmmss")
$mergefile = "$logloc" + "Merged_$date.csv"
New-Item $mergefile -ItemType File | Out-Null
(get-childitem $logloc -filter "*.csv").FullName | Import-csv | Export-csv $mergefile -NoTypeInformation
```

The output of this is shown in the following screenshot:

```
PS C:\> $logloc = "C:\temp\POSHScript\CSVDEMO\"
PS C:\> $date = (Get-Date -format "yyyyMMddmmss")
PS C:\> $mergefile = "$logloc" + "Merged_$date.csv"
PS C:\> New-Item $mergefile -ItemType File | Out-Null
PS C:\> (get-childitem $logloc -filter "*.csv").FullName | Import-csv | Export-csv $mergefile -NoTypeInformation
```

The generated merged CSV file is shown in the following screenshot:

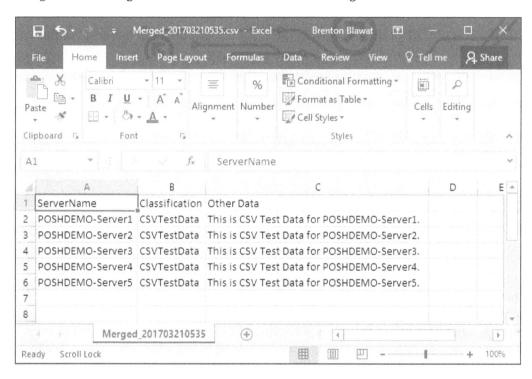

In this example, you merge all of the created CSV files into a single CSV file:

1. You first start by defining the log location by declaring `"C:\temp\`
   `POSHScript\CSVDEMO\"` and placing it in the `$logloc` variable.

2. You then continue to generate the date timestamp by using the `Get-Date`
   cmdlet with the `-format` parameter set to the `"yyyyMMddmmss"` argument.

3. You store this value in the `$date` variable.

4. You build the merge file string by placing `"$logloc" + "Merged_$date.`
   `csv"` into the `$mergefile` variable.

5. You then create the merge file by leveraging the `new-item` cmdlet with the
   `$mergefile` argument, and the `-ItemType` parameter set to `File`.

6. You pipe these results to Out-Null to suppress the file creation notification.

7. You proceed to gather all of the files from the $logloc directory to merge them in the pipeline using the Import-csv.

8. You start by calling the Get-ChildItem cmdlet with the $logloc as the argument and the -Filter parameter set to the "*.csv" argument.

9. You place the results into a parenthetical statement and call the .FullName property to obtain all of the full path names to the files.

10. You pipe all of these results to the Import-csv cmdlet to merge all of the CSV files in memory.

11. You then pipe the output from that cmdlet to the Export-csv cmdlet with $mergefile as the argument and -NoTypeInformation as a parameter.

After executing this script, you will have gathered all of the CSV files in the $logloc directory, merged the CSV files, and exported the merged results to the $mergefile CSV file.

Summary

In this chapter, you reviewed an overview of the Windows server scanning script. You learned that you need to follow a workflow to implement the script in your environment. You started by developing a script to generate randomized strings to create the encryption passwords, salt, and init. You then encoded the results, in the same script, to further secure the values. After creating the encoded password, salt, and init, you created an encryption script with those values to start encrypting strings. After encrypting strings, you continued to learn about the required answer file for the script. You learned what items you need to include in the answer file to ensure that the Windows server scanning script remains flexible. You then proceeded to explore termination files and how they are used to gracefully stop the scanning script remotely. You created a script to create and remove the terminal file locally as well as with a PSSession. Finally, you developed a script to merge the CSV results from the Windows server scanning script into a single file for review.

In the next chapter, you will learn how to create the Windows server scanning script. You will create the comment block, parameter block, the answer file reading function, and the decryption function, and then populate the answer files and create the script logs and logging functions. You will create functions for scanning disks, scheduled tasks, processes, Windows services, software, user profiles, Windows features, and directories for files. You will complete the chapter by learning about post-execution cleanup considerations.

13
Creating the Windows Server Scanning Script and Post-Execution Cleanup

When you are running systems in a large enterprise, you often need to identify information about different servers in your environment. While you could manually evaluate items on each server to determine its role, you most likely will want to automate that process. As you worked through this book, you learned multiple facets to scanning and identifying non-standard configurations on servers using PowerShell. You also learned how to optimize code to significantly increase the performance of your scripts. These examples led you up to this chapter, which combines all of the concepts that you learned into a single Windows server scanning script.

The Windows server scanning script was developed to provide a deep insight into a server's roles and functions in an environment. When you execute the Windows server scanning script against your environment, you can quickly view non-default configurations that make the server unique. This is also powerful when you are performing large-scale server discoveries to determine commonality amongst servers in your environment. It's encouraged to take this existing script and build upon it for the unique needs of your environment.

In this chapter, you will:

- Obtain an overview of the overall script structure
- Implement the comment block, parameter block, `answer` file `reading` function, and `decryption` functions
- Populate variables and arrays from the `answer` file

- Create a `logging` function to log to a data collection file, a `log` file, and the event log
- Implement a script termination function to gracefully exit the script
- Integrate and call multiple functions to scan different areas of a system
- Invoke the script's functions and copy the `log` files to a file share
- Explore how to start the script from a command line
- Learn the post-execution script cleanup activities

Windows server scanning script creation

As you start building your version of the Windows server scanning script, you will want to follow a script structure. When you use a standardized script structure, you organize your code into different sections. This allows you to quickly find components in your scripts and add to the individual sections. It also provides an easy platform for others to quickly learn and modify your scripts.

The following sections make up the Windows server scanning script:

Comment block: This is where you describe the function of the script.

Parameter block: This is where you can pass in variables and data into the script, such as the Runtime Decryptor.

Answer file reading function: This enables you to dynamically read the different values in the answer file.

Decryption function: This enables you to decrypt encrypted strings during runtime.

Populating script answers into variables and arrays: This will take the output from the answer file reading function to populate variables and arrays. This also enables you to dynamically build regular expressions from the answer file data.

Create log files and logging functions: This will enable you to log the different actions of the script, record data found by the script, write output to the screen, and even write events to the event log.

Creating a termination function: The termination function will enable you to check multiple times if a termination file is placed on the system. This will terminate the scanning script if present.

Multiple script functions: This is where you define all of the functions to scan different components of the system.

Invoking the functions: When all of the other functions and components are defined, you complete the chapter by invoking the functions, if enabled in the answer file.

Comment block

The first lines of your Windows server scanning script should be the comment block. The comment block will describe the script's function and provide revision details and information about the required **Runtime Decryptor** (**RTD**). This section should provide an example on how to run the script, and any additional notes about the script's execution.

The following screenshot displays a properly created comment block that integrates with the help system:

```
<#
.SYNOPSIS
This is a server discovery script which will scan different server components to determine
the current configuration.

.DESCRIPTION
This script will scan processes, Windows services, scheduled tasks, server features, disk information,
registry, and files for pertinent server information.

Author: Brenton J.W. Blawat / Packt Publishing / Author / email@email.com

.PARAMETER RTD
This script requires a run time decryptor as a parameter to the script.

.EXAMPLE
powershellscript.ps1 /RTD "Run Time Decryptor"

.NOTES
You must have administrative rights to the server you are scanning. Certain functions will not work properly
without running the script as system or administrator.#>
```

Parameter block

After the comment block of your script, you will want to immediately declare the parameter block. The parameter block is required for the RTD to be captured in the script. Since the decryption process relies on the RTD, you will exit the script if that parameter is not available.

To create a parameter block and to check to see if there is a value, you can perform the following:

`param($RTD)`

`if (!$RTD) { exit }`

There is no output from declaring the parameter block. In this example, you define a parameter block with the `param` command, and populate the `$RTD` variable with the input to the script. You also create an `if` statement that if the `$RTD` variable is `$null`, it will exit the script.

Answer file reading function

You continue with the scanning script by defining the answer file reading function, loading the XML into memory, and removing the `answer` file. You may choose to comment out the `Remove-Item` cmdlet step. This will provide for testing in your environment without having to recreate the XML file in the script directory.

To create an XML `reading` function, load the XML into memory, and delete the XML file, you can perform the following:

```
Function read-xmltag { param($xmlextract)
return $xml.GetElementsByTagName("$xmlextract")
}
$xmlfile ="$PSScriptRoot\Scan_Answers.xml"
$test = test-path $xmlfile
if (!$test) {
    Write-Error "$xmlfile not found on the system. Select any key to
exit!"
    PAUSE
    exit
}
[xml] $xml = get-content $xmlfile
Remove-Item $xmlfile -force
```

There is no output to display from creating this function.

In this example, you define the `answer` file `reading` function:

1. You first start by defining the `read-xmltag` function with a parameter block of `param($xmlextract)`.

2. You then leverage the `$xml.GetElementsByTagName()` method to obtain the xml tag specified in the `$xmlextract`.

3. You take the result and return it to the portion of the script that called the function. You then continue to gather the current path of the script by calling `$PSScriptRoot` and combining the value with `"\Scan_Answers.xml"`. You store the result in the `$xmlfile` variable.

4. You continue to determine if the file exists by leveraging the `test-path` cmdlet with the `$xmlfile` argument.

5. You declare an `if not exist` statement on the `$test` variable and, if the file does not exist, you use the `write-error` cmdlet to display "`$xmlfile not found on the system. Select any key to exit.`

6. You then issue a `PAUSE` statement to stop the script, and an `exit` statement to exit the script after a key is pressed on the keyboard. If the `answer` file exists, the script will continue to load the XML file into memory.

7. You use the `get-content` cmdlet with the argument of `$xmlfile`.

8. You then place this value into an `$xml` variable with the data type of `[xml]`.

9. After loading the XML file in memory, you remove the XML file by leveraging the `Remove-Item` cmdlet with the `$xmlfile` argument and the `-Force` parameter. The answer file will be removed from the system.

Decryption function

The next step after you are done loading the XML file into memory is defining the decryption function. Since the `answer` file has encoded and encrypted values, you will need this function to translate the encrypted values into strings.

To declare the `decryption` function, you can perform the following:

```
Add-Type -AssemblyName System.Security
function Decrypt-String { param($Encrypted)
    if($Encrypted -is [string]){
        $Encrypted = [Convert]::FromBase64String($Encrypted)
    }
    $r = new-Object System.Security.Cryptography.RijndaelManaged
    $pass = [System.Text.Encoding]::UTF8.GetBytes($pass)
    $salt = [System.Text.Encoding]::UTF8.GetBytes($salt)
    $init = [Text.Encoding]::UTF8.GetBytes($init)
    $r.Key = (new-Object Security.Cryptography.PasswordDeriveBytes $pass,
$salt, "SHA1", 50000).GetBytes(32)
    $r.IV = (new-Object Security.Cryptography.SHA1Managed).
ComputeHash($init)[0..15]
    $d = $r.CreateDecryptor()
    $ms = new-Object IO.MemoryStream @(,$Encrypted)
    $cs = new-Object Security.Cryptography.CryptoStream $ms,$d,"Read"
    $sr = new-Object IO.StreamReader $cs
    try {
```

```
        $result = $sr.ReadToEnd()
        $sr.Close()
        $cs.Close()
        $ms.Close()
        $r.Clear()
        Return $result
    }
    Catch {
        Write-host "Error Occurred Decrypting String: Wrong String Used In
Script."
    }
}
```

There is no output to display from creating this function.

In this example, you declare the `decryption` function:

1. You first start by leveraging the `Add-Type` cmdlet to load the `System.Security` assembly.

2. You then declare the `Decrypt-String` function with the parameter block of `param($encrypted)`.

3. You proceed to check if the `$encrypted` value is a string and then convert it to bytes if it is.

4. You then create a `System.Security.Cryptography.RijndaelManaged` object and place it in the `$r` variable.

5. You get the bytes of `$pass` and place it in the `$pass` variable, the bytes of `$salt` and place it in the `$salt` variable, and the bytes of `$init` and place it in the `$init` variable. You continue to generate a key with the `$pass` and `$salt` variables and place this value in the `$r.Key` property.

6. You generate an IV with the `$init` and place the value in the `$r.IV` property.

7. You proceed to create the decryptor object and place it in the `$d` variable, the memory stream object with the `$encrypted` value in the `$ms` variable, the `CrypoStream` object using the `$ms` and `$d` variables in the `$cs` variable, and the stream reader object using the `$cs` variable in the `$sr` variable.

8. You then issue a `try...catch` command to catch any errors during the decryption process.

9. You continue to use the `ReadToEnd()` method on the stream reader and place the decrypted text in the `$result` variable.

10. You close the `$sr`, `$cs`, and `$ms` objects.

11. You clear the `$r` variable and return the result of `$result` to the portion of the script that called the function.

12. If there is an error during the decryption process, the script will leverage the `write-host` cmdlet to display `"Error Occurred Decrypting String: Wrong String Used In Script"`.

Populating script answers in variables and arrays

The next step in the Windows server scanning script is to populate the data from the answer file into the variables and arrays. When you access the answer file data in memory, you will need to manipulate the data for use in the script. For example, the search data will have encrypted values that need to be decrypted, the ignore lists will need to be made into regular expressions, and the search extensions will need to be put into an array.

Since you will be dynamically making more than one regular expression for the script, it is best practice to make a function that generates the regular expressions. The script will be able to run without values in the file search data, the file ignore list, the search ignore list, and the built-in user list. You will need to verify that the list being passed into the function is not blank. A regular expression that is blank, or populated with no values, will match all values as true. This will cause execution issues in your script and this should be avoided.

To work around this issue, if you detect that the list is blank, you set the list value to a string that would not be matched on the system, such as `No_Input_Provided_For_List_Item`. When the regular expression is evaluated with that expression, it will be highly unlikely that the expression will match the criteria.

To create a function to dynamically create regular expressions, you can do the following:

```
function create-SearchRegEx { param($list)
    if (!$list) { $list = "No_Input_Provided_For_List_Item" }
    $RegEx = '(?i)^.*(' + (($list | % {[regex]::escape($_)}) -join "|") +
').*$'
    return $regex
}
```

There is no output to display from creating this function.

In this example, you create a new function named `create-SearchRegex` with the parameter block of `param($list)`:

1. You create an `if` statement to determine if the `$list` variable has no values. If it is blank, it will set the `$list` variable to `"No_Input_Provided_For_List_Item"`.

2. The function will continue to dynamically generate a regular expression that is case-insensitive, and will match any of the values listed in the `$list` variable.

3. After creating the regular expression, the value is stored in the `$regex` variable.

4. The script will return the value in `$regex` to the portion of the script that called the function.

Like the regular expression, you will be decoding more than once in the script and you need a function for decoding. To create a function for decoding values, you can do the following:

```
function decode-string { param($string)
    $encbytes = [System.Convert]::FromBase64String($string)
    $string = [System.Text.Encoding]::Unicode.GetString($encbytes)
    return $string
}
```

There is no output to display from creating this function.

In this example, you create a function for decoding values:

1. You first start by defining the decode-string function with the parameter block set to `param($string)`.

2. You then convert the string to bytes and store the output in the `$encbytes` variable.

3. You then decode the bytes by calling `[System.Text.Encoding]::Unicode.GetString($encbytes)` and storing the output in the `$string` variable.

4. The script will return the value in `$string` to the portion of the script that called the function.

After you create the function for the regular expression generation and decoding a string, you can start placing the answer file data in variables and arrays. To place system configuration information into variables and arrays, you can perform the following:

```
$ssd = "LAAyAGwAdQBRAG8AZABMAEwAJgA"
$afd = (read-xmltag "afd") | Select id
$encpass = $ssd + $afd.id + $rtd
$pass = decode-string $encpass
$salt = (read-xmltag "salt") | % { decode-string $_.id }
$init = (read-xmltag "init") | % { decode-string $_.id }
```

There is no output to display from creating this code.

In this example, you set the system configuration information into multiple variables:

1. You first start by defining the SSD and setting the value in the $ssd variable.
2. You then leverage the read-xmltag function with the argument of "afd".
3. You pipe this value to Select id and store the result in the $afd variable.
4. You then combine the script side, answer file, and runtime decryptors into the $encpass variable.
5. You leverage the decode-string function with $encpass and the script decodes the decryption password and places the result in the $pass variable.
6. You leverage the read-xmltag for the salt argument, pipe it to %, and leverage the decode-string function to decode the pipeline string.
7. The decoded value is placed in the $salt variable.
8. Finally, you leverage the read-xmltag for the init argument, pipe it to %, and leverage the decode-string function to decode the pipeline string.
9. The decoded value is placed in the $init variable.

You then continue to define the logging and feature information, by performing the following:

```
$logloc = (read-xmltag "logloc") | Select id
$verboselog = (read-xmltag "verboselog") | Select id
$filelog = (read-xmltag "filelog") | Select id
$evntlog = (read-xmltag "evntlog") | Select id
$csvunc = (read-xmltag "csvunc") | Select id
$scanDisks = (read-xmltag "scndisks") | Select id
$scanSchTasks = (read-xmltag "scnschtsks") | Select id
$scanProcess = (read-xmltag "scnproc") | Select id
$scanServices = (read-xmltag "scnsvcs") | Select id
$scanSoftware = (read-xmltag "scnsoft") | Select id
$scanProfiles = (read-xmltag "scnuprof") | Select id
$scanFeatures = (read-xmltag "scnwfeat") | Select id
$scanFiles = (read-xmltag "scnfls") | Select id
$scnloc = (read-xmltag "scnloc") | Select id
$killfile = (read-xmltag "killfile") | Select id
```

There is no output to display from creating this code.

In this example, you are gathering the logging and feature information from the XML file data that is in memory. For each of these values, you leverage the `read-xmltag` and use the corresponding tag name as the argument. You pipe the result to `Select id`. The logging and feature information is then stored in a variable that corresponds to the data being stored.

After declaring the logging and feature information, you proceed to create the search extensions. To create the array of search extensions with a wildcard, you can perform the following:

```
# Search Extensions
$srextlist = @()
$srext = (read-xmltag "srext") | % { $srextlist += "*" + $_.id }
```

There is no output to display from creating this code.

In this example, you create the search extension array including a wildcard:

1. To start, you declare `$srextlist` as an array.

2. You then leverage the `read-xmltag` function with the `srext` argument to gather the search extensions from the XML file in memory.

3. You pipe the result to `%`, or the alias of `foreach`, where you append an `*` to the beginning of the current extension, which is in the `$_.id` XML property.

4. After execution, you will have an array of wildcard extensions in the `$srextlist`.

The last part of this section is creating the regular expressions from the XML data in memory. To create multiple regular expressions from the XML data, you perform the following:

```
# File Search Data
$srterms = read-xmltag "srterm" | % { decrypt-string $_.id }
$srtermsRegEx = create-SearchRegEx $srterms


# File Ignore list
$flign = (read-xmltag "flign") | Select id
$flignRegEx = create-SearchRegEx $flign.id


# Search Ignore List
$srign = (read-xmltag "srign") | Select id
$sringRegEx = create-SearchRegEx $srign.id


# Built-in User List
$blst = (read-xmltag "blst") | Select id
$blstRegEx = create-SearchRegEx $blst.id
```

There is no output to display from creating this code.

In this example, you create multiple regular expressions from the XML data in memory:

1. You first start by gathering the file search data from the XML file, and decrypting the values.
2. To do this, you call the `read-xmltag` function with the `srterm` attribute.
3. You pipe this result to `%` and decrypt each encrypted value with the `decrypt-string` function and the `$_.id` XML property.
4. The decrypted values are placed in the `$srterms` variable.
5. You then leverage the `create-SearchRegex` function with the `$srterms` argument.
6. The regular expression generated by the `create-SearchRegex` function is then placed in the `$srtermsregex` variable.
7. You continue to obtain the `File Ignore list`, or `flign`, the `Search Ignore List`, or `srign`, and the `Built-in User List`, or `blst`, by leveraging the `read-xmltag` function.
8. After you obtain the results, you pipe the values to `Select Id` to select the ID attribute of the XML file.
9. You store the results in their respective variables.
10. Finally, you call the `create-SearchRegex` function for each of these variables, and the generated regular expressions get stored in each of the lists' respective regex variables.

Creating the log files and logging function

The final core scripting components are the `log` files and `logging` functions. When you are creating your `log` files, you typically want to include the server name and the timestamp in the filename. This allows you to determine what machine the `log` file is for and when the scan was run. Since the Windows server scanning script also collects data about the system, you will also need to create a CSV file for logging pertinent information.

To create the `log` and CSV files with the server name and timestamp in the filename, you can do the following:

```
$date = (Get-Date -format "yyyyMMddmmss")
$compname = $env:COMPUTERNAME
$logloc = $logloc.id
```

```
$scanlog = "$logloc\$compname" + "_" + $date + "_ServerScanScript.log"
new-item $scanlog -ItemType File -Force | Out-Null


# Create the CSV File
$scnresults = "$logloc\$compname" + "_" + $date + "_ScanResults.csv"
$csvheader = "ServerName, Classification, Other Data"
new-item $scnresults -ItemType File -Force | Out-Null
Add-content $scnresults -Value $csvheader
```

There is no output to display from creating this code.

In this example, you create the `log` and CSV file with the server name and a timestamp in the filename:

1. To start, you leverage the `Get-Date` cmdlet with the `-format` parameter with the `"yyyyMMddmmss"` argument and place the value in the `$date` variable.

2. You then call the `$env:COMPUTERNAME` environment variable and place the computer name in the `$compname` variable.

3. You also select the XML file's `.id` attribute for `$logloc`, and place it back into the `$logloc` variable.

4. The resulting value will be the string of the log location.

5. You continue to create the log filename by declaring the `$logloc` variable from the `answer` file, `$compname` with an underscore, the `$date` timestamp with `"_ServerScanScript.log"`, and then set the string in the `$scanlog` variable.

6. You then leverage the `new-item` with `$scanlog` as the argument, the `-ItemType` parameter as file, and the `-Force` parameter.

7. You pipe this value to `Out-Null` to suppress the file creation output.

8. After you execute the section of code, create a `log` file with the `computername`, `timestamp`, and `"_ServerScanScript.log"` as the filename.

After creating the `log` file, you continue to create the CSV file:

1. You use the `$logloc` variable from the `answer` file, `$compname` with an underscore, the `$date` timestamp with `"_ScanResults.csv"`, and set the string in the `$scnresults` variable.

2. You then declare the CSV header by specifying `"ServerName, Classification, Other Data"`, and then place the values in the `$csvheader` variable.

3. You continue to create the CSV file by calling the `new-item` cmdlet with `$scnresults` as the argument, the `-ItemType` parameter set to the `File` argument, and the `-Force` parameter.

4. You pipe this value to `Out-Null` to suppress the file creation output.

5. Finally, you leverage the `Add-Content` cmdlet with the `$scnresults` argument, and the `-Value` parameter set to `$csvheader`.

After you execute this section of code, the CSV file will be created with `computername`, `timestamp`, and `_ScanResults.csv` as the file name and will have `"ServerName, Classification, Other Data"` as the contents.

The CSV header cannot be added with the `-Value` parameter in the `new-item` cmdlet. The `new-item` cmdlet does not append a return after placing the data in the file. This means that when you add additional lines with the `Add-Content` cmdlet, the data will be placed as an addition to the header. To correct these issues, you separate adding the data from creating the file.

In the instance that you are going to be writing to the event log, you will need to create the event log source. To create a new event log source, if the `$evntlog` variable is set to true, you can do the following:

```
if ($evntlog -eq "True") { New-EventLog –LogName Application –Source
"WindowsServerScanningScript" -ErrorAction SilentlyContinue }
```

There is no output to display from creating this code.

In this example, you create an event log source if the `$evntlog` variable is set to True:

1. You start by creating an `if` statement to determine if `$evntlog` is `-eq` to True.

2. If the variable is true, you then leverage the `New-Eventlog` cmdlet with the `-Logname` parameter set to `Application`, the `-Source` parameter set to `"WindowsServerScanningScript"`, and the `-ErrorAction` set to `SilentlyContinue`.

3. After execution, the system is ready to write to the new event log source.

After you create your `log` files and event log source, you can create the `logging` function. The `logging` function will enable you to write information to a variety of places with a single command. The `log` function accepts three different parameters, the default parameter is when no values are included other than the `$string`. This will assume you want to write to the CSV file and will append additional data to the CSV. If you include a `$string` with a single `"y"`, it will attempt to log to the `log` file. If the `log` file is not enabled, the logging mechanism skips adding to the `log` file. The third parameter is to write to the event log. This is invoked by including a `$string`, a `Y`, or an `N` for the second parameter, and a `Y` for the third parameter in the function. If the event log writing is enabled, it will write the `$string` to the event log. Finally, the function will evaluate if verbose logging is turned on. If verbose logging is enabled, it will write the current action to the screen.

To create a `log` function that can write to a `log` file, CSV file, and the event log, you can perform the following:

```
function log { param($string, $scnlg, $evntlg)
    if ($scnlg -like "Y") {
        if ($filelog -eq "True") { Add-content $scanlog -Value $string }
    }
    if ($evntlg -like "Y") {
        if ($evntlog -eq "True") { write-eventlog -logname Application
-source "WindowsServerScanningScript" -eventID 1000 -entrytype
Information -message "$string" }
    }
    if (!$scnlg) {
        $content = "$env:COMPUTERNAME,$string"
        Add-Content $scnresults -Value $content
    }
    if ($verboselog -eq "True") { write-host $string }
}
```

There is no output to display from creating this code.

This example creates a `logging` function that can write data to a `log` file, event log, and a CSV file:

1. You start by defining the `log` function with the parameter block of `param($string, $scnlg, $evntlg)`.

2. You then create an `if` statement to determine if the `$filelog` setting is equal to `"True"`.

3. If the `$filelog` is set to True, then the script will continue to the second `if` statement to determine if the `$scnlg` is `-like` Y.

4. If the second parameter into the `log` function is Y, and the `$filelog` setting is `"True"`, it will leverage the `Add-Content` cmdlet with the `$scanlog` argument, and the `-Value` parameter set to `$string`. The script continues to the second set of `if` statements.

5. The script will determine if the `$evntlg` variable is `-like "Y"`.

6. If the variable is true, it will continue to another `if` statement to determine if the `$evntlog` variable is equal to `"True"`.

7. If the second parameter into the `log` function is Y, and the `$filelog` setting is `"True"`, the script will leverage the `write-eventlog` cmdlet with the `-logname` parameter set to `Application`, the `-source` parameter set to `WindowsServerScanningScript`, the `-eventID` parameter set to `1000`, the `-entrytype` parameter set to Information, and the `-message` parameter set to `$string`.

This will add a new value in the `Application` event log. The third evaluation is determining if the script should write to the CSV file:

1. If there are no additional parameters passed in with the `log` function, or if the `$scnlg` parameter is null, the `log` function will append the computer name to the beginning of the `$string` value and place it in the CSV file.

2. This is done by leveraging the `Add-Content` cmdlet with the `$scnresults` argument, and the `-Value` parameter set to `$content`.

3. Finally, you evaluate if the `$verboselog` is equal to `"True"`.

4. If it is set to `"True"` it will use the `write-host` cmdlet to display the `$string` on the screen.

After creating the `log` function, it is common to timestamp the start of the execution time in the `log` files, event logs, and on the screen. To timestamp the start of the execution of the script, you can perform the following:

```
$date = (Get-Date -format "yyyyMMddmmss")
log "Starting Windows Server Scanning Script at $date ..." "Y" "Y"
log "ScriptStart,$date"
```

The output of this is shown in the following screenshot:

```
$date = (Get-Date -format "yyyyMMddmmss")
log "Starting Windows Server Scanning Script at $date ..."
Starting Windows Server Scanning Script at 201703201039 ...
log "ScriptStart,$date"
ScriptStart,201703201039
```

In this example, you timestamp the start of the execution of the script:

You start by leveraging the Get-Date cmdlet with the -format parameter set to the "yyyyMMddmmss" argument.

You then leverage the log function with "Starting Windows Server Scanning Script at $date ..." as the first parameter, "Y" as the second parameter, and "Y" as the third parameter.

The output is "Starting Windows Server Scanning Script at 201703201039…".

You then call the log function with "ScriptStart,$date" as the first parameter. The output is ScriptStart,201703201039.

Creating a termination function

When PowerShell scripts execute on systems, they consume memory and CPU resources. This is especially true if you are scanning directories and leveraging the Get-Content cmdlet to evaluate files. PowerShell has to load the directory listing in memory, and place the entire contents of the file in memory for processing.

One of the common concerns with deploying a PowerShell script enterprise-wide is being able to terminate the script mid-scan if necessary. While you could use the stop-process cmdlet or the taskkill.exe to terminate the PowerShell processes, you may also inadvertently terminate all running PowerShell processes on a system. Without fully executing the script, you may be leaving sensitive scan data on the system.

An alternative to killing the PowerShell processes is to create a function to check to see if a `kill` file exists on the system. If that `kill` file exists on the system, the script will gracefully terminate. This will allow the script to stop the current process, copy the partially created scanned data to a UNC path, and exit the PowerShell script. This will provide a much more robust script termination experience. You insert the function throughout your Windows server scanning script to check the file's existence. The general rule of thumb is to check for the existence of the `termination` file as the first line of each function. You will also want to check for the file in-between iterations of long scanning operations, such as scanning files on a system. After each file scan, you should run the file check. While this may slightly slow down your script, it provides quick termination of scripts that are in process.

To create a `termination` function, you start by defining a function named `check-kill`. You then leverage the `test-path` cmdlet to verify that the `kill` file doesn't exist on the system. The `kill` file should be stored in a common area, such as `c:\temp\`, with a unique name, such as `KILL_SERVER_SCAN.NOW`. If `test-path` returns `True`, you generate a date timestamp, record that the `kill` file was detected, and copy the data-collected `log` files and data to its destination. You then exit the script.

To create a function to check if a `kill` file exists, report that the file is detected, and then exit the script. You can perform this as follows:

```
function check-kill {
    if (test-path $killfile.id) {
        $date = (Get-Date -format "yyyyMMddmmss")
        log "Kill File Detected at $date. Terminating Script." "Y" "Y"
        log "KillFile, Kill File Detected at $date.. Terminating Script"
        copy-item -Path $scnresults -Destination $csvunc.id -Force
        copy-Item -Path $scanlog -Destination $csvunc.id -Force
        exit
    }
}
```

There is no output from this script as it exits the PowerShell instance.

In this example, you create a function to detect if a `kill` file exists, report that the file is detected, copy the files to the `$csvunc`, and exit the script:

1. You start by declaring the `check-file` function. You create an `if` statement with the `test-path` cmdlet to determine if the `$killfile.id` exists.

2. If it does, you obtain a date timestamp leveraging the `Get-Date` cmdlet with the `-format` parameter set to the `"yyyyMMddmmss"` argument.

3. You then leverage the `log` function with the `"Kill File Detected at $date. Terminating Script." "Y" "Y"` value.

4. This records the `kill` file termination to the event log and `log` file, if enabled.

5. You then leverage the `log` function again with the `"KillFile, Kill File Detected at $date.. Terminating Script"` value.

6. This logs the `kill` file detection in the CSV file.

7. You then leverage the `copy-item` cmdlet to copy the `$scnresults` file to the `$csvunc.id` path with the `-Force` parameter.

8. You also leverage the `copy-item` cmdlet to copy the `$scanlog` file to the `$csvunc.id` path with the `-Force` parameter.

9. Finally, you will need to leverage the `exit` command to exit the script.

After defining the function, you call the function with `check-kill`. When the function evaluates, the file does not exist, so it allows the script to continue to the next operation. If the file exists, it will terminate and copy the scan results and scan log to the UNC/file path provided.

Multiple Windows server scanning script functions

After you finish creating the entire core scripting components, you start defining the individual scanning functions for the script. The scanning functions will evaluate multiple aspects of the system and record all the results in the CSV file. You will create functions for scanning disks, scheduled tasks, processes, Windows services, software, user profiles, Windows features, and directories for files containing strings. You will also create a `measure-diskunit` function for converting disk storage units.

To create the `measure-diskunit` and `scan-disk` functions, you can perform the following:

```
function measure-diskunit { param($diskspace)
    switch ($diskspace) {
        {$_ -gt 1PB} { return [System.Math]::Round(($_ / 1PB),2),"PB" }
        {$_ -gt 1TB} { return [System.Math]::Round(($_ / 1TB),2),"TB" }
        {$_ -gt 1GB} { return [System.Math]::Round(($_ / 1GB),2),"GB" }
        {$_ -gt 1MB} { return [System.Math]::Round(($_ / 1MB),2),"MB" }
        {$_ -gt 1KB} { return [System.Math]::Round(($_ / 1KB),2),"KB" }
        default { return [System.Math]::Round(($_ / 1MB),2),"MB" }
    }
}
```

```
function scan-disks {
    check-kill
    $disks = get-wmiobject win32_logicaldisk
    Foreach ($disk in $disks) {
        $driveletter = $disk.DeviceID
        $freespace = $disk.FreeSpace
        $size = $disk.Size

        if ($freespace -lt 1) { $freespace = "0" }
        if ($size -lt 1) { $size = "0" }

        $freetype = measure-diskunit $freespace
        $convFreeSpc = $freetype[0]
        $funit = $freetype[1]

        $sizetype = measure-diskunit $size
        $convsize = $sizetype[0]
        $sunit = $sizetype[1]

        switch ($disk.DriveType) {
            0 { $type = "Type Unknown." }
            1 { $type = "Doesn't have a Root Directory." }
            2 { $type = "Removable Disk" }
            3 { $type = "Local Disk" }
            4 { $type = "Network Drive" }
            5 { $type = "Compact Disk" }
            6 { $type = "RAM Disk" }
            default { $type = "Unable To Determine Drive Type!" }
        }
        log "DiskConfiguration, Drive $driveletter | Drive Type: $type |
Size: $convsize $sunit   | Freespace: $convFreeSpc $funit"
    }
}
```

There is no output to display from creating this function.

In this example, you create a function to measure disk units of measure and scan the individual disk configuration on a system:

1. You first start by defining the `measure-diskunit` function with the parameter block of `param($diskspace)`.

2. You then create a `switch` statement evaluating the `$diskspace` variable.

3. The script evaluates for petabytes, terabytes, gigabytes, megabytes, and kilobytes listed in descending order.

4. If the script returns `True` for a unit of measure, it will divide the value by the unit measure and round the value to the tenths place.

5. It will return an array with both the converted disk space and unit of measure label. You then define the `scan-disks` function to evaluate the disks on a system.

6. You call the `check-kill` function to determine if the script should continue or terminate.

7. If the script can continue, you leverage the `win32_logicaldisk` class to determine each disk's drive letter, free space, and disk size.

8. You leverage the `measure-diskunit` function to determine the unit of measure and the value in that unit of measure.

9. You then leverage a `switch` statement to evaluate the drive type number.

10. The corresponding number will return a string value for the type of disk.

11. You complete the `scan-disks` function by leveraging the `log` function with `"DiskConfiguration, Drive $driveletter | Drive Type: $type | Size: $convsize $sunit | Freespace: $convFreeSpc $funit"`.

Scheduled tasks function

To create a function to scan scheduled tasks that are not running as built-in users, you can perform the following:

```
function scan-schtasks {
    check-kill
    $schtasks = Get-ScheduledTask
    foreach ($Task in $schtasks) {
        $tskUser = $Task.Principal.UserId
        if($tskUser -eq $null) { $tskuser = "SYSTEM" }
        if (!($tskUser -match $blstRegEx)) {
            $tskname = ($task.TaskName).replace(","," ")
```

```
            $tskpath = $task.TaskPath
            log "ScheduledTsksData, Scheduled task with the name of
$tskname in the location of $tskpath is running as $tskuser"
        }
    }
}
```

There is no output to display from creating this function.

In this example, you create a function to scan scheduled tasks that are not running as built-in users:

You start by defining the scan-schtasks function.

You call the check-kill function to determine if the script should continue or terminate.

If the script can continue, you leverage the Get-ScheduledTask cmdlet to gather all scheduled tasks.

You evaluate each scheduled task and determine if the Principal.UserID property is matched to the built-in user regular expression.

If the user is not matched by the $blstRegEx regular expression or, !($tskuser -match $blstRegEx), you gather the scheduled task name and scheduled task path.

You complete the function by leveraging the log function with the "ScheduledTsksData, Scheduled task with the name of $tskname in the location of $tskpath is running as $tskuser" value.

Windows processes function

To create a function to scan the processes on the system for users that are not built-in, you can perform the following:

```
function scan-process {
    check-kill
    $processes = Get-WmiObject win32_process
    foreach ($process in $processes) {
        $procuser = $process.GetOwner().User
        if (!($procuser -match $blstRegEx)) {
            $procname = $process.Name
            $procdom = $process.GetOwner().Domain
```

```
    $procuser = $process.GetOwner().User
    log "WindowsProcessData, $procname is running with the
$procdom\$procuser account."
    }
  }
}
```

There is no output to display from creating this function.

In this example, you create a function to scan processes that are not running as built-in users:

You start by defining the `scan-process` function. You call the `check-kill` function to determine if the script should continue or terminate.

If the script can continue, you leverage the `win32_process` WMI class to obtain the current running processes.

You continue to evaluate each process to determine if the `.GetOwner().User` property is matched to the built-in user regular expression.

If the user is not matched by the `$blstRegex` regular expression or, `!($procuser -match $blstRegEx)`, you gather the process name, process user's domain, and process username.

You complete the function by leveraging the `log` function with the `"WindowsProcessData, $procname is running with the $procdom\$procuser account."` value.

Windows services function

To create a function to scan services on the system for users that are not built-in, you can perform the following:

```
function scan-services {
    check-kill
    $service = get-wmiobject win32_service
    foreach ($service in $services) {
        $svcAuthUser = $service.StartName
        if (!($svcAuthUser -match $blstRegEx)) {
            $svcdisplay = $service.DisplayName
            log "WindowsServicedata, Service with $svcdisplay name is
running with $svcAuthUser account."
```

```
        }
    }
}
```

There is no output to display from the creation of this function.

 To obtain a detailed explanation of interacting with Windows services, you can refer to *Chapter 5, Interacting with Services, Processes, Profiles, and Logged on Users.*

In this example, you create a function to scan Windows services that are not running as built-in users:

1. You start by defining the `scan-services` function.

2. You call the `check-kill` function to determine if the script should continue or terminate.

3. If the script can continue, you leverage the `win32_service` WMI class to obtain information about the Windows services.

4. You continue to evaluate each service to determine if the `.Startname` property is matched to the built-in user regular expression.

5. If the user is not matched by the `$blstRegEx` regular expression or, `!($svcAuthUser -match $blstRegEx)`, you gather the service `DisplayName`.

6. You complete the function by leveraging the `log` function with the `"WindowsServicedata, Service with $svcdisplay name is running with $svcAuthUser account."` value.

Installed software function

To create a function to scan the software installed on a system, you can perform the following:

```
function scan-software {
    check-kill
    $RegLocations = "HKLM:\Software\Microsoft\Windows\CurrentVersion\
Uninstall\*","HKLM:\Software\WOW6432Node\Microsoft\Windows\
CurrentVersion\Uninstall\*"
    foreach ($reg in $RegLocations) {
        $softwareKeys = get-ItemProperty $Reg | Select DisplayName | Sort
DisplayName
        foreach ($software in $softwareKeys) {
```

```
            if ($software.DisplayName -ne $null) {

                $value = "InstalledSoftware," + $software.DisplayName

                log $value

            }

        }

    }

    $progpaths = "\Program Files\","\Program Files (x86)\"

    $disks = (Get-WmiObject win32_logicaldisk | where {$_.DriveType -eq
"3"}).DeviceID

    foreach ($disk in $disks) {

        foreach ($progpath in $progpaths) {

            check-kill

            $progfile = $disk + $progpath

            $test = test-path $progfile

            if ($test) {

                $files = Get-ChildItem -file $progfile -Recurse | where
{$_.FullName -like "*.exe"} | Select Fullname

                foreach ($file in $files) {

                    $productName = (get-itemproperty $file.FullName).
VersionInfo.ProductName

                    if (!$productName) { $productName = "Product Name
n/a" }


                    $productVersion = (get-itemproperty $file.FullName).
VersionInfo.ProductVersion

                    if (!$productVersion) { $productVersion = "Product
Version n/a"}

                    $value = "InstalledSoftware," + $file.Fullname + " |
Name: $productName | Version: $productVersion"

                    log $value

                }

            }

        }

    }

}
```

There is no output to display from the creation of this function.

In this example, you create a function to scan the installed software on a system:

1. You start by defining the `scan-software` function.

2. You call the `check-kill` function to determine if the script should continue or terminate.

3. If the script can continue, you populate the two main registry keys that contain the display names of installed software and place them in the `$reglocations` variables.

4. For each of these registry locations, you leverage the `get-ItemProperty` cmdlet to obtain the display names of the installed software.

5. If the display name has a value, you build the string of `"InstalledSoftware,"` + `$software.DisplayName` and place it in the `$value` variable.

6. You then leverage the `log` function with `$value` to record the individual software titles in the CSV file.

You continue to evaluate the executables in the `\program files\` and `\program files (x86)\` directories on each disk drive:

1. You leverage the `win32_logicaldisk` WMI class to obtain the drive letters of the disks that are local disks.

2. You evaluate each disk for `program files\` and `\program files (x86)\` and recursively query all of the files ending with the `.exe` extension.

3. You then call the `check-kill` function again to determine if the script should continue or terminate.

4. If the script can continue, you query the executable file's `VersionInfo.ProductName` property and place it in the `$productname` variable.

5. If no product name is found, you replace the `$productname` variable with `"Product Name n/a"`.

6. You continue to obtain the `VersionInfo.ProductVersion` property and place it in the `$productversion` variable.

7. If no product version is found, you replace the `$productversion` variable with `"Product Version n.a"`.

8. You then create the string of `"InstalledSoftware,"` + `$file.Fullname` + `" | Name: $productName | Version: $productVersion"` and place it in the `$value` variable.

9. You then leverage the `log` function with `$value` to record the individual software executable product name and product versions in the CSV file.

User profiles function

To create a function to scan the profiles on a system to identify the user profiles, you can perform the following:

```
function scan-profiles {
check-kill
$profiles = get-wmiobject Win32_UserProfile
    foreach ($profile in $profiles) {
        $currentdate = Get-Date
        $lastusetime = $profile.LastUseTime
        $lastusetime = [Management.ManagementDateTimeConverter]::ToDateTi
me($lastusetime)
        $age = [math]::Round(($currentdate - $lastusetime).TotalDays)


        $sid = $profile.SID
        Try {
            $usersid = New-Object System.Security.Principal.
SecurityIdentifier("$SID")
            $username = $usersid.Translate( [System.Security.Principal.
NTAccount]).Value
        }
        Catch {
            log "There was an error translating SID value $sid to a
username. Account may not exist." "Y"
            $username = "(Deleted Account)"
        }
        log "UserProfileData, User with name $username and SID $sid last
logged in $lastusetime. ($age Days Old)"
    }
}
```

There is no output to display from the creation of this function.

In this example, you create a function to scan the user profiles on a system:

1. You start by declaring the `scan-profiles` function.

2. You call the `check-kill` function to determine if the script should continue or terminate.

3. If the script can continue, you leverage the `win32_userprofile` WMI class to gather the user profiles from a system.

4. You then evaluate each function on the system for the last use time.

5. You calculate the number of days from when the profile was last used.

6. You continue to identify the profile's `.SID` property and store it in the `$SID` variable.

7. You attempt to translate the `$SID` variable to a username. If the username translates properly, it will place the username in the `$username` variable.

8. If it does not translate, the `try...catch` method will handle the error and use the `log` function with the `"There was an error translating SID value $sid to a username. Account may not exist."` `"Y"` value.

9. This will record the error message to the `log` file, if enabled.

10. The script will also set the `$username` variable to `(Deleted Account)` if the SID cannot be translated.

11. Finally, you leverage the `log` function with the `"UserProfileData, User with name $username and SID $sid last logged in $lastusetime. ($age Days Old)"` value. Depending on the quantity of profiles, multiple values will be logged in the CSV file.

Windows features function

To create a function to scan the installed Windows features, you can perform the following:

```
function scan-features {

    check-kill

    $crntFeatures = Get-wmiobject win32_serverfeature -ErrorAction
SilentlyContinue -ErrorVariable err

    if ($err) { log "ServerFeatureInfo, Cannot get server feature
information from WMI. System may not be a server or access is denied to
WMI." }

    foreach ($feature in $crntFeatures) {
```

```
        $featurename = $feature.Name
        log "ServerFeatureInfo, $featurename feature is installed on the
system."
    }
}
```

There is no output to display from the creation of this function.

In this example, you create a function to query the system for installed Windows features:

1. You first start by defining the `scan-features` function.
2. You call the `check-kill` function to determine if the script should continue or terminate.
3. If the script can continue, you obtain all of the currently installed features on the system by leveraging the `win32_serverfeature` WMI class.
4. If there is an error obtaining the server features, you leverage the `log` function with the `"ServerFeatureInfo, Cannot get server feature information from WMI. System may not be a server or access is denied to WMI."` value.
5. If you are able to obtain feature information, your script continues to evaluate each of the features installed on the system.
6. You obtain the feature's `.Name` property and place it in the `$featurename` variable.
7. Finally, you leverage the `log` function with the `"ServerFeatureInfo, $featurename feature is installed on the system."` value.

Scan files and folders function

To create a function to scan directories for files that contain specific strings, you can perform the following:

```
function scan-directory {
    $errors = @()
    foreach ($directory in $scnloc) {
        check-kill
        $content = get-childitem $directory.id -Include $srextlist
-recurse -ErrorAction SilentlyContinue -ErrorVariable +errors | select-
string -Pattern $srtermsRegEx -ErrorAction SilentlyContinue
        if ($errors) {
            foreach ($err in $errors) {
```

```
            if ($err.Exception -like "*Could not find a part of the
path*") {
                $filepath = ($err.Exception).ToString().split("'")[1]
                log "FileScanData, Error Accessing Path:
`"$filepath`" may be over 248 Characters."
            }
            if ($err.Exception -like "*is denied.*") {
                $filepath = ($err.Exception).ToString().split("'")[1]
                log "FileScanData, Error Accessing Path:
`"$filepath`" Access Is Denied."
            }
        }
    }
    foreach ($match in $content) {
        $filename = ($match.Path).Trim()
        if (!($filename -match $flignRegEx)) {
            $lineno = $match.LineNumber
            $linecontents = (($match.Line).Trim()).Replace(",","")
            log "FileScanData, String match found in file named
$filename with the line number of $lineno and the line contents of
$linecontents."
        }
    }
}
}
```

There is no output to display from the creation of this function.

In this example, you create a function to scan directories for files that contain specific strings:

1. You first start by defining the `scan-directory` function to query the directories defined in the `$scloc` variable.

2. You call the `check-kill` function to determine if the script should continue or terminate.

3. If the script can continue, you leverage the `Get-ChildItem` cmdlet including the file extensions specified in the `$srextlist` variable.

4. You pipe these results to the `select-string` cmdlet with the `-Pattern` parameter and the regular expression in `$srtermsRegEx` as the argument.

5. The files that have the appropriate extensions, and contain strings that match `$srtermsRegEx` will be placed in the `$content` variable.

6. In the event that the `Get-ChildItem` cmdlet has errors obtaining content, you catch each of the errors and store them in the `$errors` array.

7. You then process each error by looking at the `Exception` property.

8. If the exception is `-like *Could not find a part of the path*`, the script will leverage the `log` function with the `"FileScanData, Error Accessing Path: `"$filepath`" may be over 248 Characters."` value.

9. If the exception is `-like *is denied.*`, the script will leverage the `log` function with the `"FileScanData, Error Accessing Path: `"$filepath`" Access Is Denied."` value. If no errors are found, the script will evaluate each of the filenames that were found.

10. If the user is not matched by the `$flingRegEx` regular expression or, `!($filename -match $flingRegEx)`, the script will obtain the match line number and contents of the match line.

11. Finally, you leverage the `log` function with the `"FileScanData, String match found in file named $filename with the line number of $lineno and the line contents of $linecontents."` value.

Invoking the functions

To check if the functions are enabled and to invoke the functions if they are, you can perform the following:

```
if ($scanDisks.id -eq "True") { scan-disks }
if ($scanSchTasks.id -eq "True") { scan-schtasks }
if ($scanProcess.id -eq "True") { scan-process }
if ($scanServices.id -eq "True") { scan-services }
if ($scanSoftware.id -eq "True") { scan-software }
if ($scanProfiles.id -eq "True") { scan-profiles }
if ($scanFeatures.id -eq "True") { scan-features }
if ($scanFiles.id -eq "True") { scan-directory }
```

The output of this function will vary if you have verbose logging enabled.

In this example, you check to see if the Windows server scanning functions are enabled and invoke the functions if they are. For each of the features, you query the `.ID` attribute of the XML file answers to determine if the value is set to `True` or `False`. If the value is `True`, the respective function will execute.

The final step of the script requires that you have a local folder shared with the named CSVFiles. The script will copy the log file and CSV file to \\localhost\ CSVFiles after execution. To tag the end of the script, and copy the log files and the CSV file to a UNC path, you can perform the following:

```
$date = (Get-Date -format "yyyyMMddmmss")
log "Windows Server Scanning Script completed execution at $date" "Y" "Y"
log "Scriptend,$date"
copy-item -Path $scnresults -Destination $csvunc.id -Force
copy-Item -Path $scanlog -Destination $csvunc.id -Force
```

The output of this is shown in the following screenshot:

```
$date = (Get-Date -format "yyyyMMddmmss")
log "Windows Server Scanning Script completed execution at $date ." "Y" "Y"
Windows Server Scanning Script completed execution at 201703211543
log "Scriptend,$date"
Scriptend,201703211543
copy-item -Path $scnresults -Destination $csvunc.id -Force
copy-Item -Path $scanlog -Destination $csvunc.id -Force
```

In this example, you tag the end of the script, and copy the log files and the CSV file to a UNC path:

1. You first start by obtaining the date with the Get-Date cmdlet and the -format parameter set to the "yyyyMMddmmss" attribute.

2. You leverage the log function with the "Windows Server Scanning Script completed execution at $date" "Y" "Y" value.

3. If enabled, this adds the string to both the log file and the event log.

4. You continue to leverage the log function with the "Scriptend,$date".

5. This writes, in the CSV file, the completion of the script with a timestamp.

6. Finally, you leverage the copy-item cmdlet to copy the $scnresults file to the $csvunc.id path with the -Force parameter.

7. You also leverage the copy-item cmdlet to copy the $scanlog file to the $csvunc.id path with the -Force parameter.

After execution, you will have fully scanned the system and the log files are in a file share for review.

Running the script

The very last step in the script process is invoking the Windows server scanning script. You will need to ensure that you have the answer file in the same directory as the script. You will also want to make sure that you keep a copy of the answer file, because the Windows server scanning script will remove the answer file after execution.

To execute the Windows server scanning script from a command line, you can perform the following:

```
powershell.exe -executionPolicy bypass -noexit -file"c:\temp\
ScanningScript.ps1" "AAZwAmAE4AMgAoAFEAVAAhAFAA"
```

The output of this is shown in the following screenshot:

In this example, you successfully launch the Windows server scanning script:

1. You first start by calling the powershell.exe executable from an elevated command prompt.

2. You bypass the PowerShell execution policy by leveraging the -executionPolicy parameter with the bypass argument.

3. You then leverage the -noexit parameter to ensure that the PowerShell session doesn't exit after execution.

4. You then leverage the -file parameter with the c:\temp\ ScanningScript.ps1 script name and location. You will need to update this value to match the name of your script.

5. Finally, you include the runtime decryptor of "AAZwAmAE4AMgAoAFEAVAAhAFAA" as the final argument for invoking the Windows server scanning script.

After executing this command, you will see that the Windows server scanning script will start executing on the system.

Performing script cleanup

Once you are done executing a PowerShell script on a system, you will need to evaluate the data footprint that you are leaving on the system. If you are creating files, you will want to make sure that they don't contain sensitive data. If you are leveraging answer files, you will want to make sure that they're removed from the system.

Some of the common script cleanup activities include:

- **Delete answer files**: Since answer files typically contain sensitive information, you will want to verify that the files have been deleted at the end of your script.

- **Delete supporting files**: Any files that are used for installation of software should be removed from the system.

- **Delete sensitive files**: If you are performing data collection for sensitive information, you will want to make sure that you delete the files from the system. In some cases, you may want to encrypt the data as its being written to ensure a secure data gathering experience.

- **Ensure all script-created processes and jobs have completed**: In some instances, your PowerShell scripts may invoke additional processes and jobs on the system. Before exiting PowerShell, you should verify that all processes and jobs have completed successfully.

Summary

In this chapter, you learned how to compose a Windows server scanning script. You started the chapter learning about the structure of the Windows server scanning script. You proceeded to the core scripting components section where you defined the comment block, parameter block, created the answer file reading function, the decryption function, populated the answer files, created the script's logs and logging functions, and created the check-kill function.

You continued creating the script by creating functions for scanning disks, scheduled tasks, processes, Windows services, software, user profiles, Windows features, and directories for files containing strings. You then created a section to query if the `scanning script` functions were enabled and invoked the functions if they were. You completed the script by commenting the end of the `script` file and copying the `log` and CSV files to a UNC path. You learned how to start the Windows server scanning script from the command line with multiple parameters. This chapter concluded with exploring the different post-execution cleanup activities.

Index

A

Advanced Encryption Standard (AES) 34
Answer File Decryptor (AFD) 161
answer files
  about 22
  data output information 22
  data sources 22
  Enable/Disable script features 22
  encrypted data 22
  inclusion / exclusion lists 22
  script logging location 22

C

Comma Separated Value(CSV) 11, 23
comment blocks
  about 9
  requisites 9

D

decryption
  with encoded password 50-53
disk information script 98-100
disk statistics
  about 90
  disk space, converting to MB and GB 94, 95
  DriveType property 92-94
  FreeSpace property 96-98
  logical disk information, retrieving 90, 91
  physical disk information, retrieving 90
Distributed Management Task Force
    (DMTF) 72
Document Object Model (DOM) 23

E

EncryptionKey 35
executables
  scanning, in program files 111-114
export process, scheduled tasks
  reference 86
expressions
  building, dynamically 151-153
eXtensible Markup Language (XML) 23

F

files
  excluding 123-128
  scanning 115-118

H

Hypertext Markup Language (HTML) 23

I

InitializationVector (IV)
  about 35
  creating 36-38
installed software detection 108-110

L

logged on users
  identifying 69, 70
logging files
  creating 11-13
logging function
  creating 15-19

www.ingramcontent.com/pod-product-compliance
Lightning Source LLC
Chambersburg PA
CBHW060547060326
40690CB00017B/3628